BLACK, RED AND DEADLY

*Black and Indian Gunfighters
of the Indian Territory, 1870–1907*

LIGHTHORSE

— Courtesy Robby McMurtry

BLACK, RED AND DEADLY

Black and Indian Gunfighters of the Indian Territory, 1870–1907

By Arthur T. Burton

EAKIN PRESS ★ Austin, Texas

FIRST EDITION

Copyright © 1991
By Arthur T. Burton

Published in the United States of America
By Eakin Press
An Imprint of Eakin Publications, Inc.
P.O. Drawer 90159   ★   Austin, TX 78709-0159

5   6   7   8   9   10

ISBN 0-89015-798-7

Library of Congress Cataloging-in-Publication Data

Burton, Arthur T.
    Black, Red, and deadly : Black and Indian gunfighters of the Indian territory. 1870–1907 / by
Arthur T. Burton.
        p.   cm.
    Includes bibliographical references and index.
    ISBN 0-89015-798-7 : $14.95
    1. Afro-American outlaws — Oklahoma — History. 2. Indian outlaws — Oklahoma —
History. 3. Peace officers — Oklahoma — History. 4. Frontier and pioneer life — Oklahoma.
5. Oklahoma — History. I. Title.
F698.B87   1991
976.6'00496073--dc20   90-44270
                                                                                                       CIP

"Desperado" cover painting by Robby McMurtry

This book is dedicated to:

The memory of my grandparents,
Mr. and Mrs. Frank B. Traylor,
lifelong residents of Arcadia, Oklahoma;

The legacy of the great peace officer,
Bass Reeves;

All who struggle for truth and justice.

Contents

Acknowledgments

Many people gave encouragement and assistance in the preparation of this book. I wish to express sincere gratitude to Dr. Nudie Williams, historian at the University of Arkansas, Fayetteville. Dr. Williams is one of the foremost authorities on African-American deputy U.S. marshals of the Indian Territory. Besides giving me permission to quote from his unpublished master's thesis, Dr. Williams supplied pertinent information and inspiration. I am also grateful to Dr. Daniel Littlefield, director of the *American Native Press Archives* at the University of Arkansas at Little Rock. Dr. Littlefield supplied many leads which assisted in locating archival newspaper sources. Richard Fronterhouse was most gracious in allowing me the opportunity to quote his unpublished seminar paper on the life of Bass Reeves. Robert R. Ernst, research consultant for the U.S. Marshal's Service, was most helpful in assisting in locating source material for the book and giving encouragement on the project.

Everyone at the Oklahoma Historical Society was considerate and helpful. William D. Welge, archivist, was very patient and tried to assist and help with my many inquiries. His knowledge of Oklahoma history is encyclopedic; he is truly a marvelous person. Also, Yvonne Madison and Mary Moran of the Society's Newspaper Department were of great assistance.

Guy Nichols, park ranger, Fort Smith National Historic Site, U.S. Park Service, was most helpful in locating photographs and information on outlaws and lawmen who came through the Fort Smith federal court. Wanda Joy Karrant, Genealogy and Arkansas Department, Fort Smith Public Library, supplied much invaluable assistance and information that was critical to the success of the research project.

Brad E. Gernand, graduate reference archivist, Western History Collection, University of Oklahoma Library, gave assistance on inquiries for source material and offered suggestions that were enlightening.

Also assisting in location of source material was Doris RedElk

Thames of the Oklahoma Territorial Museum in Guthrie.

There was correspondence with a large number of public libraries throughout the state of Oklahoma. The individuals and their respective libraries listed below were most helpful:

Betty Germany, reference librarian, Ralph Ellison Branch, Oklahoma City Public Libraries; Mary Cary, reference librarian, Ardmore Public Library; Hazel Gosey, reference librarian, Wewoka Public Library; Peggy Royster, director, Guthrie Public Library; Vicky Nigh, reference librarian, Muskogee Public Library. Within this same category, Mary Sieigler, Texas State Library, Austin, Texas, would have to be included.

Local historians who gave insight into territorial Oklahoma were Pliny Twine of Muskogee, and James E. Stewart and J. W. Simmons of Oklahoma City.

In my trips to Oklahoma, my cousin, Mayor Marilyn Murrell of Arcadia, assisted with lodging, logistics and moral support. I also received encouragement and assistance from all of my Oklahoma family.

This book would not have been completed without the assistance and encouragement from my wife, Patrice. Besides accompanying me on research trips, she typed and proofread the manuscript and offered suggestions which improved the final product. Her love and understanding were critical and needed to the fulfillment of this project. To all I didn't mention, a big thanks — I won't forget you. And above all I thank the Creator for giving me the vision.

Preface

Regrettably, some of the accomplishments and sagas of the African-American and Native American western gunfighter have never been told in book form. There is a need for the total history of the American West to be told so there will be a more complete picture. Minorities have played a crucial role in the development of our nation, and the West is no exception. This is one of the few studies, if any others exist, exclusively about black and Indian gunfighters of the American West. The evidence uncovers the facts that there were black and Indian gunfighters in prestatehood Oklahoma that deserve a place in our nation's history. These men, both good and bad, were as dangerous as any found in the history of the West.

As a result of movies, television, and literary works, a large segment of our population believes the settling of the American West was done primarily by whites. Historians have recognized the fact that there were more than 5,000 African-American cowboys during the cattle trail era, but sadly they have been sorely neglected. In our popular history only Western lawmen such as Wyatt Earp, Bat Masterson, Wild Bill Hickock, and Pat Garrett are known. But there were black and Indian lawmen whose exploits would rival or top the gentlemen mentioned. The African-American peace officer of the western frontier is another neglected area and one of the least known of occupations recorded. These men set a high standard of law enforcement in the Indian Territory (prestatehood Oklahoma).

In popular history only outlaws such as Jesse James, Billy the Kid, Butch Cassidy, and Sam Bass are known. Again there were black and Indian outlaws of the Indian Territory whose crimes and criminal activity were second to none.

African-American peace officers served in other states, such as those in the Texas State Police between 1871 and 1875, and a few town lawmen in areas of Kansas, New Mexico, and Colorado. There were also African-American outlaws such as Isom Dart, the famous horse rustler of Colorado and Wyoming, and the harmless confidence man Ben Hodges of Dodge City, Kansas. But nowhere, for such an extended period of time, were African-American lawmen and outlaws as numerous as those that existed in the Indian Territory.

The sociological, political, and legal aspects made the Indian Territory unique. African-Americans had originally made the trek with Native Americans (known as the Five Civilized Tribes from the South) to this territory. This episode became known as the "Trail of Tears." The Native American lawman and outlaw were, for the most part, from one of the "Five Tribes." They had embraced a large share of white civilization, from customs and clothing to laws. For many years this land had an unduplicated, integrated social structure unlike anywhere else in America after Reconstruction. Black, white, and red men and women, outside of outlaw intrusion, lived in reasonable harmony. The conflict of outlaw and lawman in places such as Deadwood, South Dakota, Tombstone, Arizona, and Dodge City, Kansas, were tame in comparison to Indian and Oklahoma Territories.

My interest in gunfighters of the American "Wild West" started when I was a child. Growing up, I was a great fan of all the popular television westerns such as *The Lone Ranger, Cisco Kid, Hopalong Cassidy, Gene Autry,* and *Roy Rogers.* I also watched the old serial movies shown on television, such as *Red Ryder, Lash LaRue,* and *Bob Steele.* As time went on, another generation of television shows captured the imagination of America; my favorites were *Gunsmoke, Rawhide, Wanted Dead or Alive, Have Gun Will Travel, Bat Masterson, Wyatt Earp,* and *The Rifleman.* Walt Disney Productions, of that era, produced television serial westerns such as *Texas John Slaughter* and *Elfeyo Baca,* which were loosely based on real characters. Except for a special appearance by Sammy Davis, Jr. (on a program such as *The Rifleman*) and a short-run program of the late sixties titled *The Outcast* (which co-starred Otis Young as a black bounty hunter), there were no stories and very few, if any, depictions of African-Americans in westerns on television or in Hollywood movies. Native Americans were, except for Tonto, characterized as uncivilized. The Indians who were lawmen and outlaws were never presented on the silver screen; there was only the depiction of the U.S. Army versus the western tribes.

While attending grade school, I watched a movie in an assembly that was titled *Harlem On The Prairie* or *The Bronze Buckaroo.* It was an all-black western musical from the 1930s similar to a Gene Autry film. My first reaction was to feel embarrassed, because everyone knew there were no black cowboys, or at least that is what I thought at that time. I had never seen, in the mainstream, any popular movies of African-Americans wearing the white hat and badge, sticking-up stagecoaches, or riding tall in the saddle.

Although born and raised in the Chicago area, my family did have Southwestern roots. My mother was born and raised in Arcadia, Oklahoma; her parents had arrived in Oklahoma Territory as small children around 1890. It is said that Choctaw and Cherokee blood are both in the family. My mother's uncle who eventually settled in California was said to have played in Hollywood movies as an Indian extra in westerns. Many summers were spent taking the "Texas Chief" to visit my grandparents. In doing so, we would always detrain in Guthrie, Oklahoma, to visit my aunt, uncle, and cousins first. My uncle, Henry Parks, always wore a cowboy hat and boots and generally kept a couple of riding ponies for his children. Uncle Henry, on more than one occasion, mentioned black gunslingers of Oklahoma's territorial days. I felt, at that time, Uncle was just trying to impress his city slicker nephew with some tall tales about black gunfighters. I just knew that these inferences couldn't be true because Uncle Henry didn't have any names, dates, or explicit details. If it was true it would have been depicted on television or the movies, as far as I was concerned.

By the time I was twelve I started reading history books on the American Wild West. I located a short statement about someone named Cherokee Bill from the Indian Territory. It asserted that he had a fraction of "Negro" blood, although his picture looked like the average person from my African-American neighborhood. There was also mention and a picture of the Rufus Buck Gang, composed of "Indians" which also looked like some folks from my neighborhood. As I moved into my teen years I realized that African-Americans played a larger role in the settling of the West than had been depicted on television and in the movies. Especially meritorious were the black U.S. cavalry units, the Ninth and Tenth Regiments, known as the Buffalo Soldiers to the Plains Indians. There was also a very fine western movie titled *Buck and the Preacher,* which was loosely based on the migration of African-Americans out of the South into the western territories during the 1870s. But still, I had no evidence of African-Americans who were bona-fide gunfighters. To my knowledge, black gunfighters never actually existed, even if there were black cowboys.

For many years the subject of black gunfighters never crossed my mind, even during the last two years of high school at Arcadia High, which was part of the Oklahoma City school system. While attending college, I noticed a book titled *The Black West* by William L. Katz, which featured a chapter on Oklahoma and included a photo of black and Indian peace officers in territorial Oklahoma. Though interesting, this did not make a big impression on me because I erroneously felt these officers were assigned to patrol only the areas where their indigenous ethnic groups lived. My paternal grandfather was a peace officer in Mississippi and had jurisdiction only where other blacks lived; in other words, he was the "Negro" lawman explicitly. Later Katz wrote another book titled *Black Indians,* which briefly mentioned an African-American deputy U.S. marshal named Bass Reeves as an Oklahoma legend. I was quite surprised to read this tidbit of information, although I am sure my grandfather mentioned the name of Bass Reeves at least on one occasion. Although intrigued, I still was not inspired to do any investigating.

A few years ago, I attended a family reunion in Oklahoma. While spending time with my cousin Jabari Parks and his former college roommate, I received some information that made an impression and gave me impetus for research. The former roommate said he grew up in a section of Muskogee, Oklahoma, which was named "Reeves Addition." He was sure it was named for Bass Reeves. This was quite fascinating to think that a former black peace officer was honored by a community in this fashion. As soon as I got back home to Phoenix (a suburb of Chicago), I started to research as much information as possible on Bass Reeves. The first information I received dispelled the rumor that "Reeves Addition" was named for Bass; it was named for a former businessman named Ira Reeves. Ironically, the subsequent information was quite astounding and illuminating. Bass Reeves was the initial inspiration for this book, and I think the most important personality within it. After further research of Reeves and other important Native American and African-American lawmen of prestatehood Oklahoma, I realized that there was information on Native American and African-American outlaws that also needed to be exposed. Therefore, some of them are included in the text.

Many of my relatives have been and are now involved in the rodeo scene in Oklahoma. Some of the greatest African-American cowboys have come from Oklahoma, including the great bulldogger Bill Pickett, who was associated with the Miller 101 Ranch near Ponca City. Many say that Marvel Rogers from Idabel was the greatest all-around black cowboy. Cleo Hearn from Seminole was the first African-American to receive a rodeo scholarship to Oklahoma State University in the 1950s. It is my hope that this research on gunfighters will help complement the legacy of the African-American and Native American cowboys of the past, present, and future.

The term gunfighter as used in the title and in the text describes those individuals who lived and died by the gun on both sides of the law. Gun buffs will notice in the text that the Winchester rifle was the "weapon supreme" of the Indian Territory, although many also used and carried the Colt revolver pistol.

In describing people of African descent in the text, I use the popular term "black" and the more ethnologically correct title African-American. In describing a mixture of black and Indian I use titles such as African-Seminole, African-Creek, etc. The only time such terms as "colored" and "Negro" are used is if they are taken directly from a source such as a newspaper, interview, etc. For indigenous people I use the popular term "Indian" or the more ethnologically correct title of Native American. The use of the term "Red" in the title is to denote red man; Oklahoma means the "Red People" in Choctaw language and as such was chosen as the name of the state.

This study will help give all Americans a deeper and more complete view of the settlement of the American West. I hope it is a revelation for you as it was for me and that you enjoy reading it as much as I did researching and writing it.

All the errors in the book are mine and I take all responsibility for any found. It is hoped that at a future date this text can be updated with more undiscovered, pertinent information on the subject matter. But for now I will holster my pen and tie up my car.

Adios . . . Vaya con Dios.

ART T. BURTON

Introduction

No part of the West was more of a legal and jurisdictional nightmare, or criminals' paradise, than Indian Territory. This immense wilderness of prairies and mountains was bounded by Arkansas on the east, Kansas on the north, a strip of no-man's-land on the northwest, and Texas on the west and south. Without a doubt, the territory offered outlaws their safest refuge and their richest field for uninhibited plunder. At one time or another, the worst scoundrels in the West accepted the open invitation to visit Indian Territory. The Jesse James Gang vacationed there between holdups, and the Dalton, Doolin, and Cook gangs roamed there, robbing and killing at will.

Into this section also came the cattlemen. Already Texas drovers had trailed more than a million longhorns across Indian country to railhead shipping points in Kansas. The streams of voracious cattle and unruly cowboys swelled to torrents, cutting broad swaths through the territory to points north. The steady influx of white settlers into Kansas and Texas pushed groups of squatters across the borders into the territory. The overland mail service required the establishment of stage stations here and there. Two railroad companies — the Missouri, Kansas & Texas and the Atlantic & Pacific — poked fingers of steel across the region, and flung up depots along the right of way.

Following the Civil War, the government agreed to pay the

1

Choctaws and Chickasaws for ceded land but said they would use the money for the benefit of relocated Africans, if the tribes did not adopt their slaves.

Both tribes opted for relocation of the former slaves, but the government neglected their removal, and the Freedmen remained in the territory. Eventually, the Choctaws adopted the freed blacks, but the Chickasaws held out permanently. The Reconstruction treaties did allow the Indians to re-establish themselves under their own government and did not require a federal territorial government.

In *Black Indians,* Katz says:

> Among the Seminoles, blacks were immediately liberated and six were elected to the forty-two-seat Seminole Council. Blacks were also elected as representatives to the Creek Council in Okmulgee. By the end of freedom's first year, African-Seminoles were building homes, churches, schools, and businesses, as well as planting and harvesting crops.
>
> Black members of other Indian Nations worked vigorously for equality, land ownership, and education. Very few left their host nation. Whatever unfairness they felt among their Indian friends could not match what they would experience among whites. They knew this and stayed. Here were a people who would never lynch or brutalize their sons and daughters.
>
> Among Creeks, Seminoles, and Cherokees, black people made economic strides they could rarely duplicate in U.S. society. African-Cherokees owned barbershops, blacksmith shops, general stores, and restaurants. Some had become printers, ferry-boat operators, cotton-gin managers, teachers, and postmasters.

By 1870, there were five black towns in Indian Territory. The towns established were Tullahassee in 1850; North Fork Colored, Arkansas Colored, and Canadian in 1869; and Gibson Station in 1870. There would eventually be twenty-seven towns and one colony in Oklahoma that would be governed and settled by African-American people. Four of the towns and the colony were located in Oklahoma Territory, while twenty-three were located in Indian Territory.

The population of Indian Territory in 1870 was approximately 68,152. Included were 16,000 Cherokees, 15,000 Choctaws, 14,000 Creeks, 4,800 Chickasaws, 2,160 Seminoles, 7,407 other Indians, 6,378 blacks, and 2,407 whites.

It is interesting to note that Indian Freedmen called blacks that migrated into Oklahoma "state Negroes." Initially there was resentment because Freedmen felt "state Negroes" were too subservient to

2

whites, but the two groups learned to work together for common cause, legal or illegal.

In Indian Territory, nothing worked in favor of firm and uniform law. The territory had no white man's towns at all in 1870. The Five Civilized Tribes — Cherokee, Choctaw, Chickasaw, Creek, and Seminole — were recognized by the U.S. government as self-governing nations within their own allotted lands, and each tribe had its laws, courts, and police force. The Native Americans' police were called "Lighthorse" because they were a mounted police force. But the Indian courts had no jurisdiction over white invaders, no power to exert even minimal restraints on fugitives from other parts. Moreover, they lost jurisdiction over every Indian who committed any crime against, or in company with, a white. Such Indians, and every white who committed any crime whatsoever within the territory, fell under the jurisdiction of the United States Court for the Western District of Arkansas, whose sole judge and handful of marshals were expected somehow to enforce law and order over some 70,000 square miles of outlaw-hunted terrain.

The presence in Indian Territory of stagecoach stations and of railroad depots and personnel was entirely legal, representing legitimate commerce under the terms of the Intercourse Act. But in the classic pattern of the frontier, these installations and the legitimate transients who passed through them attracted countless other individuals whose business was strictly illegal, and whose rush into the territory was greatly accelerated by the total absence of local law enforcement agencies. With the arrival of gamblers, prostitutes, whiskey peddlers, and drifters who lived by the gun, criminal violence took a drastic leap upward.

By the early 1870s, cries of alarm and indignation were rising from Indians in the territory and from bordering communities. The *Western Independent* of Fort Smith, Arkansas, prophesized that "if crime continues to increase there so fast, a regiment of deputy marshals cannot arrest all the murderers." An Indian Territory newspaper, the *Indian Progress* of Muskogee, published "a calendar of the operations of the knife and pistol," listing fifteen murders, most of them uninvestigated, that had been committed in a "peaceful" thirty-mile radius in just two years.

These reports and vociferous complaints from terrorized travelers did not escape the notice of the men charged with administering justice and enforcing law in Indian Territory. In 1871 one small step was taken to meet the deepening crisis: the judge, the marshal, and the

3

district attorney moved their headquarters southwestward from the town of Van Buren to the town of Fort Smith on the Arkansas River, only 100 yards from the eastern edge of Indian Territory. But at the same time, the judicial workload in Arkansas itself increased as more settlers flowed in and business boomed. To add to the problem, in 1872 a corrupt incompetent named William Story was appointed to the federal judgeship. After slightly more than 100 murders were committed in Indian Territory, Story had to resign to avoid impeachment for bribery.

By 1875, the federal court of western Arkansas was in such a scandalous disarray that Congress might have abolished it altogether, except for two factors. In the first place, there was no better alternative available and no time to devise one. In the second place, a thoroughly viable nominee for the vacant and unwanted judgeship was suddenly put forward. He was not only honest, capable, and vigorous but actually distinguished. To make this paragon even more incredible, he had volunteered for the $3,500-a-year post. His name, already well-known in government circles, was Isaac Charles Parker, but he was soon to win greater fame as the "Hanging Judge" of Fort Smith.

Parker was only thirty-six in 1875, but he had behind him a long and varied career. He had served as city attorney in his hometown of St. Joseph, Missouri; as a presidential elector for Abraham Lincoln; as a judge for a backwoods district of Missouri; and as a two-term Representative to the U.S. Congress. But when he applied for the Fort Smith judgeship in a letter to President Grant, more was involved than dedication to the law. As a member of the House Committee on Indian Affairs, he had become deeply concerned with the Indians' plight; his sponsorship of measures to give them economic aid moved his congressional colleagues to dub him "the Indians' best friend."

Parker sentenced eighty-eight men to be hanged, but only seventy-nine came to their death on the gallows. One was killed while trying to escape; one died while awaiting sentence; seven won reversals, after that became possible in 1891, and received lesser sentences on being retried.

The racial background of the men hanged at Fort Smith by Parker for crimes against society were thirty whites, twenty-six Indians, and twenty-three blacks. Obviously, the distribution between the racial groupings was fairly close. Two black criminals had erroneously been notated as Indian: Rufus Buck and Cherokee Bill (Crawford Goldsby).

Between May 10, 1875, and September 1, 1896, Judge Parker

4

tried 13,490 cases and won better than 8,500 convictions. Approximately one in every hundred of those found guilty was sentenced to death; for the others, it was terms of imprisonment from one to forty-five years in one of the state penitentiaries that accepted federal prisoners by arrangement with the government. His court was in session six days a week, from 7:30 A.M. to noon and 1:00 to 6:00 P.M.

Of the cases he heard, more than eighty-five percent were for offenses committed in Indian Territory. It was his theory, often expressed, that certainty of punishment rather than punishment itself was the only combat to crime. He put his theory into practice, and with the boundless vigor of a dedicated zealot, he inaugurated the greatest outlaw hunt in history. When the territory's hardest criminals heard his name, they shuddered, for it was synonymous with the gallows.

Never before in American jurisprudence was there such a court as his. From 1875 until 1889 there was no appeal from his decision; his word was final except on those very rare occasions when the president intervened.

Judge Parker's special, private bailiff, except for eight months of his tenure, was a black man named George S. Winston. He was born February 5, 1846, near West Point, Georgia, but on the west side of Chattahoochee River, which, beginning at West Point, forms the dividing line between Georgia and Alabama to the Gulf of Mexico. He was the slave of George Winston, son of "Captain" Tom Winston. Both father and son owned large plantations on both sides of the river.

After the Civil War, Winston traveled to Atlanta and obtained a job as a waiter in a hotel. On May 15, 1867, Winston, as a private in the U.S. Army, and about 200 other ex-slaves (recruits) were taken to Jefferson Barracks, near St. Louis, Missouri, and after about two weeks to Fort Riley, Kansas. He was later sent to Fort Harker, where he was assigned to Company B, 38th Infantry Regiment. He served in various garrison and escort duties on the frontier. In the summer of 1869, his command marched to Fort Griffin, Texas, and Winston was detailed to escort the wagons passing between Forts Griffin and Concho. He continued in this capacity until he was discharged May 15, 1870, from Company E, 24th Infantry Regiment. The consolidation of the 38th Regiment, in 1869, with the 24th Regiment, caused his transfer to the latter.

After leaving the army, young Winston sought employment in Fort Smith, Arkansas. He found some menial employment on a couple of jobs before he was hired by U.S. Marshal Root's chief clerk. Winston was given the job of being a custodian of bankrupt stock of a general store that was put under federal custody. In the spring of 1872, Winston was appointed one of the six bailiffs to serve in the federal courtroom under Judge Story.

During his first year as bailiff, Winston gained favor with the court by his diligence and close attention to details, and in 1873 Judge Story appointed him as his private bailiff. He was not removed by Judge Caldwell, in the autumn of 1874, after Judge Story resigned. When the new appointee, Judge Parker, took his seat the following May, he appointed Winston as his private bailiff on the recommendation of all the court officers.

One of Judge Parker's early moves was to appoint 200 deputy marshals to police the area over which he had jurisdiction and bring in the lawbreakers. It was actually the idea of his marshal, D. R. Upham, to hire several hundred deputy marshals and send them out with John Doe warrants, which could be served on anyone whom they might have reason to suspect of being engaged in a criminal activity. Parker reopened investigations into many old, unsolved murders and other felonies, issued warrants for the arrests of the most notorious criminals and their gangs, and told these marshals: "Bring them in alive — or dead!"

It was a big order. Two hundred men were a mere handful to cover an area of 74,000 square miles, where the outlaws knew every trail and hideout and the deputies had little protection other than their own discretion and skill in serving these processes of law. A year's imprisonment was the only penalty attached to resisting a federal officer. "To a man who will risk his life to avoid arrest," commented the attorney general, "a year's confinement is a small matter."

The problem was made even more difficult by the practice of some of the settlements to furnish known criminals "a sort of asylum in exchange for immunity"; often whole gangs of outlaws "bore themselves so quietly among the citizens of the town while their lurid escapades filled the border press." Here also was a large class of citizens who "hated marshals and hampered them in every possible turn." Decent citizens were afraid to let a marshal stay overnight or otherwise accommodate him for fear of reprisals the next day. S. W. Harman stated, "Many a wanton, unprovoked and unpunished murder had shown that there was a real basis for that fear."

The outlaws had committed themselves to crime and fled to the

Indian country for the protection and opportunity it afforded to further satiate their keen appetites. Marshals were "intruders" in their criminal empire, and the outlaws connived and banded together to prevent them from performing their duty. From the prairies in the wild country to the west, high knobs or hills were used as lookout points. Lights at night or flashing signals in the daytime, relayed from one knob to another, often warned fugitives miles away that officers were in a certain locality, told the size of their force, and even gave their identity. Many a deputy had to conceal his identity and sometimes associated with his quarry for weeks to obtain enough evidence to insure a conviction and to await an opportunity to make a successful capture.

The task of ridding the territory of outlaws would not be an easy one.

Part I

OUTLAWS

CHAPTER 1

No Sunday West of St. Louis, No God West of Fort Smith

Indian Territory can be considered the "wildest" of the Wild West. Black and Indian outlaws were prevalent throughout the territory. A great percentage of the gangs were integrated, and this would also include the leadership of such units. There were three principal classes of outlaws: murderers, horse thieves, and bootleggers. Added to the Indians and mixed African and Indian were the white outlaws who had fled from Texas, Kansas, and other states. Young blacks and Indians probably turned to a life of crime for the same reason whites did: the lure of easy plunder, notoriety, excitement, and the feeling that their legitimate options for a livelihood were limited.

One of the first black criminals to appear in the territory during the 1870s was Aaron Wilson. He was a discharged soldier who was living among Penateka Comanche on the Anadarko Agency in September 1875. The next month he would meet his fate as an outlaw.

Fifty-six-year-old James Harris and his twelve-year-old son were crossing the Indian country en route to Texas with a wagon, three horses, and the remnants of a stock of goods from a clothing store he had operated at Beatty, Kansas. On October 12, 1875, they camped near the Wichita Agency, twelve miles from Fort Sill. Not far from the fort the travelers passed a camp of Comanches, among them Aaron Wilson. An hour later, the African mounted an old gray horse and left camp, going in the direction taken by the wagon.

He followed for two days, and finally stopped at their camp and partook of their hospitality. After eating a hearty supper, he lay down to sleep by their fire and wrapped up in one of his host's blankets. At midnight he crept from his blankets and killed Harris with an ax. Harris's death cry awakened his son. The boy begged for his life; Wilson calmly withdrew a double-barreled shotgun from the wagon. The boy fled, but Wilson pursued him and killed him with a charge of buckshot 175 yards from camp. He then removed the old soldier's uniform he had been wearing and dressed himself in a new suit of clothes from the wagon, removed the scalps of his victims, and rode off with them wrapped in a handkerchief.

Stopping at the Wichita Agency, he exhibited the scalps and told the Indians he had taken them from two white men whom he had killed. The chief recognized the horses as belonging to the victims who had passed a few days before. The Comanche did not approve of such a violation of hospitality and reported him to the agent. Wilson became frightened and rode away, but was apprehended the next day by a squad of United States troops that had been dispatched from Fort Sill. In the left boot of the elder Harris was near $350 which Wilson had missed. Wilson was tried by Judge Parker and hanged at Fort Smith, April 21, 1876.

In May 1880, a couple of bloody murders were committed by a gang of Indians with a black leader. The gang numbered five and was led by an African Seminole named Charley Bowlegs, who was the son of Billy Bowlegs of Florida notoriety. The crimes were committed on the line between the Chickasaw and Seminole nations.

On the night before the murders, the five men crossed the Canadian River into the Chickasaw Nation, on pretense of gathering cattle, in the neighborhood where two white men lived, Scott Davis and one Bateman. It must have been known to them that Scott Davis would also be out hunting cattle on the next day, and they posted themselves on a sandbar where they could see some distance about them. They soon saw Davis, in company with Thomas Factor, approach. Bowlegs and his party at once crossed over and secreted themselves in a ravine, commanding a view of the trail traversed by Davis and Factor. The two men came leisurely along, Factor being just in advance. As Davis came within range Bowlegs gave the order to fire and Davis fell from his horse, still alive. One of the attacking party ran up to him and, placing the muzzle of his gun to the head of the prostrate man, blew out his brains. They told Factor to "go on home." After concealing the body in a hollow tree near the scene of the murder, they went to the field, several miles distant, where Davis's partner, Bateman, was at work plowing. They crept to within a short distance of Bateman and Bowlegs again gave the order to fire, but the others refused, saying, "We killed one, you kill this one." Accordingly, Bowlegs crept to the fence, raised his Henry rifle to his shoulder, brought it to bear on the unsuspecting victim, and shot him.

Tulwa Harjo was the only gang member captured. Bowlegs committed suicide, another was killed in a quarrel, and the others kept themselves out of the reach of law officers.

These crimes were interesting in that two white men were murdered for no obvious reason. At the trial in Fort Smith, Harjo admitted having fired one shot, but said he did not know what the gang was intending to do. He said that he was with them as interpreter, supposing they were looking for strayed cattle. Harjo went on to say that he was not with the others when Bateman was killed. Factor was arrested on the supposition that he conspired with the murderers to lead Davis into a trap, but he produced evidence to cause doubt in the minds of the jury and he was acquitted. Tulwa Harjo was sentenced to be executed by hanging on June 24, 1881, but on application of his attorneys, a new trial was granted and Tulwa Harjo was discharged.

April 20, 1882, is remembered as the day when one of the most sensational crimes in territory history was committed.

Two blacks named Henry Loftus and Martin Joseph (Joseph had two aliases — Bully July and Bully Joseph) made arrangements with a white man, Bud Stephens, a fugitive horse thief from Texas, to go with them to steal some horses in the Chickasaw Nation. Bully July was a Chickasaw Freedman and was very knowledgeable of the area.

Stephens, who was thirty-five, in escaping from Texas brought with him a sixteen-year-old white girl named Dora. The pretty girl had run away from home with him over the protests of her parents. They lived together in a cabin in the Arbuckle Mountains and presented themselves as married, although no marriage between them had occurred. Their cabin was located near Bywater's Store, south of Desporado Springs and Fort Arbuckle.

Loftus and Joseph had actually been employed for a while by Stephens. He had been so impressed with Loftus that he made him his

12

wrangler. Horses sold for good prices, because they were the chief means of travel. In Texas, Bud and Dora, and sometimes one or both of their black cowhands, would ride out on the range and round up their choice of horses. They quickly improvised a corral by stretching ropes from tree to tree, assembled their herd, and drove them across the Red River into the Arbuckles. There the horses were loose-herded for a few weeks until other rustlers showed up with similar herds from Kansas, Missouri, Arkansas, and West Texas. Two or three days of trading went on until each rustler was in possession of strange horses which he could sell in his own neighborhood without arousing any suspicion.

Stephens's crime in Texas had been a robbery committed in Grayson County, Texas. A posse from Texas invaded the Indian Territory and went into the Arbuckles to search for Stephens. With the help of local nesters, they found where he had holed up in an old cabin at Sorghum Flat, north of what is now Dougherty. In the gun battle which followed, Stephens killed and wounded some of the posse and then escaped under cover of darkness. Later, he was captured, but he shot the deputy who was taking him to Texas and got away again. He made his way back into the Arbuckles, where a man could safely hide from the law.

On that day in April 1882, Stephens and his two black hired hands went on a horse-stealing expedition; Dora also went along. They were some distance away from the girl, and engaged in running the horses into a rope corral, when Loftus shot Stephens in the back, killing him. Evidently, the two blacks had decided they would split the proceeds between them and be the richer for it.

Loftus and Joseph next rode back to the girl and told her that her husband had fallen from his horse and was seriously injured. He wanted her to come to him, they added. She did so. They took her to a sequestered place and, pulling her from her horse, violated her.

Now they were in a dangerous situation, for if the girl testified against them, both might be hanged. Rape was an offense with a death penalty attached. They decided to shoot the girl. They carried her into a narrow cavern in the rocks, at the far end of which was a deep pit or "well." Into the pit they dropped her body, and after it threw her saddlebags filled with clothes, a bed quilt, and other identifying articles and departed in haste.

Henry Loftus, while drunk not long afterward, told of the triple crime of rape and two murders to his brother, William Loftus, who

13

was law-abiding and hard-working. When Bully July learned of this, he killed Loftus and left the country.

William Loftus notified officers, and the bones of Stephens were found where he was killed. Meanwhile, Bully July was arrested by Deputy Marshal J. H. Mershon and placed in the Fort Smith jail. According to the story of the surviving Loftus, and Bully (July) Joseph's account also, Stephens had been murdered by Henry Loftus, now dead.

To prosecute the prisoner, it was necessary to obtain evidence of his crimes against the girl. Deputy Mershon was dispatched with a party to the deep hole in the mountain. John Spencer volunteered to go down and bring up the bones. The others tied a rope about his waist and lowered him into the dusky pit.

What Spencer didn't know was that a den of rattlesnakes had set up housekeeping in the bones of the victim. As his feet touched the bottom, there was a sudden rattling and hissing. In the dim light Spencer saw the skeleton crawling with the mass of scaly reptiles.

"For God's sake, pull me up quick!" he screamed. A moment later he stood back on the floor of the cave, white-faced and trembling. His nerves soon steadied, however. Then, with a lantern in one hand and his revolver in the other, he asked to be lowered into the pit a second time. Taking advantage of the blinding effects of the light upon the reptiles, he aimed at the shining eyes of the largest and nearest snake as it reared to strike, and fired.

The result was indescribably hair-raising. At the explosion of the gun, the lantern went out. In the same moment, the snake which had been decapitated by the bullet flung its writhing body out and coiled itself around one of his arms.

He lighted the lantern again, and told the men above to lower him into the bottom. His bravery was rewarded. The blast of the revolver shot, in the narrow space of the "well," so frightened the rattlesnakes along the walls that they drew back into the cracks and crevices between the rocks as far as they could get. Holding a grain sack, Spencer rapidly gathered up all the grisly remains that had once been a young girl, along with her clothes, the saddlebags, and other articles thrown by her murderers down into the pit.

When he appeared above the mouth of the well with one end of the great rattler attached to his wrist and the other wrapped about his neck, he presented an appearance that nearly caused a stampede among the posse.

But the corpus delecti had been secured. Martin Joseph, also

14

known as Bully July, was convicted by Judge Parker's court. He was hanged at Fort Smith, Arkansas, on June 29, 1883.

Jackson Crow's father was a Creek Indian; his mother, an African. He was raised in the Choctaw Nation and was a bad citizen.

On the morning of August 7, 1884, the dead body of Charles Wilson, a prominent citizen of the Choctaw Nation, was found in the road a few miles from Kully Chaha. The find created a great sensation, as Wilson was a well-known merchant. He had been assassinated while returning from an election, and the murder was charged to Jackson Crow, Robert Benton, Peter Coinson, Ned McCaslin, John Allen, Dixon Perry, Charles Fisher, Jim Franklin, Corn McCurtain, Joe Jackson, and John Slaughter. With the exception of Crow, all were Indians and could only be tried in the Choctaw courts. Crow had, up to this time, failed to take advantage of the Choctaw Freedmen's registration law, which declared the ex-Indian slaves to be "bona fide" citizens, after having properly registered under the law. He was therefore amenable to the Fort Smith court for his crime and he went on the scout. Some of the others were arrested by the Indian officers, but being prominent citizens they were released, and the jury failed to find an indictment.

Crow was at large until the winter of 1886, and in the meantime his friends had registered him as a citizen. In December 1885, Deputy Marshal Charles Barnhill and posse trailed him to a house in the Poteau Mountains. Crow refused to surrender until the posse set fire to the building. When arrested, he had Charles Wilson's pistol in his possession.

At the trial, in September 1887, Crow tried to interpose his Choctaw citizenship between himself and justice, but the court held that the crime was committed prior to registration and therefore could not affect the federal court's jurisdiction of his crime. Two of Crow's comrades in crime, Joe Jackson and John Slaughter, were witnesses for the government. They said that the party of Indians met Wilson on the road and Robert Benton accosted him about a misunderstanding that arose between them at the election. Benton shot Wilson three times. Wilson fell, but quickly rose and grappled with Benton, at which Crow shot him in the back with a Winchester, killing him, then beat his brains out and left the body where it was found.

During the trial Crow claimed he could not speak English, but after the president's refusal to grant him a pardon, he could speak good English. Crow died as he had lived — a wicked, unrepentant man, at

15

whose door was laid many other crimes. Only a few years prior to the killing of Wilson, a white man named Uriah Henderson left a store on the line between the Indian Territory and Arkansas, in company with Crow, and was never seen again. Crow met his fate on the gallows of Fort Smith, April 27, 1888.

On November 29, 1886, George Moss, Sandy Smith, Foster Jones, and Dick Butler, all African-Americans, conspired to steal beef on the range in Red River County, Choctaw Nation. It was agreed among them that if anyone caught them in the act they would murder whoever he might be. They proceeded to the Red River bottoms and shot a fine steer, the property of George Taff, a citizen of the Choctaw Nation. Taff happened to be in the vicinity looking after his stock when he came upon the black thieves. Upon being recognized, Taff was shot immediately by Moss. During the shooting, Moss's horse got away and Moss was unable to catch him. Discovery of his horse and the dead body of Taff led to the arrest of all four conspirators. Moss was arrested and he confessed; along with Smith he was taken to Fort Smith by deputy marshals. But Jones and Butler, being citizens of the Choctaw Nation, were released; the Fort Smith court had no jurisdiction. The infuriated citizens, knowing that the murderers would probably never be punished in the Choctaw courts, took them to the place where Taff was slain. After hearing their confessions, they completely riddled them with bullets; their bodies were left on the open prairie as prey for buzzards and wolves. Sandy Smith died before the trial, from wounds received while en route to Fort Smith. He was attempting to escape from the deputy marshal. Moss was hanged the same time as Crow on the gallows of Fort Smith.

CHAPTER 2

Dick Glass:
The Notorious Whiskey Runner

According to Katz in *Black Indians* . . .

> One lively source of trouble, since the Civilized Nations first adopted slavery, was the struggle between bigoted "mixed bloods" and black Indians. By 1878, Cherokee mixed bloods were in a shooting war against black Creeks across their invisible border. Cherokee gunmen targeted Creek Lighthorsemen, their local police.
>
> Cherokees rode into Creek lands to defy police authority and fire into Creek homes. By early 1880, Creeks claimed Cherokee desperadoes had slain four and wounded six people for racial reasons.

When they demanded legal action, nothing happened. A letter of appeal was sent to the Creek chief:

Muscogee, I.T., Feb. 23, 1880

Hon. Sam'l. Checote
Chief, M.N.

Dear Sir:

> We appeal to your honor to extend to us your protecting arms for our grievances:
>
> On the 20th inst. five Cherokee citizens, namely: Dick Van, George Laura, Tom French, Jeff Beam, and one unknown, did make a raid on the residence of one Ben Burnett, col., a Creek citizen (whilst peacefully sleeping, without fear of molestation) committing much depradation. They set his house afire, discharged their revolv-

ers through his door, two of the balls penetrating the tender flesh of his niece (a member of his family). He escaped death by leaping through the back window while they were engaged in kindling a fire to the front of his house.

When they found he had escaped, they followed, shooting at him, and might have ended his life but for the timely arrival of some of his neighbors, when the said Cherokee dispersed; leaving him and his friends to extinguish the flames of his burning home. This was done without any provocation from the said Ben Burnett.

Upon a previous occasion to this one, Syrus Herrod was forced to leave his home in Muscogee from the too frequent attacks upon his home by members of the above named desperadoes; he is now living as best he can in the charity of his relations as he cannot return to his home for fear of being murdered.

Still, that is not all: there is threats and insults to our people made from time to time which will be put into execution if something is not done.

Our citizens are kept continuously on the watch lest they be surprised in so much that they can't pursue their daily avocations.

This state of affairs has been pending for many months. As law abiding citizens we have chosen to be termed cowards rather than return like for like.

We can bear this no longer. Already four people have been killed and six wounded. *Nothing done.* "Tis niggers." We cry for justice. In one accord, "Give us justice."

We, the undersigned representatives of our people do solicit your kind att'n. (you being the head of our government) in this matter of our grievance. We solicit it in the manner that you exert your influence with the Chief of the Cherokee Nation to turn over the above named men to be dealt with justly by our law.

If our country will give us no aid, we are firmly resolved to seek the aid of some other authority.

Yours respectfully,

Scipio Sango, Town Chief	Simon Brown
Jessie Franklin	Wm. Durant
Ned Robins	Gov. McIntosh
Monday Durant	Perle W. G.
Jno Kernel	Sugar George
Ben McQueen	H. C. Reed

According to Katz, for some reason, Dick Glass, a notorious African-American outlaw whose outlaw band ruled nearby Marshalltown, decided to help out. When two black Creeks, implicated in stealing horses, were kidnapped and lynched on Cherokee soil, Glass leaped to action. Perhaps the two were friends or members of his gang.

On the morning of July 27, 1880, Glass led his outlaws across the border into Cherokee territory and a gunfight began. Several men on both sides were wounded. One Cherokee named William Cobb died, and Glass was shot through the cheekbone and lost his horse to Cherokee fire.

Feelings escalated on both sides, almost causing a full-fledged war between the Creeks and Cherokees. A Cherokee court found the suspects in the Creek lynchings innocent. Rewards were posted for Dick Glass, wanted dead or alive, and he had to abandon Marshalltown and the Cherokee region.

In 1885, Dick Glass sent a letter to Hon. J. C. Atkins, commissioner of Indian affairs, Washington, D.C. The letter was mailed on April 24 from Sasakwa, Seminole Nation, Indian Territory. Glass made a plea for help and sought to give his side of the story of what happened on July 27, 1880, in hopes of receiving a fair trial. Following is the complete letter:

Dear Sir,

I take occasion to lay a case before you asking that you in your official capacity have me given justice in the courts of the Indian Nations if it lies within your power. I have been hounded for nearly five years with a reward on me, dead or alive. I have been obliged to hide or scout around and men knowing that I dare not show myself have taken occasion to commit all manner of crimes and lay it on me, knowing that I dare not come forward and prove my innocence for fear someone might assassinate me for the reward on my head, as has been done to two of my companions, that were with me at the time I herein describe. I have hoped to secure a fair trial for years but now give up hope unless I can interest you in my case. I will briefly give you the circumstances.

About July 26, 1880, a party of Cherokees having an old grudge at some of us Creek colored people which grudge was born of caste prejudice and fostered by little disputes over the ownership of unmarked cattle, came to Marshalltown Creek Nation at night and representing themselves as U.S. Deputy Marshalls, demanded the surrender of Monday Roberts and Robert Jones. These two men believing they were U.S. Deputy Marshalls surrendered at once. These Cherokees took their prisoners a short distance and hung Robert Jones to a tree over the road and fired 17 shots into his body. They took Monday Roberts a piece further and went off in the thick brush and hung him. A man living near where the first man was hung, heard the shooting and went the next morning to see what it was about. He found the body of Robert Jones and came back to the colored settlement and reported the facts. A party of us went out to bury the dead and investigate the cause. Not finding the other man and naturally supposing him to be dead too, we began searching for the body. As we did not find it, we concluded to divide up into parties and follow the tracks of the perpetrators of the outrage hoping to come across the other body.

Myself and three others followed up one part until we came to where cattle had crossed the trail and obliterated the tracks, so we turned back. This was across the Cherokee line. After we got back about a half or three quarters of a mile over in the Creek Nation, I met a white man I knew driving a wagon. I stopped a moment to speak to him while my companions rode on. After they passed a short distance they saw four Cherokees riding toward them. I saw them also and hastened to catch up to my party. As I got up, I saw the Cherokees had drawn their pistols and were threatening my party. I called out not to shoot, but Billy Cobb, one of their party swore he would kill every black . . . of us. As he spoke, he fired; killing my horse under me. I got clear of my horse only to receive a shot through my coat at the shoulder. I had not drawn my pistol until then. After that I drew and began firing at their party. We emptied our pistols at each other and both parties rode away. Billy Cobb falling off his horse and dying as he got near home. During the fight, I was shot through my cheekbone and knocked insensible. My party helped me off the ground.

The Cherokees raised a great excitement over it and demanded my arrest by the Creeks. The Creek authorities knowing that it was on their soil, refused to extradite me. The matter was brought before the U.S. Indian Agent, Union Agency, and argued by leading men of both nations without an agreement. The Agent then took a committee from each nation and visited what was represented to be the place of the fight. The Creeks felt that it was about 100 yards over in their country and the Cherokees claimed about that far in their country. Neither party was right as the dead horse that fell dead in the fight showed plainly the spot at least a half mile over in Creek Nation. The Cherokees claimed it ran there after the shot. Another thing caused the Creeks to say little was that the Cherokees threatened them with violence if they sided with negroes.

After the Agent decided according to the representations made him, the Creeks still refused to surrender us knowing it was made by the facts being misrepresented. The Cherokees then put a large reward on us, dead or alive, and shortly afterwards some Cherokees (not officers) came over into the Creek Nation and killed one of our party, Jim Samson, while resisting arrest. We knew it would be death if the Cherokees captured him. Afterwards, some unauthorized Creeks, in trying to arrest Ben Roberts, another of our party, for the reward killed him while he was resisting arrest. There is only one more besides myself now living and we are both perfectly willing to be tried before the Creek authorities for the offense if it can be called one.

I feel that we did nothing but what men might do who were attacked by others. We did not seek the fight and only defended ourselves. I do not know that I killed Billy Cobb. No one could tell when so many shots were fired. I do know that he shot my horse and shot me. The weapons we used were six shot revolvers and each party emptied theirs. Had I been an Indian and my companions the same, nothing would have been said, but because I am a negro I am blamed as much as if I was the aggressor. I know that I could not get a fair trial in the Cherokee Nation. The authorities would be powerless to protect me or to prevent violence or the intimidation of my witnesses. The trial would be a farce surely ending in my death. As I have stated before, I am weary with hiding and scouting and bearing the blame for every crime anyone wishes to do. They speak of me as having a gang and committing thefts, etc. They have put that out of my power, did I so wish. The men that follow stealing etc. would only be too glad to reap the large reward ($1000) put on my head and I know too much to trust myself in their company. I cannot stay anywhere but must roam about continually.

I now most respectfully and hopefully ask that you intercede in my behalf and secure me a fair trial among the Creeks where it belongs, and I will surrender to the authorities at once as they know well I have always wanted to do. If any other court wants me, I am ready to be tried except in the Cherokee Nation, there it would be death, I know.

I ask you as a man, who was borne and suffered much, in the cause of humanity and for the sake of my family to make some effort in my behalf, that I may not be for the sake of a reward, put up by private parties in the Cherokee authorities hands, killed as were my companions.

I remain

Very respectfully,
(Signed: Richard Glass)
called Dick Glass

This letter was a very eloquent one for an outlaw, written shortly before he was killed in a gun battle with peace officers. But Glass was a lawbreaker, known throughout the territory for his infamous deeds. Not long after the shootout in the Creek Nation, Glass took up trading stolen horses in Denison, Texas, for liquor which he sold in the dry Indian Territory at high prices. There was a $300 fine for selling liquor to Native Americans, but it flowed freely anyway.

In *Black Indians,* Katz says:

> In 1882, Glass had a wild shootout with Creek Lighthorsemen that left him so badly wounded, he was reported dead. Later that year, he was captured by a Kansas sheriff seeking the $600 reward. But Glass mysteriously escaped, possibly by bribing the lawmen.

An article that appeared in the *Vinita Weekly Indian Chieftain,* on September 29, 1882, described the jailbreak:

> Dick Glass has not gone to the pen yet, but the officers would like to know where he has gone. On last Saturday he filed his irons in jail at Winfield, Kansas, and escaped amid a shower of bullets.

At the year's end, Glass was again on the trail in defense of his people, leading a column of African-Creeks in the Green Peach War against mixed bloods. The Green Peach War was one of the five insurrections among the Creeks in the Indian Territory after the Civil War. All were efforts to resist the attempts being made to impose changes upon their mode of living and prompted by a desire to return to the conditions prevailing prior to their removal from the east. These outbreaks were led by the full-blood Creeks whom the blacks recognized as their allies. The Green Peach War was the bloodiest of all the rebellions; it is also referred to as Isparecher's War.

Chief Samuel Checote had caused Isparecher to be deposed as a district judge of the Creek Nation. Isparecher and his friends were disgruntled, believing Checote's action to be unwarranted. Meeting almost daily at Isparecher's home, their dissatisfaction eventually took the form of a "society" with the avowed purpose of restoring the original Muskogee government.

Information of the budding insurrectionist society reached the principal chief, and the Lighthorse was dispatched to arrest the leaders. A bloody clash occurred in which several men were killed on each side. Isparecher quickly mobilized a force of about 350 warriors, Indians, and blacks, which was encamped at Nuyaka Springs in the western edge of the Creek Nation. Intimidation of Indians that adhered to the Creek tribal government was a regular occurrence. Pleasant Porter was called back from Washington and placed in command of a force of about 850 mounted Indian Lighthorsemen.

22

In one night, Porter's forces surrounded Isparecher's group, confiscating all the provisions in the area. Isparecher was starved into breaking out of the encirclement. A dash was made, on a cold night, for the Sac and Fox Agency located to the west. Porter was forced to give up the chase when the fugitives departed from the Creek Nation. Federal troops took Isparecher's group into custody shortly afterward near Fort Reno. They were detained until they signed an agreement to return home and abide by prevailing laws.

Isparecher was an able man and subsequently took an active part in all matters affecting the welfare of his people, and true to his word he walked the road to peace.

Dick Glass no doubt had a great empathy for his people, the Creek Freedmen, but after this war he was back on the outlaw trail dealing in liquor and stolen horses and cattle. On June 5, 1884, the *Muskogee Indian Journal* ran the following article:

> It is rumored that a gang of eleven men, five negroes, four Indians and two whites were seen hid in the mountains near Dave Carr's ranch, across Deep Fork, Friday. They are supposed to be Dick Glass & Co. from the Chickasaw Nation.

A few months later, on October 16, the same newspaper ran the following story:

Dick Glass Again

> A gentleman in from the west says that Dick Glass, Geo. Mack and several more hard cases, fully bad as the two shining lights named above, are camped at the extreme southeast corner of the Potawatomie country. They have a tent and are openly selling whiskey and stealing horses. Only two days before the gentleman visited there they relieved an emigrant of four head. They have friends all through there who through fear or admiration stand in with them, and who on the approach of a marshal or officer gives them notice by firing off pistols. They are only two or three houses from Sacred Heart Mission and the good people in that neighborhood are very anxious to have the gang cleared out. If any marshal wants them bad enough to go there they can be easily found, and as there are several with charges booked against them it might be a profitable trip.

There were even reports that fellow gang members were striking out on their own after being educated in the Glass gang. The *Muskogee Indian Journal* ran this story on November 20, 1884:

Bob Williams and another party some time ago passed through Wealeka with eighteen head of ponies which they are supposed to have stolen, and they succeeded in disposing of them at Catoosa. They then went to Arkansas City where they either stole or bought a flat boat and loading it with provisions and whiskey, floated down the Arkansas with it, selling as they went. When they reached Tulsa on Sunday an effort was made to effect their cargo. A crowd took possession and the drunks in that town could hardly be counted for two or three days. Williams is said to be one of the Dick Glass gang while they were in the Pottawatomie Country.

There were reports in the territory that outlaws and lawmen used steel breast plates on occasion. Wyatt Earp was quoted as saying: "Certain outlaws and their friends have said I wore a steel vest under my shirt. There have been times when I'd have welcomed such a garment, but I never saw one in my life outside of a museum, and I very much doubt that any other frontiersman has either." The following event involving Dick Glass is one of the earliest reports of using such protection. The story comes from the *Muskogee Indian Journal,* April 2, 1885.

Dick Glass Can Cut
Two More Notches in His Gun Stock

Dick Glass is getting for himself a name that will soon rival Jesse James. His home is the "Point" about seven miles north of Muskogee but circumstances have compelled him to sleep out nights and he has been roaming from this place through the Seminole, Pottawatomie and Chicasaw Nations to the Texas line. He has been mixed up with deviltries innumerable but seems to have repented for lately a letter appeared in the *Journal* from him stating that he wished to become a law abiding citizen if the officers would not molest him. But his repentance came too late and the heavy rewards aggregating over $1000 offered for him led Sheriffs John A. Culp and Ex-Constable Rush Meadows of Cook County, Texas, to attempt his capture. Learning he was hiding in the neighborhood of the Arbuckle Mountains, the officers were there to capture him while preceding to make the arrest were met by Glass who was riding a horse. Culp ordered him to throw up his hands, when the negro reached for his pistol. The officers opened fire and Glass fell from his horse as if badly wounded. The officers, presuming they had killed him, laid aside their arms and approached their supposed victim, when he suddenly drew his pistol and shot both officers mortally. Information gleaned from the dying men developed the fact that Glass wore a breast-plate, which successfully wards off the bullets from the officers pistols. A posse was soon organized and gave pursuit, but they do not stand much show of getting him, as he knows every inch of the country and has many friends who will hide him or fight for him as the case may require.

A few months later, the infamous black outlaw Dick Glass was killed in a shootout with Indian police led by the famous lawman Sam Sixkiller.

H. W. Hicks, who was the station agent for the M.K. & T. Railroad at Colbert, Indian Territory, gave the following story of Dick Glass's demise:

Dick Glass was quite a notorious outlaw of the 80's. He had been forced to leave the neighborhood of his native Creek Nation, near Wagoner, following his cattle stealing, the killing of young Billie Cobb, and the wounding of Alex Norman of the Cherokee side of the line. The latter resulted in a near Cherokee-Creek War.

After being run out of the Creek Nation he took up his abode in the Choctaw and Chickasaw Nations, and with his other lawlessness, took to bootlegging on a large scale. He sold by the barrel instead of the pint or quart. His base of operation was in the neighborhood of Stonewall. The same prohibition laws were in force then as we had when statehood came, and it was Uncle Sam's business to keep out all intoxicating liquors from the limits of the Five Civilized Tribes. For this purpose, an Indian Police force was maintained with headquarters at Muskogee, and Sam Sixkiller was the chief of the force.

One day word was telegraphed to Muskogee that a covered wagon with several darkies in it, leading a horse behind, had passed Colbert, the last station on the M.K. & T. Railroad north of Red River going toward Denison.

A hint to the wise was sufficient, and the next day there unloaded from the Katy train several Indian Police officials. Two or three local officers were waiting to meet them, and had horses saddled and all ready to go.

When they started out to way-lay the covered wagon, they found that it had already passed, and on the return the posse picked up a colored man from the neighborhood and deputized him to act as scout and guide. With the colored man riding ahead, they trailed the wagon all afternoon, and until they located their camp on a creek about thirty miles northwest of Colbert. Then, without showing themselves, the posse passed around the outlaws' camp and secreted themselves in the timber on each side of the road where the outlaws would pass, and waited until morning.

After the outlaws had eaten their breakfast they resumed the journey, two of them walking behind the wagon and two riding in the seat in front. Thus, they went right into the trap of the officers, and the first hint of it was when the call to surrender and throw up their hands came.

Instead of obeying the command, each man went for his gun, which they had strapped around them. When the smoke of battle had cleared away, the two who had been walking in the road were dead, another had been wounded and was running through the brush along the creek. The other man in the wagon had fallen down inside the wagon bed and they naturally thought he was dead, too. They all took in after the man who ran down the creek, capturing him and bringing him back to the wagon.

When the officers returned, they found that the man they thought dead in the wagon, had unhitched the team and had gone, riding one horse with the other still hitched to it.

The only man already mounted was their colored scout, and he took the trail expecting to follow it on foot if necessary, but found that instead of staying in the timber where he would have had a good chance to elude the posse, he was evidently excited and stayed on the wagon road. Being burdened with an extra horse, harnessed and fastened to its mate, he made very poor time and the colored scout soon overtook him. The only way to save his life was to stop and surrender, which he did.

The posse returned to the wagon, loaded the two dead men and the badly wounded man in the wagon, and with the one captured alive, returned to Colbert before the night.

I had seen Dick Glass before. He was run out of the Creek Nation. He had a bad scar across the side of his neck, running from his ear down to his chest, caused by a burn of some kind, over which the skin had grown red instead of black. He also had a scar on one hand, made by a bullet which had passed through it when he was in one of his shooting scrapes. Dr. Williams of Muskogee, told me he had met Glass in the middle of the Arkansas river, north of Muskogee, and had dressed his hand for him.

When I examined his body, there was no mistaking the identity as both scars were there as described above. Glass was filled with buck-shot from waist line to neck, and had been hit in the side of the head, back of the eyes.

The other darkey killed was not identified. He was copper colored, and had a bullet in the center of his chest and another through his head.

The wounded man had been sitting in the seat beside the driver, and one of the officer's bullets had gone through the wagon box before striking him and had thus been deflected, and kept from killing him. I think he later died from the wound.

There was a full sized barrel of whiskey in the back end of the wagon, several Winchesters, one pearl handled .45 revolver, two ivory handled pistols and one or two plain old frontiers. The firearms were divided among the posse.

Glass had a fine shooting Winchester Carbine, a .40-60, which was left with me for more than a year before the officer who fell heir to it had me ship it to him. This was the end of the outlaw, Dick Glass.

The *Vinita Indian Weekly Chieftain* ran the following story on June 11, 1885, concerning Glass's death:

Dick Glass Killed. — Information reached here last Saturday of the sudden "taking off" of Dick Glass that morning at Postoak Grove, thirty miles west of Colbert. Captain Sam Sixkiller with Policemen Laflore, Murray, and Gooding and C. M. McClellan of Oowa-la, were in pursuit of a band of negroes headed by Glass who had been to Denison for a load of whiskey and were on their way back to the Seminole nation. The officers were accompanied by a negro spy to locate them. After this was done, the officers left the main road and got around ahead of them and selected a place near the roadside to await their approach. About 7 o'clock the negroes came along, one driving the wagon and Glass and two others following close behind. When within ten feet, Sixkiller stepped into the road and commanded them to surrender. Instead of doing so, they started to run. After Glass ran a few steps, he succeeded in getting his pistol out and as he turned to shoot the police party fired on them. Dick Glass and Jim Johnson were killed and the driver slightly wounded. Thinking the latter dead, the officers started in pursuit of the remaining desperado and succeeded in capturing him after a chase of half a mile. Returning to the place where the shooting occurred, they found the driver and the horses gone, the wagon having broken down. After a six mile chase, the driver was recaptured. After returning with the prisoner to the scene of the first encounter, the bodies of Glass and Johnson and the two prisoners were loaded into a wagon and taken to Colbert where Glass was fully identified by a number of parties.

And so came the end of Dick Glass. He was undoubtedly one of the worst African-American outlaws to ride the trails of prestatehood Oklahoma. The defense of his race was noble but his criminal activities were inexcusable. As described by the narrative, his operation was well organized and covered quite an extensive area.

Historian Kenneth W. Porter has suggested, "If Robin Hood, legendary outlaw-champion of the Saxon peasantry, ever existed as a historical character, he probably resembled Dick Glass more than he did the Robin Hoods of ballads, novels and movies."

CHAPTER 3

Ned Christie:
Last of the Cherokee Warriors

Ned Christie was the most feared Indian outlaw in the Indian Territory during the late nineteenth century. His war against officers of the U.S. government lasted almost five years.

Ned was the son of a full-blood Cherokee known as Uncle Watt Christie, a blacksmith by trade. He was born on December 14, 1852, and was a highly respected member of the Cherokee government, serving on the council for one term, even though he had no formal education. Ned preferred to speak in Cherokee, but could communicate in broken English and he understood the language well. An excellent marksman, the six-foot, four-inch Indian served as a bodyguard to Principal Chief Dennis Bushyhead. He was, by trade, a blacksmith and a gunsmith.

When Ned was a young man, he had some quarrel with another Indian boy by the name of Palone. In the ensuing struggle, Christie killed the young Indian. He was tried in the Indian courts and acquitted. He then settled down and became a law-abiding citizen.

Christie had no more serious trouble with the law until the murder of U.S. Deputy Marshal Dan Maples on May 5, 1887. The event was recapped in an article in the *Northwest Arkansas Times,* November 16, 1964:

> Dan Maples and his wife, Maletha Jane Campbell Maples, came

29

to Benton County shortly after the close of the Civil War from their native Carroll County. After serving as deputy sheriff for the county, Dan was appointed U.S. Deputy Marshal and worked under Chief Marshal Thomas Boles and John Carroll, who succeeded Boles, in 1886.

To understand the situation in the Indian Territory at that time, it must be remembered that this was practically a haven for criminals. The Indian government had no control over white men and the Cherokee government and courts of Arkansas and Kansas were far away and their jurisdiction rights frequently questioned in cases arising in the territory. The men who lived here, mostly cowboys who guarded the herds in the Cherokee Strip, guaranteed their personal safety by their accuracy with a gun . . .

It was into this area then that Dan Maples was sent on May 4, 1887. He, like all the marshals, was considered an intruder. The citizens banded together to prevent those officers from performing their duty. If the marshal was successful, he earned $2 for bringing in his man plus the enmity of the man's friend.

Maples was sent to Tahlequah at the request of residents who asked for a man who was not afraid because the lawless element had gotten out of hand . . .

Other reports say he carried a whiskey warrant for an Indian named John Parris and that he was sent to arrest the noted desperado Bill Pigeon. [Pigeon was wanted for the slaying of Deputy Jim Richardson but disappeared into the Flint Hills and was never found.]

Maples had worked mostly in the Cherokee country as he was familiar with the tribe and its language and was praised as "part of the cream" of Marshal Carroll's staff.

His wife begged him not to go. Her premonition of impending disaster was intensified as he bade her farewell and prepared to get into the wagon when a bird fluttered around his head and landed on his shoulder.

The next she heard was when the news of his death came over the wires.

The following report was published in a local paper (undated clipping kept by family) shortly afterwards:

"Deputy Marshal Dan Maples of Bentonville, on Monday left for the Cherokee Nation to arrest the noted desperado Bill Pigeon. He was accompanied by J. M. Peel and George Jefferson. On Thursday the news came over the wires that Dan was shot and badly wounded. A later dispatch brought the news that he was dead. No further particulars are known as yet. Dan Maples was well known in Benton County and no man had more or warmer friends."

Later: "The body of Mr. Maples arrived and was buried yesterday at Bentonville." (The dates on the tombstone, as copied by his granddaughter, are born, January 17, 1846, killed, May 5, 1887.)

The following week a more complete report was published again with no date or name on the paper:

"This community was thrown into a great state of consternation by the arrival of the son (Sam Maples who himself was deputized as a marshal, September 9, 1893) of Deputy U.S. Marshal Dan Maples, accompanied by one of the posse, last Thursday night announcing the killing of Maples at Tahlequah, Indian Territory on the preceding (Wednesday) night.

"The particulars as near as we can learn are as follows:

"Marshal Maples accompanied by his son, Mac Peel, George Jefferson and a young man engaged as cook, all of Bentonville passed through our city (probably Fayetteville) last Monday week, en route for the Nation, arriving at Tahlequah the next day.

"Maples and one of the posse, George Jefferson, started to go up in town to do some trading and after transacting their business they started back to camp and while crossing the creek within a hundred yards of camp, were fired upon by an unknown party. It was near dark when the shooting occurred.

"It seems that Jefferson was on the lookout and discovered the gleam of a pistol in the hands of the murderer, who was secreted behind a tree, and he (Jefferson) called to Marshal Maples to 'Watch Out!' But the warning came too late, and the first leaden messenger from the assassin's weapon caused the death of Maples, it being the only ball that took effect.

"The murderer, however, not being satisfied with his already bloody and cowardly work emptied the remaining chambers and reloaded and emptied his second round at Jefferson.

"Jefferson, strange to say, being an open target, stood and emptied his pistol at the murderer, escaping without a single scratch. Maples also fired four shots after being shot clear through the body.

"The remaining parties at camp, Mac Peel, the cook and Maples' son, hearing the shooting went to the rescue as quickly as possible, but the affray was of short duration, and by the time they procured their weapons and arrived at the scene, the murderer had fled to the bush.

"Maples was at once conveyed to a residence in Tahlequah where he received the best care and attention at the hands of the worthy citizens of that place. He died the next day. No clue has yet been announced, only that a dispatch had been received at Bentonville, from Chief Bushyhead stating that an arrest had been made and was thought they had the man who murdered Maples."

31

This report is essentially as the descendants recall their grand-mother telling the story and as Jefferson related to them. Mrs. Maples lived until 1934 and never forgave the Indians for killing her husband . . .

The *Indian Journal* of May 16, 1887 said that Heck Thomas was one of the marshals sent out to capture the slayer. "Should he get the right man he would make a very profitable haul — there is a $500 reward for the murderer."

Heck Thomas was sent out to capture a young Indian named Charley Bobtail, who had been a constant companion of John Parris, one of the suspects in the Maples killing. He arrested Bobtail the night of May 20 and took him to Fort Smith. Four men were suspected of having a part in the ambush. Also arrested were Parris (also spelled Parish) and Bud Trainor. The fourth, Ned Christie, remained at large. Bobtail denied any knowledge of the crime and Parris confessed that Bobtail wasn't there and said, "The man who killed Maples is Ned Christie."

Ned had no way of proving his innocence; he decided to go on the scout. The $500 put up for the capture of the murderer was done by the citizens of Bentonville, Arkansas. The governor of Arkansas also offered a reward.

Ned went to his father's home and got two .44-caliber Colts his father had carried during the Civil War. Ned studied the technique used by the Colt factory to convert cylinders from muzzle-loading to breech-loading. The Indian gunsmith worked carefully and before the day was out, the Model 1860 army revolvers would fire the modern metallic cartridges.

Christie used a reliable .58-caliber Springfield musket as a shot-gun, and later bought a new model '73 Winchester in .44-40 caliber from Eli Wilson, a close friend. Ammunition for his new rifle was interchangeable with that of his pistols.

After the warrant was sworn out for him, Ned refused to speak another word of English.

Deputy Joe Bowers rode into Rabbit Trap of the Going Snake District to serve Ned Christie with the murder warrant. As he neared, the Indian fugitive fired from the dense undergrowth of forest and struck the lawman's leg. A charge of assaulting a federal officer was now filed against Christie.

There was conflict in the Indian sense of justice and the white man's standard of law and order. Not long after Deputy Bowers made his attempt, Deputy John Fields arrived early in the morning. Ned lunged out of the cabin door, his Winchester in his hand, and the sincere lawman turned his horse for a hasty retreat. The eagle-eyed marksman shot once, striking Fields in the neck. When he saw that the deputy kept on riding, Christie did not fire again. A third charge was filed.

A great deal of available information on Christie is conflicting. Some of the charges about him being a horse thief and bandit are nebulous. He did become a fugitive, and his skill with firearms kept the law at bay for many years.

Later that same year, the deputies tried to serve their warrants. A resumé of the number of deputy marshals killed was carried in the *Fort Smith Weekly Elevator* dated December 9, 1887. It stated: "Dan Maples murdered at Tahlequah, presumably by Ned Christie, Charles Bobtail, John Parris and Bud Trainor. The three latter are in jail here, while Christie is at large."

And Christie remained at large — in fact, Harry Sinclair Drago, in *Outlaws on Horseback,* says he gave the deputies the longest and most determined battle they ever fought. He also indicates it was never established who fired the shot but Christie was presumed guilty because he fled.

Ned was one of the most dangerous outlaws the marshals had to go after, and he fought a greater number of battles with government officers than any outlaw in the history of Judge Parker's court.

Back in Fort Smith, U.S. Marshal Carroll advised his deputies to "Quit trying to take him alive." Aware of the coming change in tactics, Christie's neighbors became his warning system. Christie knew of a stranger's approach an hour before he arrived.

At these times, Ned's wife brought up extra water from the rock-girthed spring, while Ned and his son filled leather pouches with extra ammunition, took positions, and waited for the attack.

Once, as they waited, a large posse rode up. The deputies in the posse included William Bouden, Milo Creekmore, David Rusk, and Charlie Copeland. During the skirmish, Ned wounded three of them, but silenced his smoking '73 to allow the possemen to remove their battered comrades out of the range of fire.

In 1889, Deputy Marshal Heck Thomas decided to get Ned Christie. Deputies L. P. "Bones" Isbel, Dave Rusk, and Salmon rode southward from Vinita, Indian Territory, to meet him. Leaving their horses in the hills, they carefully moved in on Ned's distant cabin. Their cautious approach lasted for three days, and they were not discovered by Ned's unseen sentries.

On the fourth morning before daybreak, they inched into position near the house. But Christie's watchdogs caught scent of them and started barking.

Ned ran to the left, kicked loose a board at the gable end, and started shooting. Thomas ordered Christie to surrender, but silence was his only answer. The marshal called for him to send his wife out, if he was going to fight, and Christie opened fire.

Heck Thomas had taken cover behind a small outbuilding Christie used as a blacksmith and gunsmith shop. The deputies set it afire, hoping that would draw Christie out into the open.

Trying to get a better look, Isbel leaned out from a tree for an instant. Ned's keen eyes spotted him and a shot sent Isbel staggering back with a bloodied shoulder. As Thomas quickly pulled his longtime friend to cover, Christie's wife sprinted for the safety of the woods.

The morning breeze blew the blaze toward the cabin and the flames danced higher as they engulfed the log structure. Christie's boy leaped from the smoke-blanketed structure and ran for the tree line. Thinking it was Ned, Rusk and Salmon gunned him down.

The deputies were attending to Isbel's wound when Christie jumped from the loft and made for the forest. Thomas leveled his rifle at Christie and it roared. Ned grabbed at his forehead and fell into the brush at the edge of the timber.

Thomas left Isbel in the care of Deputy Salmon while he and Dave Rusk searched the woods in vain for the fugitives. Indian friends located the wounded pair and took them to an Indian doctor.

Deputy Isbel lost the use of his right arm as the result of Christie's accuracy. Ned's boy suffered from wounds in the lungs and hips, but eventually recovered; his own injury was the most serious. Thomas's bullet shattered the bridge of his nose and put out his right eye, then lodged itself just above the temple.

Christie was taken to a prominent hill now known as Ned's Fort Mountain. It was a mile north of his home, and there they kept him until he recuperated. Ned's loyal tribesmen built a stout stone and wood structure, camouflaged from view by massive boulders and dense foliage. From the shelter at the crest of the hill, Ned and his allies could watch the only trails winding into the area. Fresh water could be easily obtained from the spring on the same plateau as Ned's makeshift hospital.

Very proud of his once-handsome features, the grotesque disfigurement of his face and his sightless right eye served as constant reminders; Ned grew vicious with his hatred of the white man.

When Ned regained his strength, he returned home, stared in silence at the ashes, crossed Bidding Creek to higher ground, and commenced to build again.

After acquiring a stream-driven saw mill, the skilled craftsman constructed a two-story log structure. Its walls were two logs thick, and lined with oaken two-by-fours. There were few openings: only a door, and on the second floor, small slits that a rifle barrel could be stuck through for shooting.

It was fear that pounded every hand-wrought spike into the sturdy logs — not a fear of death, but of the humiliation and shame of Parker's gallows and the hangman's noose.

Ned carefully cleared away brush and stones from around the area that might afford a man cover. Ned told his family and friends: "I no give up, I die here fighting."

On November 27, 1890, the *Vinita Weekly Chieftain* described an attack on Ned's "fort" led by the legendary black U.S. Deputy Marshal Bass Reeves. Quite a bit of fire damage was done to the house and Christie was believed wounded but escaped. Christie swore he would get even with Reeves and his posse for burning his house. (More on this raid is included in the chapter on Reeves).

Of all the lawmen, U.S. Deputy Marshal Dave Rusk was the most persistent in his attempt to capture Ned Christie. It was humiliating for Rusk and the other deputies that a single Indian had held off the entire force of Indian Territory lawmen for four years.

Rusk, in 1891, tried his hand at apprehending the wily outlaw Indian. He formed a posse of Indians known to be loyal to the federal government. As the posse took positions in the forest around the clearing, a barrage of rifle fire emanated from the cabin-fort. It was apparent Christie was receiving help from some cohorts.

Shortly after the shooting began, four Indian possemen fell wounded. A strange gobbling sound could be heard over the intermittent rifle blasts. The possemen recognized it immediately as the Cherokee death call. Rusk looked at his four injured men as the gobbling sound continued. There was no choice but to call off the fight.

On two other occasions, in a lone effort, the stubborn deputy crept into spying distance of Ned's fort. In each instance, the crack shot Cherokee teasingly sent a bullet tearing through the crown of the old man's black hat.

Aware of the identity of the pesky deputy, Ned sent a young Indian boy to Tahlequah with a message for editor Robert Fletcher Wyly to be printed in the *Cherokee Advocate:* "I thought I saw a big black potato bug in my garden, but it turned out to be the hat of that 'little marshal' — Dave Rusk!" Rusk wisely gave up his single-handed pursuits, knowing full well that Christie could have as easily put the bullet through his head instead of his hat.

For added income, Rusk owned a general store in Oaks, a small community north of Tahlequah. Rusk's family lived in the town, and he began to fear for their safety. He moved them to Joplin, Missouri, to stay with relatives — and just in time. While the deputy was away, a group of Cherokees rode up to the store and dismounted, except for Ned Christie, who rode his horse straight into the building.

The men ransacked the store while Christie held William Israel, a Cherokee clerk, at gunpoint. The startled clerk was then forced out the back door. One of the desperadoes discovered a barrel of tar in the yard and came up with the idea to make good use of it. They tarred and feathered the helpless clerk and poured raw whiskey down his throat, sampling a little as they did. The bandits' shots chased the drunken clerk into the woods. Christie then proceeded to put the store to the torch.

He turned and rode away down the dusty road, whooping. From this time on, Christie was accused of many crimes he never committed.

Somehow through it all, Christie held to his intent not to kill. He continued to near-miss, or to graze a man, hoping only they would go away and leave him alone. He did not understand that each injured man and each passing year that he remained at large was a major disgrace to the lawmen. Even they began to wonder when he would come to understand, and change his point of aim.

The relentless marshals regrouped at Ned's Fort Mountain on October 11, 1892. Deputies Rusk, Charlie Copeland, Milo Creekmore, and D. C. Dye were among the attackers.

Two officers were quickly wounded by Ned's sharpshooting. The posse fell back and then began to load brush into a lumber wagon Christie had used in constructing his fort. The brush was set afire, and the wagon was shoved toward the fort, but the burning vehicle careened into an outhouse and stopped short of its target. Several sticks of dynamite were hurled at the walls but bounced harmlessly onto the ground, and the posse retired in disgust. Following this onslaught, Ned lived in peace for three weeks.

The final attack on Ned's fortress began on November 1, 1892. Deputy Marshal Paden Tolbert led a sixteen-man posse, which included one black member who doubled as cook, that wound along the rocky trail, hidden by huge copper-leafed oaks. Tom Johnston and Ben Knight, Sr., were guides for the large posse. This time, they brought a three-pounder cannon which was shipped by train from Coffeyville, Kansas; they hauled laboriously by wagon into the rolling, rocky hills of the Going Snake District. This was the first and only time that a cannon was used against a civilian in American law enforcement history.

In addition to this, they carried thirty tins of black powder for the piece, fuses, three boxes of matches, and six sticks of dynamite. The posse arrived by nightfall, unnoticed. On November 2, in the dim light of the predawn hours, the men encircled the clearing and sought protection behind any available obstruction.

Then, through the murky light, they saw the cabin door open and a figure step out with a bucket in his hand. The lawmen centered him in their rifle sights and called for his surrender. It wasn't Ned but an Indian fugitive named Arch Wolf. He dived back for the door as rifle fire came pouring in from the posse.

The battle raged on throughout the day, with more than 2,000 shots being fired, but the lawmen's bullets dropped harmlessly as they smashed into the tough log walls. Then the deputies readied their cannon, taking deadly aim. Again, luck was with Ned. The projectiles left the cannon barrel with impressive force but hit the fort with a deafening crack and bounced back into the clearing, leaving the logs skinned but the structure unmolested. After the thirtieth shot from the cannon, the tired breech split.

When darkness arrived, the lawmen retired deep into the woods to plan for the coming day. In their retreat, they happened upon the charred remains of the rear axle and wheels of Ned's old wagon used in the October 11 fight. The deputies came up with an idea for their last ditch effort. With oak planks found by the abandoned sawmill, the desperate posse built a thick wall buffer and mounted it upon the wagon axle. Taking another board, they made a tongue to guide the rolling barricade. The makeshift shield was completed shortly after midnight and the officers pushed it to the edge of the clearing.

Deputies Paden Tolbert, G. S. White, Bill Smith, Bill Ellis, and Charlie Copeland, who was carrying six sticks of dynamite, manned the rolling wall as the remainder of the posse took positions around the clearing and commenced firing to provide diversion. The dynamiters reached the cabin and began firing at the yellow flashes which surged from the gunports on the second floor. Meanwhile, Copeland leaped for the wall of the cabin and placed the lethal bundle with its sizzling fuse against the bottom log.

In a moment, after the deputies reached safety along the tree line, the dynamite exploded, shattering the wall and setting the structure on fire. Christie and Wolf tried to make it to the woods by running through the thick smoke, but Ned suddenly found himself face to face with Wess Bowman. Christie jerked up his Winchester and fired hastily but succeeded only in powder-burning Bowman's face. Bowman spun and got off a shot as Christie ran past. The rifle slug hit the tall Indian behind the ear and killed him on the spot. Young Sam Maples, vengeful son of Dan Maples, came forward and emptied his revolver into Ned's body. Wolf somehow managed to escape, but later was apprehended and sentenced to a prison term.

Ned's body was placed on the door of his cabin, which had blown free with the blast. He was loaded onto the lawmen's supply wagon and hauled down the lonely trail to Fayetteville, Arkansas. At Fayetteville they were joined by Alvin Beatty, who was sheriff of Washington County, Arkansas, and Dr. H. W. Wood issued a death certificate. The triumphant group with their trophy boarded a train and headed for Fort Smith.

Upon arrival, they took the body to the federal building and presented it to Marshal Jacob Yoes. A civic group asked if Christie's body could be put on display for the schoolchildren of Fort Smith. The deputies placed it on the federal building porch and there it remained for the afternoon. Ned's family came that evening and claimed the body.

His body was shipped by rail to Fort Gibson and hauled by wagon back to his home. There he was turned over to his father, Watt Christie. Ned was interred in the Christie Cemetery, which is now Wauhillau, Oklahoma. He was about forty-five years old at the time of his death.

In 1922, Fred E. Sutton, a former deputy marshal and freelance writer, wrote that Dick Humphrey, an African-American blacksmith, told him that he was a witness to the Dan Maples murder and that Ned Christie was not the guilty man. Humphrey stated that on the night of the murder, he was on his way to Jennie Schell's house for his customary drink of whiskey when he spotted Bud Trainor taking a coat off Ned Christie, who was lying in the grass in a drunken stupor. Suspecting foul play, Humphrey said he hid behind a large tree to see what was going to happen.

As Humphrey waited in the dark, Dan Maples came along, presumably on his way to arrest Jennie Schell for selling whiskey. Humphrey said that as Maples crossed the stream on a footlog, Bud Trainor emptied his two guns into Maples and ran into the darkness. He said Maples fired four shots at Trainor as he fell.

Humphrey stated that he did not give his testimony because he was afraid of Trainor and his outlaw friends. Even after he learned of Trainor's death at the hands of renegades in the Cooweescoowee district, he was still afraid of Trainor's friends. He kept the story until he was an old man, after Trainor's friends had all died.

The Clark interview as well as the Humphrey story would have probably cleared Ned Christie of the murder if they had been made known at the time and confirmed his claim that he was innocent, saving additional lives as well as considerable embarrassment on the part of the United States government.

The legend of Ned Christie will live forever in the folklore of eastern Oklahoma. Ned was the toughest foe that Judge Parker's deputies ever faced. He made good his vow that he would never be taken alive; he felt there was no justice for Native Americans in the white man's courts of law.

CHAPTER 4

Cherokee Bill:
Toughest Of Them All

The most famous outlaw in Indian Territory history was a young black man named Crawford Goldsby, better known by his nickname, Cherokee Bill.

Cherokee Bill was born at Fort Concho, Texas, on February 8, 1876. His father was George Goldsby, a soldier of the Tenth Cavalry, one of the famous "Buffalo Soldiers." There has been some confusion about George Goldsby's lineage. George had served as a first sergeant in D Company of the all-black Tenth Cavalry; only the officers were white. On his enlistment papers, he put himself down as a Negro in 1867.

In 1878 trouble occurred in Fort Concho between black troops and white cowboys. The trouble came in the nearby village of Saint Angela at Morris's saloon. A party of cowboys and hunters surrounded a sergeant from D Company, cut the chevrons from his sleeves, the stripes from his pants, and had a good laugh over his predicament. They did not laugh for very long. The soldier returned to the post and gathered up some fellow troopers. Armed with carbines, they went to the saloon and a blazing gunfight at close quarters followed in which one hunter was killed and two others wounded. Pvt. John L. Brown was killed and another trooper wounded. Capt. G. W. Arrington came to the post with a party of Texas Rangers intent on arresting 1st Sgt.

George Goldsby of D Company for allowing the troopers to get their carbines, but commanding officer Col. Benjamin Grierson challenged their authority on a federal post. This gave Goldsby time to go AWOL, where evidently he headed for Indian Territory. Goldsby, who was originally from Selma, Alabama, set up shop as a farmer at Cleveland, Oklahoma Territory. Goldsby was evidently a very light-skinned black, because he told people he was of Mexican, white, and Sioux Indian blood. It was not unusual for light-skinned blacks to pass for other ethnicities, if possible, in the late nineteenth century. The fact that he was from Selma makes it very doubtful that he was part Mexican or Sioux, who were from the far Northern Plains Indian domain.

Crawford's mother was Ellen Beck, a black woman who had some Cherokee Indian and white blood in her ancestry. Crawford had a brother named Clarence who was two years younger. After being abandoned at Fort Concho, the mother moved with the two young boys to Fort Gibson, Indian Territory. Ellen was a Cherokee Freedman and had originally met George Goldsby at Fort Gibson. Crawford's mother left him in the care of an older black woman known as "Aunty" Amanda Foster. He lived with Aunty Foster until he was seven years old. At that time his mother sent him to the Indian school at Cherokee, Kansas, for three years, and he was then sent to the Catholic Indian School at Carlisle, Pennsylvania. When Crawford reached the age of twelve, he came home to Fort Gibson.

Upon returning home, he found his mother had married a local black barber, William Lynch, who had a shop in Fort Gibson for many years. As is often the case with steprelationships, Crawford and his stepfather did not get along, and he began laying out and associating with the worst of companions, developing a taste for liquor and rebelling against authority.

At the age of fifteen, Crawford went to live with his older sister, Georgia Goldsby. She had married Mose Brown and lived near Nowata on claims gained by her mother's Freedman status. Mose took a dislike to Crawford and continually mistreated him to the extent that Crawford left and returned to Fort Gibson. In Fort Gibson, Crawford made his home with a Cherokee Indian by the name of Bud Buffington.

Crawford did oddjobs by the time he was seventeen. Alex R. Matheson, in an interview, said, "He cleaned up and swept out our store. He was the best working, the most honest Negro boy that worked for us." On another occasion right before he got in trouble with the law, Crawford worked on a small ranch owned by James W.

41

Turley and his father. Crawford came looking for work, barefooted, coatless, and wearing a ragged cap. He did his chores for his room and board and later was paid wages for his work. Turley said Crawford "was a quiet, good-natured, hard-working boy, well-liked by all who knew him."

Crawford's first serious trouble occurred when he was eighteen, in the early spring of 1894. While attending a dance, in an area of Fort Gibson, the slum known as "old town," he and Jake Lewis, a black of about thirty-five years of age, got into a quarrel. The trouble started when Crawford tried to take up for his younger brother. He was severely beaten by Lewis and some of his friends. His mother had always told him, "Stand up for your rights; don't let anybody impose on you." Smarting under the blows, Crawford determined to have revenge. One morning, two days later, as Jake went to the barn of his employer (C. L. Bowden of "old town"), he was met at the door by Goldsby, who flourished a six-shooter and threatened to kill him. Soon after, Crawford shot Lewis. The victim started to run and Goldsby shot him again. Lewis fell; Crawford left him for dead and mounted his horse and fled. Lewis did recover from his wounds. The Cherokee authorities tried to arrest him, but Goldsby was on "scout," left the Cherokee Nation, and went into the Creek and Seminole Nations, where he became acquainted with mixed-blood Cherokees Jim and Bill Cook, who later became noted outlaws.

In the early summer of 1894, a memorable event took place in the Cherokee country. After long negotiations, the government had purchased from the Cherokees their right to the Cherokee Strip, which was opened to settlement September 16, 1893, with the great Cherokee Strip Run. Certain portions of the payment were reserved for the Cherokee tribal treasury, but a total of $6,640,000, known as "strip money," remained to be paid out in shares to all who could make legitimate claims to having the required one-eighth Cherokee blood to qualify. Individual payments amounted to $265.70.

The distribution was made amid scenes bizarre and lawless. With all that money to be given out, sharpers, gamblers, bootleggers, highwaymen, even murderers gathered from every quarter to defraud the Indians of their money. When the Cherokee treasurer, E. E. Starr, arrived at each of the several points in turn where the distributions were made, the collectors were there with their stacks of bills to take the top

42

off the monies the Cherokees received.

At every distribution point a circus atmosphere prevailed, with merry-go-rounds, dance halls, "cat wagons," and all the usual carnival devices to take money from the Indians. Through the crowds slipped pickpockets, and many a Cherokee never knew how his funds disappeared. Liquor sellers, despite the law, did a huge business. Gamblers labored night and day to "peel" the Indians at crooked poker, chuck-a-luck, loaded dice, and other games. There were many holdups, and even murders.

The first payment was made at Tahlequah, where more than $1,000,000 was distributed, beginning June 4, 1894.

Goldsby and the Cooks started for Tahlequah to obtain their shares of the money, $265.70 each. But they did not want to be seen in Tahlequah; Goldsby on account of his trouble with Jake Lewis and Jim Cook on account of his larceny charge. They stopped at "Halfway House," an eating house and primitive hotel on Fourteen Mile Creek. Travelers between Fort Gibson and Tahlequah could stop there for meals. It was operated by Effie Crittenden, who employed Bob Hardin, a brother-in-law of the Cooks, as a cook in her establishment. His wife, Lou, was a half sister of the Cook brothers. The three boys gave the Crittenden woman an order and she proceeded to Tahlequah and drew their money. Effie was the wife of Dick Crittenden, of Cherokee extraction, who with his brother Zeke held deputy marshal's commissions. They were separated and on unfriendly terms. The gunfight that occurred at her house on the evening of July 18, between Sheriff Ellis Rattling Gourd and a posse of seven men on one side and Goldsby and the Cooks on the other, was alleged by some to have been planned by the ex-husband, in the hopes that Effie would be killed.

Goldsby and the Cooks, through the efforts of Effie Crittenden, drew their pay on the last day of the treasurer's stay at Tahlequah. A posse under Sheriff Gourd had followed Effie back to the house with the intention of capturing the fugitives. Goldsby and the Cooks had planned on leaving the vicinity on Monday, July 18, after dark. Just as nightfall came, Goldsby sat outside the door, under a tree. They were able to hear the posse approaching due to some of them drinking and talking loudly. The sheriff had a Cherokee warrant for Jim Cook, on the larceny charge. His posse included Sequoyah Houston, Dick Crittenden and his brother Zeke, Bill Nickel, Isaac Greece, Hicks, and Bracket. Goldsby and the Cooks hastily grasped their Winchesters and, as the posse opened fire, they were met with deadly fire. A hot fight ensued, during which Houston was killed and Jim Cook wounded seven times. After Houston fell, the sheriff and four of his posse fled, leaving the Crittendens to face the danger. The brothers, knowing that to turn their backs meant death, held their antagonist at bay, behind the house, until they (the Crittendens) escaped in the dark.

John J. Hannon, an early resident of the Creek Nation, gave an account of what happened to Goldsby and Cook after they left the fight:

> It was a little later Jim and Bill Cook and Bill Goldsby (Cherokee Bill) got into some kind of scrape over in the Cherokee Nation and Jim Cook was wounded. They forded the Arkansas River at Rabbit Ford, rode right by our place and stopped and left Jim at Mary Elliott's to be cared for until he recovered from his wound. (where he was later captured by the posse. ed.)
>
> Bill Cook and Cherokee Bill went up on top of Kaler Hill, unsaddled their horses, stretched some blankets up on some poles for a shade, and lay down to rest while their horses grazed and rested. Pretty soon a Deputy U.S. Marshal came and spied them up there. Cherokee Bill's horse had grazed off down the hillside quite a way from them. The marshal crawled in the grass up to the horse and got him started down to a house where a man named Addington lived. Before he got there, though, Bill saw him, grabbed his Winchester and started after him. The marshal ran in and told Addington what was up and deputized him to help him. Mr. Addington's folks were sick so he said, "We can't fight here, let's go to the barn." They slipped out and got behind the barn, and as Bill came by, the marshal commanded him to put up his hands. Bill dropped to one knee, fired several shots into the corner of the barn, right at them, then ran for his horse. The marshal, instead of shooting him, shot the horse. When Bill saw the horse fall, he turned and went after the marshal who fled. Cherokee Bill and Bill Cook then got the other horse, went down to a farm house, took a horse and rode on.

It was here that Crawford Goldsby is said to have gained the alias that before his death even his mother came to use in speaking of him. The next day after the killing of Houston, the officers were questioning Effie Crittenden. When asked if Crawford Goldsby was in the fight with the sheriff's posse, she said, "No it was not Crawford Goldsby, but it was Cherokee Bill."

By the summer of '94, Cherokee Bill stood not quite six feet tall. He was a burly, broad-shouldered man possessing great physical

44

strength. Only the color of his skin revealed his Indian blood; his features were distinctly Negroid, including thick lips and kinky black hair.

With his rifle he could burst a squirrel eye as far as he could see — every shot — and he said that he could shoot from his waist on a level and hardly ever miss his target.

Those who knew him best say that he would take long journeys through the woods and that his mental alertness during his sleepless nights while playing the game with his shrewd foes left him almost limp, silent, morose. He would talk in monosyllables and would get on the move again. When he rode into any town, he would plunge into wild, lawless acts and spend very freely the "hot money" for drinking and gambling. In such company as he was in most of the time, fights were common. He never seemed to be afraid of anyone or anything.

Soon after the fight at Fourteen Mile Creek, the famous Cook Gang was organized, with Cherokee Bill as a member. The Cook Gang was integrated but most of the members were black men, the majority being Cherokee Freedmen. The band of outlaws received credit for numerous robberies and murders in the Cherokee and Creek Nations. On July 14, 1894, the Muskogee Fort Gibson stage was held up by six masked robbers in the Arkansas River bottoms. Passengers were relieved of their money and watches. An hour later, William Drew, a prominent Cherokee, was held up on the other side of the river and robbed of eighty dollars, an expensive belt, and pistol. Two days later, Bill Cook, Cherokee Bill, Lon Gordon, Sam McWilliams, Henry Munson, and Curtis Dayson held up the Frisco train at Red Fork.

At 10:00 on the morning of July 31, the Cook Gang rode into Chandler, Oklahoma Territory, across the Creek Nation line, and dismounted in the rear of the Lincoln County Bank. Three rushed inside while the remaining two stood watch at the door with Winchesters. Two men covered President O. B. Kees and his brother Harvey Kees, the cashier, and demanded that they "cash up purty damn quick." The third man ran into the private office where teller Fred Hoyt was lying sick. The outlaw ordered him to go to the safe and unlock it. Hoyt, already weak from his illness, fell on the floor in a faint, and the bandit fired at him. The bullet just missed him and tore into the floor.

The outlaws outside called that it was time to go, and the three men grabbed between $200 and $300 that lay on the counter and ran to their horses. J. M. Mitchell, a barber across the street, sounded the alarm and was killed by one of the outlaws. The bandits left the city

45

with a posse of citizens and two deputy sheriffs in pursuit. Numerous shots were fired. One of the gang, Elmer Lucas, was shot in the hip and captured. The others were able to elude the posse in the hills.

On the night of September 21, the gang stuck up the J. A. Parkinson & Company store at Okmulgee, taking over $600. On October 5 they crossed the Arkansas River at the ferry between Muskogee and Fort Gibson and held up a traveler near Fort Gibson, relieving him of nineteen dollars. The following day they robbed Ed Ayers, a Cherokee, of $120 on the road. The gang robbed the Missouri Pacific depot at Claremore on October 11, and within two hours the Katy Railroad agent at Chouteau was robbed. They wrecked and robbed the Kansas City and Memphis Express of the Missouri Pacific Railroad at Coretta.

Coretta was a blind siding five miles south of Wagoner. The robbery of the Missouri Pacific express which took place on Saturday night, October 20, was described by the *Daily Oklahoma* newspaper on October 23, 1894:

The train was going at a speed of about twenty-five miles per hour and within 100 feet of the switch, a man sprang from behind an embankment and threw the switch for the side track, running the train into a string of empty box cars. Engineer James Harris applied the air and reversed his engine, but did not have time to jump before the engine struck the cars on the siding. Two of the robbers ran to the engine and commanded Engineer Harris and Fireman Cottrell to come down, and as soon as they had dismounted, marched them to the baggage and express cars, where, by firing through the doors, they forced Messenger Ford to admit them. Meanwhile, two more of the robbers had taken up positions at the rear of the train to prevent anyone escaping through the rear doors of the sleeper, two more mounted the platform between the smoker and the baggage car and two more, the platform between the first and second coaches; all keeping up a continual firing. During this time, the two in the express car were ransacking it. They got all the money in the local safe and Messenger Ford's gun, and then commanded him to open the through safe. He told them it was impossible, and after hearing his explanation as to how it was locked, they left the express car.

The two robbers on the front platform started through the second coach demanding money and valuables. As soon as they reached the rear of the coach, the two men on that platform started through the second coach. When they were about half way through this car, a freight train following close behind whistled and Bill Cook, the leader who had all the time remained outside issuing commands, swearing at the passengers and shooting, called for all hands to come

46

out. The men on the cars jumped out, and when all were outside, fired a last volley at the train and disappeared in the darkness.

Jack Mahara, an advance agent for Mahara's Minstrel Company, was struck in the forehead by a bullet and seriously injured. Walter Barnes of Van Buren, Arkansas, was slightly injured by a piece of bullet striking him in the cheek . . . Special officers Helmick and Dickson of the Missouri Pacific were on the train, also Deputy Marshals Heck Bruner and Jose Casaver, but the attack was so sudden that they were all covered by Winchesters in the hands of the bandits before they had time to make a move. Casaver lost a watch and his six-shooter in the fracas . . . The train was backed to Wagoner for assistance and to give medical attention to the injured. The entire train was completely riddled with bullets, every window being broken and the engine cab shot to pieces, even the steam gauge and gauge pump, being shot away.
[The author will present evidence later that black outlaw Buss Luckey was possibly the leader of this train robbery, not Bill Cook.]

By this time, panic reigned in the northern half of Indian Territory, and Union agent Dew M. Widsom sent a wire to the Office of Indian Affairs in Washington as follows:

> My police force is not equal to the emergency, and Marshal Crump at Fort Smith writes that he has not the money to keep marshals in the field for a campaign. Affairs here are in a desperate condition; business is suspended, the people generally intimidated and private individuals robbed every day and night. I renew my recommendations and earnestly insist that the government, through the proper channel, take the manner in hand to protect its court and citizens of the United States, who are lawful residents of the territory. Licensed traders are especially suffering, and they are here under suspense. The state of siege must be broken and something done to save life and property.

Marshal Crump was summoned to Washington to give a full account of the operation of the gang. The attorney general pledged the government's full cooperation. The secretary of war threatened "to abrogate the treaties, abolish the tribal relations and establish a territorial government." The attorney general authorized the posting of the rewards for the capture of any or all of the gang, as did Chief J. C. Harris of the Cherokees.

Some of the early settlers who lived and worked in the area the Cook Gang operated in have related stories about Cherokee Bill and the gang. The aforementioned James W. Turley gave the following story about Cherokee Bill:

> At one time he rode up to where Jim and his father were walling up a well, got off his horse, and said to Jim, "You know you are liable to get shot?" Jim said, "What have you got it in for me for?" Crawford said, "I haven't got it in for you; I'd rather shoot anyone else than you. Your father is all right down in the well. There are posses over at your house, looking for me, and there is liable to be a shooting match here. If I could see to pick out Heck Bruner, I'd like to get him."
>
> He stood there motionless, and unafraid with his eyes on the deputies and their posse, until they left the house, and crossed Flat Rock Creek and were out of sight on their way toward Tulsa, whereupon he turned and asked Jim for food. Jim told him that he or anyone else was welcome to eat at the Turley home, so Cherokee Kid (Bill) got himself a sandwich and rode off toward the North, eating as he rode.

Ashley Guffey gave the following account about a surprise visit from Cherokee Bill:

> While we lived here, Cherokee Bill made us a visit, came one night and wanted to spend the night with us. Of course, we didn't refuse him. He was very courteous, and seemed to appreciate our hospitality. His reason for coming to our place, he explained, was that he was being chased by the U.S. Marshals, who had run him out of the Osage country, where, he said, he had been selling whiskey.

Burl Taylor, a black man who lived in the Creek Nation, had several encounters with Cherokee Bill; the first is another version of what occurred after the Fourteen Mile Creek fight:

> While I was working at the Nevins ferry, my horse strayed and I was out looking for it. I met Bob Elliott just west of Telephone ferry. He asked me where I was going, I told him I was looking for my horse; he then asked me to go with him and warn Cherokee Bill and Bill Cook that Bill Stout had gone to Muskogee to tell the U.S. marshal where they were hiding and he would help me find my horse. I asked him where they were hid and he pointed upon the hill where the school for the blind is located. And said, "See where those yellow slickers are spread over the bushes for shade? Well they are under them." We started in behind Bill Stout, when we got just north of the hill we turned south up the hill to where Cherokee and

48

Bill were. When we arrived, Cherokee said, "Come on under and cool off." Bob Elliot answered, "We don't have time." Then said, "See Bill Stout going yonder." Bill Cook answered, "Yes." Bob told him that Stout was on his way to Muskogee to tell the marshal where they were hiding. Cherokee said he could not believe it, every time he and Bill made a good haul, they always gave Stout a hand full of money and gave his wife a lot of money to cook meals for them.

Pretty soon we saw a dust cloud coming from Muskogee, it was not long until we counted thirteen in the marshals' posse. Bob and I went south across the hill after we got about even with the old Will Robinson place; Bob stopped and said, "Let's wait here and see the fun." The posse went on around the hill to Will Robinson's place and hid in the crib and barn. They told Mr. Robinson and his wife to go across the road to the Madden home so they would not get hurt. Cherokee and Bill Cook rode down toward the crib, a man in the crib fired at Cherokee and killed his horse. Cherokee grabbed his Winchester and stood up where his horse was shot, firing at the officers. Cook kept telling him to come on and they would get another horse; Cherokee answered that he would go as soon as he finished the round of shells in the Winchester. After he finished firing, he got on the horse behind Cook; they started south at a fast gait and Cherokee lost his hat in the strong wind. He jumped off the horse and started back after it. He had his Winchester gripped in both hands, raised over his head. He was running as fast as he could, letting out a loud whoopie and curses each step. The posse thought he was coming back after them, they all jumped on their horses and ran for it. Cherokee had a big laugh over it, they went on toward Coody Creek and met a man driving a horse and buggy.

Cherokee got off and taken the man's horse from the buggy and went back and got his saddle. Just a few days before this Jim Cook was captured at Bill Stout's place on the river. Jim had been wounded a few days before he was captured, he saw the officers coming and run from the house and hid in the brush. The officers combed the brush until they found him. I taken them across the river as they took him to the Fort Smith jail. They had to turn him free at Fort Smith because what he was charged with was not a federal offense and happened in the Cherokee Nation. That night Cherokee and Bill came to Muskogee and went to Captain Sever's place, located about where the Severs' hotel is now located. They then went to the barn and got two sorrel horses that belonged to Captain Severs. They were fine horses. They then went to the Stout home on the river to kill Bill Stout, but Bill was hiding out. They made several trips there looking for him. One night they slipped into the chicken-coop and stayed all night but Bill never did show up.

One day just before noon while I was working on the Nevins ferry, I was bringing the ferry from the east landing. I heard someone calling me, looking around I saw a group of men on horse-back on the little strip of land running to a point between the Verdigris and Grand rivers. They wanted me to come over after them, which I did. It was Cherokee Bill, Jim and Bill Cook, Jim French, Sam McWilliams, who was known as the Verdigris Kid, Texas Jack and Skeeter.

Just as we landed for them to get on the ferry, twenty-five U.S. marshals rode up on the west bank of the Arkansas River where Hyde Park is now located. The outlaws asked me who they were and I told them it was a marshal's posse. The outlaws tried to get us to take them over to where the posse was but we told them we were afraid to do it. That when the shooting started we would be killed, they said alright then to take them to the east bank on the Fort Gibson landing. As soon as we landed them the posse began shouting for us to come over and get them, when we got there they wanted to know who the men were that we had ferried across. I told them who they were, they told me they did not want any foolishness, they went into a huddle a distance to where I could not hear what they were saying; then they came back and asked me if I was sure it was who I had told them it was. I told them it was and they went into another huddle, then came back to me and wanted to know how to get to the Rabbit Ford and how far it was. I told them (they knew as well as I did). The outlaws had been in hiding across the river, when the posse left, Cherokee came out and motioned for me to come over. When I got there they were waiting for me and asked, what the damn laws had to say; I told them what the posse was going to do. As the posse had further to go, Cherokee said, "Thanks, we will be there to meet them." Just as they left, Jeff Nevins called me back to the other side, when I got there Jeff asked me what was going on. When I finished telling him he said, "Let's saddle the horses and go see the fun." We got our horses and went down the bank of the river on the west side.

We got to where we could see the ford real good and stopped and waited, it was not long until we saw the outlaws ride around the Rogers' home and hide. Pretty soon the posse rode into the river, stopped and let their horses drink. After they finished drinking, the posse started on across the river, just as they got started good, the outlaws all started to running their horses into the river and firing their Winchesters at the posse. The posse did not fire a shot but turned their horses and made a run for it; I never saw a bunch run as fast as they did, they did not come back after the outlaws another time.

50

I saw a gun battle between a posse and Cherokee Bill, Sam McWilliams, and Texas Jack. This happened at my half-brother's house, whose name was Frank Daniels. He lived on Caney River about five miles from Ramona. Deputy U.S. Marshal Heck Thomas, out of Fort Smith with sixteen deputized in his posse, came to Frank's home and told him that Cherokee Bill, Sam and Texas Jack were coming there, (don't know how they knew of their coming) and that Frank, his wife and I had better go somewhere as there was going to be plenty shooting and we might get hit. Frank told him that we could just go to the cellar, that it was safe there, it was a big two-story log house with a big cellar, there were several out-buildings also built of log. They hid the horses and stationed themselves in the house and out-buildings. It was not long until Cherokee and his friends showed up; they rode to the horse-lot, just as they got to the gate one of the posse outside got excited and fired at them, just hit the edge of Cherokee's leg, killing his horse. When the possemen fired this shot, they all began firing at the outlaws; Texas Jack's horse was hit but not killed.

Texas Jack made a break for the timber and never did show up anymore. When Cherokee's horse was shot from under him, he got his Winchester and stood there in the wide-open pumping shots from his Winchester at the possemen. Sam McWilliams' horse was shot down and Sam was shot through the leg but not bad. He lost his Winchester when his horse was shot down; he crawled around in the high grass until he found it, then came to Cherokee's side, raised up and began firing — helping Cherokee out. Cherokee told Sam that he just had one more shot left in his gun and that there was a damn Law kept sticking his foot around the corner of the smoke-house and he was going to get it the next time he stuck it out, and then they would make a run for it. Sure enough, the fellow stuck his boot out again and Cherokee made a good hit. The fellow let out a cry and started hobbling toward the house, when he did this, Sam shot at him three times, knocking him down with the last shot but did not kill him. Cherokee and Sam then made a run for the timber, the way the bullets were hitting the dust around them as they crossed the road; we were looking for them to be shot down any minute, but they made it safely. The posse was afraid to go in the woods after them.

After the posse left, Cherokee and Sam came back to the house and got their saddles and bridles, borrowed two horses from Frank, went about two miles and roped two horses from a pasture belonging to a neighbor of Frank's and brought his horses back. We asked what became of Texas Jack, they told us that they had a pretty good bunch

51

of money and it was in Jack's saddle bags, and they told him to beat it with the money.

Clarence O. Warren, a white resident of the Creek Nation, gave an account of how the Cook brothers and Cherokee Bill got their ammunition:

> And something else about the Cook Bros. and Cherokee Bill. They of necessity had to have ammunition, a lot of it, guns and shells, sometimes they had money and sometimes they didn't, but they had a way of getting the ammunition which worked if they were out of funds. As I said, my uncle Jim Kgan, had a store at Sapulpa. The manager of this store was another uncle of mine, Bert Gray. He said it was he who sold ammunition to these outlaws. They would come in usually when my uncle was alone and tell him what they wanted and how much. So, of course, they got it, and on short order, for he was anxious to get rid of them as soon as possible. But they always asked how much the bill was, and for my uncle to keep account of it for they would return later and pay it; and the unusual thing about it, they always slipped in when they had money and paid their bill.
>
> Well, later, I think it was after the capture of Cherokee Bill, and during his trial at Fort Smith, that the question of where and how they got their guns and ammunition came up. This led to an investigation and it was found that they bought it at Sapulpa, and at the Kgan store. So, Bert Gray, being manager of the store was summoned to appear at Fort Smith, by Judge Parker, the Federal Judge of that district, as a witness, and to tell just what he knew about the matter. Well, he related to the court the story as told here and wound up by saying, "Judge when fellows like that come in and put their six shooters on you, that makes their credit mighty good with me." This created quite a lot of laughing and seemed to be a good explanation as to how and why the Kgan store sold them ammunition. It seemed anybody, especially the Cook Brothers and Cherokee Bill, could open an account with six shooters.

For women, Cherokee Bill seemed to have had irresistible charm. He was said to have a sweetheart in nearly every section of the territory. He was often protected from harm by loyal friends and a violent reputation. Lawmen who pursued him, hearing of his fast six-shooter action, kept a safe distance and many times avoided engaging in battle. Because he was on good terms with Cherokees, Creeks, and Seminoles, he moved easily through their villages and lands, something his pursuers could not do.

52

From the time Cherokee Bill joined the Cook brothers, he acted as though he was destined to die in two years and wanted to kill as many men as he could. Some of the other fugitives who allied themselves to the Cook Gang that summer of 1894 were killed in desperate fights with deputy marshals; others were captured and given penitentiary sentences.

The robbery at Chandler of the Lincoln County Bank on July 31 was Bill's first bank job. In the course of the robbery, he shot to death a barber named J. M. Mitchell. It was also assumed that Cherokee Bill was the killer of posseman Sequoyah Houston at the Fourteen Mile Creek fight. Also in the course of robbing a train, Cherokee Bill murdered a Missouri Pacific conductor named Sam Collins, when he insisted Bill pay his fare or get off the train. Not seeing eye to eye with the Cook brothers, he pulled a few jobs on his own. Cherokee, with three men, their identity unknown, held up the Missouri Pacific Iron Mountain depot at Nowata. During the holdup Cherokee Bill shot and killed the station agent Dick Richards for no cause or reason whatsoever. All of his crimes are not notated; the number of his reported or purported killings ranges from seven to thirteen, the lower figure probably being more accurate.

One of the most talked about killings by Cherokee Bill was that of his brother-in-law. His sister, Georgia Goldsby, had married Mose Brown, who, as stated earlier, couldn't get along with Cherokee at all. Most historians have his name as George, but his daughter said his name was Mose. Most historians also state Cherokee killed him in 1894 over an argument about some hogs. Cherokee Bill's niece gave the following story of what happened between her father and uncle:

> . . . Shortly after this trouble, and Crawford had returned to the home place where he was staying, he wrote to my mother asking her to come to see him, which was only natural as she was his only sister and closest advisor. Father learned of her intended trip to see Crawford and objected to her going, and when he saw he could not prevent her from going he told her he was going with her. Mother tried to persuade him not to go and told him, "You know that you always mistreated Crawford and was the cause of him leaving that home once, and he told you that he would kill you some day if you didn't leave him alone, and you had best not go about him or molest him again."
>
> However, when Mother went aboard the train at Fort Gibson, Father also boarded the same train at another place without Mother knowing of his presence on the train. When she got off the train at

Nowata where she was to take livery conveyance out to the place, to her surprise there stood Father on the station platform. Mother again tried to persuade him not to go out to the farm, or about Crawford, but he was determined and got into the buggy with Mother and went on out to the farm with Mother. Upon their arrival at Crawford's place, Crawford asked him why he came, and during the altercation that followed, Crawford shot and killed my father. That sad occurrence happened in September, 1894, when I was only nine months old. Shortly after the death of my father, I was taken into the home and care of my grandmother, Ellen Lynch, at Fort Gibson where I was reared.

The crime which finally led to Cherokee's incarceration, and for which he died on the gallows, was committed November 8, 1894. On that date, Lenapah, a little town on the Kansas & Arkansas Valley Railroad, later to become the Missouri Pacific, was the scene of the criminal act which cost Cherokee Bill his life. The town, located twenty-four miles south of Coffeyville, Kansas, and just north of Nowata, Oklahoma, is a historical place in the annals of the Indian Territory, as it was the scene of one of the first "holdups" committed by the Indian outlaw Henry Starr. It was near here, also, that Starr killed U.S. Deputy Marshal Floyd Wilson in 1892. At that time the principal store in Lenapah was operated by Schufeldt & Son. John Schufeldt, the junior member of the firm, was also postmaster. Just before noon, on the day noted, two men rode rapidly into Lenapah, from the south, but attracted little attention as their appearance differed little from the hundreds of cowboys who came there to trade. The general consensus is that the two men were Cherokee Bill and Sam McWilliams, alias the "Verdigris Kid." As soon as they dismounted they brought their Winchesters to bear upon the men in the store and commanded, "Hands up." At this point Bill entered the store, while the other remained outside on guard and fired an occasional volley up and down the street to warn the citizens to keep a safe distance. Cherokee Bill's first act, after entering the store, was to march John Schufeldt back to the safe, which he ordered him to open. Quickly securing all the cash contents, Bill started for the front when he saw the clothing on display in the rear room of the store, as well as a rack of guns and a shelf of ammunition. He decided that this was an excellent opportunity to replenish his wardrobe and pick up a supply of cartridges. Rifle in hand, he forced young Schufeldt into the rear room and made him lay out the articles he wanted. Schufeldt was no fool. He knew with whom he was dealing and he did as he was told.

There was a narrow vacant lot between the Schufeldt store and the restaurant next door, the interior of which was being wallpapered. A man by the name of Ernest Melton was doing the work along with several others. When they heard the shots fired by the outlaws, all rushed to the windows to see what the noise was about.

Cherokee Bill flicked a glance at the window and saw Melton staring at him. Enraged at the painter's audacity in spying on him, he threw his rifle to his shoulder and slapped a shot at Melton that pierced his brain and killed him instantly. After the crime, the outlaws rode rapidly out of town in the direction from which they had come.

During the next two months, the section of country about Lenapah and south into the Creek Nation was scoured by deputy United States marshals in search of the one desperado who, in spite of his youth, was more generally feared than any other in the Indian country. He could shoot faster than two ordinary men and few marshals had the bravery to attempt a capture, but when a reward of $1,300 was offered for him, "dead or alive," soon after the Lenapah murder, it motivated some of the deputy marshals to go one step further.

Melton's murder marked the beginning of the end of the Cook outlaws. The search for them became so fierce, they were forced to separate. Elmer Lucas was captured in a bank robbery at Chandler, Oklahoma Territory. Lon Gordon and Henry Munson were shot and killed and Curtis Dayson captured as they fled from a farmhouse in the Creek Nation near Sapulpa; Thurman Baldwin, Jess Snyder, and Bill Farris were captured by Texas Rangers in Clay County near Wichita Falls; Sam McWilliams, the Verdigris Kid, was slain by Indian deputy sheriffs at Braggs, a small town on the railroad nine miles east of Fort Gibson; and Jim French was killed by a night watchman while burglarizing a store at Catoosa. Cook was finally captured January 11, 1895, on an isolated cattle ranch southeast of Fort Sumner, New Mexico, where Pat Garrett had killed another famous outlaw, Billy the Kid. Sheriff C. C. Perry, of Chares County, and two deputies surprised him in a sod house and took him without a fight. On January 17, he was arraigned before Judge Parker. He was indicted on twelve counts of armed robbery, convicted of ten, and sentenced to forty-five years in the penitentiary at Albany. Lucas, Dayson, Baldwin, Snyder, and Farris drew ten- to thirty-year terms in prison at Detroit. Buss Luckey, another confederate, would be brought to trial later for killing a U.S. deputy marshal.

Two of Parker's deputies, W. C. Smith and George Lawson, working out of Sapulpa, combed that country for two weeks without cutting Bill's trail. However, they made a proposal to a Cherokee half-blood named Charles Patton, a Verdigris River native who was personally acquainted with Cherokee Bill. If he could locate Bill and get word to them in Sapulpa, they would split the reward money. Patton was agreeable to such an arrangement. He found Bill and the "Verdigris Kid" skulking about the hills and stayed with them from 3:00 in the afternoon until 9:00 at night. Had they imagined Patton to be a spy, Bill would doubtless have added another to his long list of victims. During this visit Bill told Patton that he had secured $164 "in a little holdup at Lenapah and had to shoot a fellow." Before he left them the "kid" gave Patton a locket which Bill took from John Schufeldt on the day of the murder, telling him to be careful or it might get him into trouble. Patton met Smith and Lawson at Sapulpa that night and turned over the locket and the information he had gained. He was a witness against Cherokee Bill at the trial and his testimony, together with the locket, which was admitted in evidence, was the most interesting of any produced by the government.

A posse that included U.S. Deputy Marshal John McGill was hurriedly organized and left for Cherokee Bill's hideout. The posse exchanged quite a number of shots with him. In the fusillade, his horse was killed but Cherokee was able to escape into the dense willow brakes. This gun battle may be the same one that Burl Taylor witnessed at his half brother's home on Caney River.

The citizens of Lenapah were really shaken up by the murder of Melton. A local newspaper reported that the Lenapah village council passed an ordinance which granted Cherokee Bill the privilege of coming and going there whenever he desired, and guaranteed him protection from molestation. This recognition of an outlaw has to be one of the most unusual in the history of the American West. But it is also a good measure of how much this man was feared in the territory.

Deputy U.S. Marshal W. C. Smith learned from a black man named Clint Scales, who sometimes worked as a handyman, that Cherokee Bill was in the habit of meeting his girlfriend, Maggie Glass, who was black, mixed with Cherokee, at the cabin of Ike Rogers, five miles east of Nowata. Soon after the Lenapah tragedy, Cherokee Bill had attended a dance at Rogers's home, and during the night he had told Ben

Vann, a black, that he did not mean to shoot the man at Lenapah, but that he shot to scare him. This incident was considered important evidence at the trial.

Ike Rogers was an African-American with some Cherokee blood; his family were Cherokee Freedmen. It is said that the family had taken the name Rogers from Will Rogers's father, Clement Vann Rogers. Rogers held a deputy marshal's commission, under U.S. Marshal Crump. He was sometimes seen in the company of the legendary black U.S. Deputy Marshal Bass Reeves, but his reputation was bad and he was not very effective as a deputy marshal.

Deputy Smith was reasonably sure that Ike would do anything for money. The proposition he made him was that he (Rogers) was to invite the girl to spend a few days with him and his wife and then get word to Cherokee Bill that she was there. Scales was to be watching the cabin, and when he saw Bill arrive, he was to drop in casually and spend the night. They were to catch Cherokee Bill off guard and capture him, in return for which Ike Rogers and Scales were each to get a third of the reward money. Maggie Glass, who was the niece of Ike Rogers's wife, would be the unsuspecting bait to trap Bill. She readily consented to the visit that was arranged by her uncle.

On Tuesday afternoon, January 29, 1895, Rogers saw Bill ride towards the house of a man named Jackson, and he sent his boy to tell Bill he wanted to see him. Shortly after dark the outlaw came to Rogers's house, dismounted, and entered. Several hours after he arrived, Clint Scales put in an appearance. Not one moment elapsed that the outlaw was not on his guard, prepared to use his Winchester. Maggie, also, was suspicious of Rogers, and she warned Bill to leave, but Bill refused to run away, telling the girl he would show Rogers how long it would take him to commit murder, his plan being to let Rogers make the first break, then shoot him in his tracks.

Rogers, in turn, was acting the part of the generous host; he watched for an opportunity to strike a deadly blow that would give him part of the promised reward. He treated the outlaw with the greatest kindness and managed to gain his confidence somewhat and urged him to stay all night. Once he suggested that the outlaw lay down his Winchester. "That's something I never do," replied the desperado. Next, Rogers offered him some whiskey doctored with morphine which he obtained from Smith, but Cherokee Bill refused to drink.

According to Rogers's account, Bill and Maggie were alone for some time before supper. When all sat down to the table, Bill kept his rifle on his lap. Supper over, the three men played cards for small stakes. Bill sat with his back to the wall. While the game was in progress, Rogers watched for an opportunity to overpower him, but Cherokee was observant of every movement. The weapons of the would-be captors were necessarily kept from sight as they didn't want to give Bill an excuse for a fight. Maggie grew weary of waiting for her lover and went to bed with Mrs. Rogers, her aunt.

The men played cards until 4:00 A.M. For hours, Scales and Rogers had been watching Cherokee Bill like hawks, but hunted animal that he was, he watched them just as warily, as though he knew what was on their minds. When they were ready to turn in, Scales bedded down on the floor and Cherokee Bill got into bed with Rogers, his rifle on the blanket at his side. Rogers lay awake for some time, hoping to catch Cherokee asleep, but whenever he would move the other would instantly rise in bed, ready to use his Winchester.

At breakfast time it began to appear as if the game would surely escape. After eating, Mr. Rogers sent Maggie to a neighbor's, a quarter of a mile away, to buy a couple of chickens. The day was cold; it was January but there was no snow on the ground. From what followed, it would appear that it made no difference whether Maggie was in the cabin or ten miles away; she had innocently served her purpose and there was nothing further she could do.

The following is testimony given by Rogers to Frank Weaver, court reporter for the weekly *Fort Smith Elevator*:

I had been instructed by Colonel Crump to get him alive, if possible, and I didn't want to kill him if I couldn't get him in any other way. Scales and I had our guns hidden where we could get them in a hurry but we didn't want to give them any show to fight. After breakfast, we talked along for some time and he began to talk of leaving. He and Scales and I sat in front of the open fireplace. I knowed that we had to make a break on him pretty soon and I was afraid the girl would take a hand in it when the trouble began, so I gave her a dollar to buy some chickens at a neighbor's so as to get her out of the way. I also sent my boys away as I had not told them of my plans. Bill finally took a notion that he wanted to smoke and he took some paper and tobacco from his pocket and rolled a cigarette. He had no match, so he stooped over towards the fireplace, to light it, and turned his head away from me for an instant. That was my chance and I took it. There was a fire stick lying on the floor near me and I grabbed it up and struck him across the back of the head. I must have hit him hard enough to kill an ordinary man but it only knocked him down. Scales and I then jumped on him but he let one yell and got on his feet. My wife grabbed Bill's Winchester and we three tussled on the floor, full twenty minutes. I thought once I would have to kill him, his great strength, with his 180 pounds weight, being too much for me and Scales, but finally we got a pair of handcuffs onto him. He then pleaded and begged me to kill him or release him. He promised me money and horses, all I wanted. Then he cursed. We put him in a wagon and Scales rode with him and I went on horseback, and started for Nowata. On the way Cherokee broke his handcuffs and grabbed at Scales' gun and Scales had to fall out of the wagon to keep from losing his Winchester, while I kept Cherokee covered with my shotgun. At Nowata, we turned him over to Bill Smith and George Lawson.

In accordance with the prearrangements, Deputy Marshals Smith and Lawson had, on January 29, gone to Nowata to await the coming of Rogers and Scales, with their prisoner.

At Nowata, Deputies Smith and Lawson took charge of the prisoner and by that night had landed Bill behind the bars of the federal jail in Fort Smith. Cherokee Bill came up for arraignment before Judge Parker, charged with the murder of Ernest Melton. Bill's mother had retained J. Warren Reed, the most famous trial lawyer in Fort Smith. It is believed Reed took the case because he had a running feud with Parker. The trial was certain to attract tremendous attention, perhaps more than any other heard by the Fort Smith court, which it did. With the evidence against the notorious outlaw so strong, Reed undoubtedly expected Parker to run roughshod over the defendant's legal rights. Sufficiently pushed, he might overstep the rules of jurisprudence flagrantly enough to convince the U.S. Supreme Court that a fair trial could not be had in the Fort Smith court, which Reed had been contending for years.

The trial became an endless series of clashes between defense counsel and the bench. Bullied, exasperated beyond endurance, Parker laid down some rules of his own; limiting the cross examination of witnesses by both the prosecution and the defense and refusing to grant Reed the delays he insisted he must have to call up additional witnesses. Those he put on the stand were "alibi" witnesses, who swore they had seen Cherokee Bill fifty miles south of Lenapah on the day Melton was murdered. The prosecution produced seven, including John Schufeldt, who positively identified Cherokee Bill as Melton's slayer. The jury was out only a few minutes and returned with a verdict of guilty.

When the verdict was read, Cherokee Bill simply smiled. But his mother and sister, who were with him in the courtroom throughout the trial, wept loudly. "What's the matter with you two?" he snapped. "I ain't dead yet." And that afternoon, at the federal jail, Cherokee Bill "was engaged in a game of poker with Bill Cook (who had been captured earlier in New Mexico) and several kindred spirits as if nothing had happened."

Immediately after the conviction, his attorney, Mr. Reed, made application for a new trial, but the motion was overlooked. On April 13 Cherokee Bill was taken to the court for sentence; June 25 was set for the day of his execution. An appeal to the Supreme Court resulted in the finding of the lower court being affirmed, and he was resentenced. March 17, 1896, was then named as the day which would end his earthly career.

Back in jail, he became morose and unruly. The lower floor where the condemned were kept was called "Murderer's Row." Cherokee Bill's conduct affected the other prisoners, with whom he was allowed to mingle during the day. Bill Cook, while en route to Albany Prison on May 2, expressed the opinion that "no bars can hold Cherokee."

J. E. Kelly, the founder of Kellyville, Oklahoma, formerly in the Creek Nation, was the postmaster and store owner. Mr. Kelly spent a portion of his early life on the frontier and was a cowboy in the 1870s, in Wyoming and Nebraska. He knew the Cooks and Cherokee Bill intimately, long before they became outlaws. He visited Cherokee Bill in the jail at Fort Smith and described an incident that showed Bill's agility and love of the gun:

> Cherokee Bill was game as a hornet, and a true friend but a bitter enemy. He was quick and active and always wide awake. He was not shamming, he was an outlaw in good earnest. I saw him at Fort Smith shortly after his arrest. George Lawson, who figured in his arrest, asked me up to the jail to see him. He brought Bill out to have his photograph taken. Bill was "hot" and was crying with madness when he appeared. Lawson said, "Bill, quit your crying; here is Kelly who has come to see you; why don't you ask him about some of your old friends?" Bill, who up to this time had not raised his eyes, looked up quickly, and as he saw me he smiled through his tears and grabbing my hand exclaimed, "Hello, old friend! I never thought you would see me down here. I thought you might see me

60

all shot to —, but I never thought you would see me here." He was handed a beautiful Winchester, the property of Post-office inspector Houk, and was asked to pose for his picture. The gun was empty. Bill's eyes snapped with the old time fire; he took a position as if he had been surprised; he brought the gun into position and every nerve seemed on the alert. Oh! how he would have loved to be out in the jail yard with the gun full of cartridges. After the photographer had finished, Bill fondled the gun and asked several questions about it; he seemed loath to give it up, and before returning it he worked the lever and the trigger until it clicked like a sewing machine. It was the wonder of all the deputy marshals, how he could shoot so fast. Bill said he knew his rapid firing was not always accurate, and he might not always hit the target, but he would shoot so — fast that he would "rattle" his antagonist "so he could not hit me."

When June 25, 1895, arrived, the day first named as Cherokee's execution day, his appeal was still in the hands of the Supreme Court, and Judge Parker issued a stay of execution to give the Supreme Court time to act. This in turn would give Bill an opportunity to plan and plot his escape from that "hell hole" called a jail.

Outlaw Henry Starr would unknowingly play a major role in Cherokee Bill's attempted jailbreak.

CHAPTER 5

Henry Starr:
Star Bandit

Before Cherokee Bill arrived in the Fort Smith jail, Henry Starr had preceded him there. Starr, born December 2, 1873, at Fort Gibson, was a son of Hop Starr, a half-blood Cherokee. His mother was only a quarter-blood, which made Henry more white than Indian, although Henry always felt more Indian than white. His grandfather was Tom Starr, the infamous Cherokee outlaw who terrorized the Indian Territory prior to the Civil War. His uncle was Sam Starr, who married the famous Belle Starr of Indian Territory legend.

Like all the young Indians in the feudist Starr clan, which was led by the fierce old patriarch Tom Starr, Henry Starr learned early to be an expert with weapons. He did not use liquor, tobacco, tea, or coffee, and he had an Indian's agility and endurance. He also had an Indian's ability to find his way through a wilderness — live on roots, berries, nuts, and game — and could become independent of ordinary food sources and correspondingly hard to locate.

As early as June 1891, he was fined for "introducing liquor into the Indian Territory," and the following year, in February 1892, he was arrested on a charge of horse stealing, but was released.

Henry described the first incident this way:

> I got a job close by herding some fine steers on the Open A.

One day I went to Nowata, and a man I had known for four or five years was on his way to the Delaware Indian payment a few miles distant and asked me to take his grip over to the payment grounds. He had come over horseback and I was in a buggy, and pleased to be of any slight service to him, so I put the grip in and started.

About two miles out, two deputy marshals overtook me and commanded with drawn guns that I get down from the buggy and allow them to search it. I readily complied, and to my surprise and consternation, the grip contained two pints of whiskey. I told them that I had no knowledge of the grip's contents, also that I did not drink.

"So," said one of them, "then you must have intended to sell it, and that makes the charge against you more serious."

It was a penitentiary offense at that time to sell liquor in the Indian Territory. I did not inform on the owner of the grip, for I was satisfied that it would not help me. I knew that those scheming officers were stuck to make fees out of my bad luck. A United States court (the first white man's court in the Indian Territory) covering whiskey and misdemeanors had been established at Muskogee the year before (1889), and they took me there. That night, I, an innocent man, felt the murder-breeding leg-irons and chains.

The man I was working for immediately signed my bond and took me back with them. They knew I was innocent, but advised me to plead guilty, pay a fine and have it over with, instead of fighting a long-drawn-out trial, with no witness to help me. When my case was called about two months later, I made a plea of "guilty." One of the deputy marshals, on being questioned by the judge, had manhood enough to say that he didn't think I was a whiskey peddler. He didn't believe that I knew anything about the whiskey being in the grip. The judge fined me $100, a stiff penalty for the offense of introducing. I paid the amount and returned to Nowata, sad at heart.

Though my friends all knew I was innocent, it did not remove the reflection from my character. I was lowered and cheapened in my own estimation. There was a tribal penitentiary at Tahlequah, the Cherokee capital. The convicts sent there by the council wore stripes, and as a child, the sight of them filled me with terror. My father and mother had brought me up to think it was an awful thing to be arrested. I felt doubly disgraced, being placed in jail and chained to a bed at the same time, and I was only a kid.

The second bad experience Henry had was his arrest for horse theft. By 1891, he had become proficient as a cowboy and developed an uncanny dexterity with a lasso, as well as adding more skill to his horsemanship. He was five feet, nine inches tall, of strong athletic

63

build, with straight black hair. His Indian features were very strong. Henry described what happened with his second run-in with the law:

While working for the Roberts' boys, two strange horses drifted into a pocket formed by two farms and a pasture joining them. As there was no water in this pocket, it was plain that they were runaways. The boys said for the first one who rode that way to let them into the gate to water, as no doubt someone would be on the hunt for them. I let them in and, not noticing that one of them bore saddle marks, I rode him several times. I also informed other ranchers that he was a stray. In something like a month, Charles Eaton, his owner, came after him, and seemed pleased to find him in such good condition, even offering to pay me for my trouble. This was in October, '91, and in December, the same year, while I was in Nowata, a vicious-looking fellow, who said he was a Deputy United States Marshal, read a writ charging me with the larceny of Eaton's horse . . . The warrant had been sworn out by Charles Eaton, the same fellow that had been so profuse in his thanks for the care I took of his horse, and that simply stunned me, nor do I know this day what made him prefer the charge, as he swore the truth later.

Being imprisoned at the Fort Smith jail for something he didn't do made Starr a very bitter person. He gained a peculiar dislike for the established judicial system in the Indian Territory. In the thirty years that followed, Starr had more bank holdups to his credit than the James-Younger and Dalton-Doolin gangs combined! In 1914, Henry was taken with an idea. The automobile, he had seen, could certainly outdistance any posse on horseback. He purchased one and used it in his next bank job, becoming the first American criminal to employ a car in a robbery. After he robbed the bank in Harrison, Arkansas, in 1921, Henry Starr's car broke down on a dusty road. A sheriff's posse, riding a string of cars, caught up to him and he was critically wounded in a wild gun battle. Henry seemed proud of his record. The day before he died, he boasted to his doctors at Harrison: "I've robbed more banks than any man in America."

Henry was courteous, acquired before his end an education which gave him an almost cultured conversational grace, liked to read good literature, and was a pleasant companion. Throughout his life he displayed a remarkable ability to make friends and keep their friendship.

Starr had tried to explain to newspaper reporters why he had become an outlaw and what the atmosphere was like in the Indian Territory. He told the *Wichita {Kansas} Eagle* in 1921:

. . . it all came as a natural consequence — as natural the moon following the sun. I was born as other men. I do not recall that there were any violent upheavals of earthly nature at the time, and of all those who remember the occurrence not one that I have plied but stoutly avers there was no unusual activity in the heavens. My early years were filled with such training and precept as a good mother will always give any only son. My sisters did their part, and right well it was done. Still, my surroundings, the very air I breathed, whispered of deeds of daring and peril and constantly called to me. I had the blood of Cherokee chiefs in my veins. Tom Starr, my ancestor, was one to conjure with in all tales of freebooting and lawlessness. In the '50s and '60s, he was known far and wide as the devil's own. In all matters where law and order was one side, Tom Starr was on the other, and his path of action lay along that scope of country where the Missouri line interfered with the Cherokee lands and stretched away south to the Red River. From my childhood, I was wont to hear the tales of his prowess and daring, how he was the one man with whom the government had made a treaty of peace, and my blood was fired and went chasing through my veins, burning and scorching me with the admiration of the thing. But even yet I do not think I had a desire to follow in his steps, though the freedom of the prairies and mountains were constantly beckoning me to the free and independent life of the road.

This much I tell you in the beginning, not as a matter of justification, for of that I make no search, but that you may better understand and weigh what followed. To you who live in the marts of the East or more thickly settled sections, it is a language that tells you nothing. Your perspective is limited to your door-yard fence — to your fields at most; ours to a distance a horse might travel in a day with a rider up, whose nostrils take in the freedom of the plains and expand in the exultation of his manhood. To me, a child of the forest and stream, it was constantly singing me a song sweeter than everything else, appealing hard and strong to my wild, rebellious heart. There was constantly visions of the wildness, the living of it all, and it took hold of me, and always I was conscious of a never ceasing warfare against it. You are prescribed in your action by the laws of your king, while we — well, it had never come to us in that way yet.

It was God overhead and nothing around. The world, our world, was ours and none to dispute. You must understand that our reservation at the time was inhabited by ourselves and there were few of our white-faced friends therein. Two railways belted our broad prairies — these, and an occasional settlement, were the only forerunners of the teeming civilization you see today. We had been taught that it was ours, to have and to hold so long as grass grew and

65

water ran, ours to hunt on, ours in which to follow in the footsteps of our fathers, to do with as we wished. That was the spirit that possessed us as a people. And certainly a small enough land it was, and is, of all the country inheritance had given us.

In his autobiography, Henry Starr explained even more about his bitterness growing up in prestatehood Oklahoma:

I had always looked upon the Indian as supreme and the white renters as trash who moved from year to year in covered wagons with many dogs and tow-headed kids peeping out from behind every wagon-bow, and who, at the very best, made only a starving crop. The Indian landowner was looked up to by his white renters, and always treated with courtesy and respect. But the years have brought about a change; the white man holds power, and the same hypocritical renter had grown arrogant and insulting; whenever the Indian, and especially the full-blood in Oklahoma, is an outcast in his own country, and it is with a feeling of sadness and apprehension that I think of his future. Broken treaties, misplaced confidence and insult have made him lose interest in life. I have more white blood than Indian, and with my knowledge of both races, I fervently wish that every drop in my veins was red!

After his first two brushes with the law, Starr found a friend in Albert Dodge, a rancher living near Nowata, who gave him a job as a cowboy. Starr was a good enough cow hand, until 1892, when he was again arrested for horse theft. This time he was released on bond, furnished by his cousin Kale Starr and J. C. Harris, the tribal chief of the Cherokees.

The same day his case was called in Fort Smith, Henry was deep in the Osage country. With some other shady characters, Henry executed robberies in the Cherokee Nation and was now seriously "on the scout." He quickly obtained a reputation as a young upstart in the outlaw country.

When Starr failed to appear for his trial at Fort Smith, his bondsmen, upset under the forfeiture of $2,000, offered a reward for his capture. At the same time, Stephen Wheeler, U.S. commissioner for the western district of Arkansas, issued a warrant for his arrest. The warrant was delivered to Henry C. Dickey for execution. Dickey, the express company detective investigating the Nowata robbery, of which Starr was a suspect, obtained a commission for Floyd Wilson as his posse. The pair set out to hunt for the youthful bandit.

66

On December 12, 1892, Dickey and Wilson picked up Starr's trail near Lenapah. They proceeded south by rail, and just at dusk arrived at Mr. Dodge's "XU" ranch, eight miles from Nowata, where it had been reported the gang was rendezvoused. Dodge denied the gang was personally known by him, but admitted he had seen Starr ride past his place several times. On being apprised of the outlaw's presence, the officers mounted their horses and scoured the country, continuing their search until after midnight. The following day, as they sat at dinner with the ranchman's family, Dodge galloped in from attending affairs on the ranch and informed them he had just seen Starr ride past again. Wilson rushed to the stable, mounted the horse, already saddled and bridled, on which Dodge had just returned, and started in the direction the ranchman had sighted the outlaw. Dickey, forced to obtain a fresh mount, was delayed several minutes, and Wilson pressed on ahead of the detective to take the fugitive alone. Wilson had obtained his gung-ho spirit from earlier serving as a U.S. deputy marshal. He came upon Starr in an opening on Wolf Creek.

The two men sighted each other the same instant, and Starr dropped from his saddle, rifle ready. Wilson halted and faced his quarry only thirty yards away, Winchester in his hands. He ordered Starr to surrender, and the outlaw tried to "work away" from the officer.

"Hold up; I have a warrant for you!" ordered Wilson, and rode up to within twenty-five or thirty feet of Starr.

"You hold up!" called Starr, who made no further effort to flee.

Wilson then sprang from his horse, threw his rifle to his shoulder, and fired over the outlaw's head to frighten him.

Starr had been standing with his gun in both hands, holding the muzzle down, but, upon Wilson's shooting, returned the fire and continued to fire rapidly. Wilson fell, badly wounded. As he levered for a fresh cartridge, the empty shell jammed in his rifle. Throwing down the weapon, he reached for his revolver, and Starr fired two more shots. Wilson sank back on the ground. As he lay there, too weak to lift the six-shooter he had drawn, the outlaw calmly strode forward and fired another bullet into his heart, holding the gun so close that the blaze spouting from its muzzle scorched the officer's clothing.

The shooting frightened away their horses, but Starr managed to catch Wilson's. Detective Dickey, meanwhile, had failed to reach his companion. The fresh horse saddled for him by Dodge had objected to a strange rider and "bucked badly, preventing the officer's arrival at the place of battle until too late." Starr mounted and leisurely rode away to safety. Dickey brought Wilson's body into Lenapah and from there took it by passenger train to Coffeyville.

On his run from the law, Henry had two close calls with black Deputy U.S. Marshals Ike Rogers and Rufus Cannon. In his first encounter Henry said he spared the life of both deputies:

> I had met my mother and sister by appointment at the home of J. O. Morrison, on the prairie nine miles northwest of Nowata, and I heard afterwards my treacherous stepfather had told the deputies to get me. As they approached the house, I was undetermined what to do. At that time I was paying attention to Mr. Morrison's daughter, May, and in her presence I would not run. Perish forever the thought! There were several ladies present, and they pleaded with me not to kill the officers. "Ladies," I replied, "it is not a question of my killing them but of keeping them from killing me!" I kept out of sight in the hall at the head of the stairs with my rifle drawn, and could have killed them as easy as shooting two rabbits had I so desired. Both knew I was in the house, for they had discovered my well known horse tied in the barn, but at the time each assured the other that I was not any place around. As they started off, I watched them from the window. Roger's hat blew off as he passed the window, and he looked up, but I had covered and he only pulled his hat over his eyes and went on without looking back. They made no attempt at my arrest, and I could tell by their action that they did not want me very bad.

On the next occasion it was a different story, when Starr, with pals Ed Newcome and Jesse Jackson, ran into Rogers and Cannon later that winter. On the evening of January 20, 1893, near Bartlesville, they came upon Rogers and Cannon and a posse of more than fifteen Indian police, armed and waiting. A running fight ensued, in which Cannon shot off Jackson's right arm and sent another bullet through his side before he was captured. Starr and Newcome managed to escape. Rogers, in his report to Marshal Yoes at Fort Smith, stated that "about 200 shots were fired," the captured outlaw would "possibly recover," and "we are now on the trail of Starr and his confederate and will yet run them down. We are determined to rid society of this gang."

Henry Starr, on June 5, 1893, embarked on a bank robbery of his own, with his own gang.

68

The Starr Gang — Frank Cheney, Bud Tyler, Hank Watt, Link Cumplin, Kid Wilson, and Happy Jack — robbed the People's Bank at Bentonville, Arkansas. The take was in excess of $11,000 besides additional silver that was lost while ushering the cashier who was carrying the loot down the street. As they passed the office of the *Bentonville Sun,* a young lady in the building reached out and jerked Starr by the shoulder into the building. The robbers were taken so by surprise that they left without trying to recover the silver. The Bentonville robbery resulted in a score or more deputies, along with the Wells Fargo special officers, putting forth a special effort to capture the gang, especially Starr. The gang rendezvoused at Cheney's farm near Wagoner and divided the loot. They then split up and were never reunited.

Henry went to get his sweetheart, May Morrison, and drove to Emporia, Kansas, in a covered wagon, with Kid Wilson as a bodyguard. The three caught a train at Emporia for California but stopped off at Colorado Springs, arriving July 1, 1893. They registered at the Spaulding House as Frank Jackson, Mary Jackson, and John Wilson, all of Joplin. On July 3, Henry was recognized by William Feuterstine, a Fort Smith merchant, who had sold him some merchandise during one of Henry's trips to Fort Smith. Feuterstine informed the hotel clerk the identity of his guest, and the clerk called the Colorado Springs chief of police, L. C. Dana. Henry Starr's reputation was widespread and Dana took every precaution possible to capture the outlaw without incident. He bided his time, waiting until Henry was eating in a cafe alone that evening. He and J. W. Gathright caught Henry by surprise, and arrested him without a struggle. Wilson was arrested a few minutes later in the red light district. "Miss Jackson" was awakened a few minutes later and interrogated. A search uncovered $1,000, a revolver under a pillow, and $500 in gold in a nearby valise. She suddenly admitted her identity when she was told the other two were in jail.

May was released and sent back to her parents in the Indian Territory, and Starr and Wilson were turned over to the U.S. marshal of Denver. A few days later, deputies from the Fort Smith court arrived and took charge of the outlaws, returning them "heavily menacled and chained" to Fort Smith. Newspapers along the route of the train had a field day reporting the exploits of the two.

Henry Starr was only nineteen when he was arrested. But he was already a hardened criminal. At his trial in Fort Smith, fourteen separate indictments, including one for the murder of Floyd Wilson, were lodged against him. He was convicted of that murder and Judge Parker sentenced him to hang by the neck until dead. The date of execution was set for February 20, 1895. Henry was fortunate enough to get a new trial set by the Supreme Court; he was an inmate in the federal Fort Smith jail when Cherokee Bill made his appearance.

CHAPTER 6

Cherokee Bill's Last Stand

J. D. Berry, former deputy sheriff of Franklin County, Arkansas, was head jailer at the Fort Smith federal jail and was as competent as any who served during Judge Parker's tenure. There were more than 200 prisoners in the jail in the spring of 1895, and hardly a day passed that there was not some scheme afoot for a single escape or a wholesale run for freedom. Berry read the mood of the prisoners and sensed trouble brewing. On July 10 he ordered a search of the entire prison. In Cherokee Bill's cell the guards found nine .45 cartridges, and in the bathroom on Murderer's Row they found a .45 revolver, fully loaded, hidden in a bucket of lime.

Sherman Vann, a black trusty serving ninety days for larceny, was suspected. Vann admitted carrying in the lime, but if the weapon and ammunition were hidden there, he never knew it. Cherokee's cohorts denied that they knew where the weapon came from. Henry Starr was one of the first questioned by Berry, but most of the guards doubted he had anything to do with it.

During the week following, it was again whispered throughout the city that Cherokee Bill would kill somebody in the jail. Although Berry and his guards remained alert, they foolishly allowed him the freedom of the Row during the day, the same as the other prisoners, unmanacled, although the press gave warning of the danger. They also failed to discover a second revolver that had been smuggled into his cell. Cherokee Bill had hidden it in the wall behind a loose stone. The inside half of the stone had been broken off and the whitewashed end replaced.

At 7:00 on the evening of July 26, Turnkey Campbell Eoff (pronounced Ofe) and Guard Lawrence Keating entered Murderer's Row. The guards at the jail usually were relieved by the night guards at 6:00, and 6:15 was the time for locking the cells on each of the three floors. Owing to the long days and hot weather, the prisoners were allowed to remain in the corridors until near 7:00. It was the responsibility of Eoff and Keating, who guarded the lower tier of cells in the daytime, to "ring" the prisoners in for the night. Night Guards Will Lawson, Bras Parker, and William McConnell had just come on duty and were sitting on the ground outside, ten feet from the corridor entrance and the stairway to the jailer's office. Captain Berry had been gone about ten minutes.

Two rows of cells ran north and south of each side of the inner corridor, or "bullpen." The whole inner part of the jail was built of chilled steel, the doors of cross-barred steel, and the corridor walls of steel bars crossed as open grates. Every prisoner had his own cell, and when the gong sounded, each was to go to his proper cell and close his door behind him. Then a guard at the entrance threw a lever, dropping a long bar, or "brake," intended to fasten the closed cell doors on either side at the top. It was Eoff's job, after the lever was pulled, to enter the corridor and lock each door separately. It was a comparatively safe procedure, but there was always the chance that prisoners might hide at the rear of the cage or otherwise deceive the unarmed turnkey. To lessen the danger, Keating, wearing his pistol, walked along outside the cage to make sure each man was in his cell and had closed his door in order that the brake should work properly.

The brake on either row could be opened, however, by a broomstick or similar instrument in the hands of a prisoner at the north end of the tier. In compliance with a concerted movement to capture the jail, it was thrown open on the west tier, where Cherokee Bill and his associates were confined, while Eoff and Keating were attending the cells on the east side. As the turnkey passed around the south end and started locking the doors of the west row, Keating kept pace outside the corridor. Cherokee Bill's door, like the others, was free to be pushed open, and he calmly waited with revolver ready.

Cherokee's cell was "No. 20" and was the third from the south

72

end. Adjoining his cell on the south was one occupied by Dennis Davis, a half-witted black convicted of murdering one Solomon Blackwell. The keyhole in the lock of his door had been stuffed with paper. When Eoff inserted the key it lodged in the lock, and he remarked to Keating, "There's something wrong here." Keating walked closer. At that instant, the door of Cherokee Bill's cell was pushed open and Bill leaped out across the short space, shoved the muzzle of a revolver through the bars at Keating, and shouted, "Throw up, and give me that pistol!"

Instead of obeying, Keating, with a great deal of courage, reached for his own revolver. Instantly, Cherokee Bill's weapon was in action, and Keating staggered back, fatally wounded.

Eoff, who was unarmed, turned when the shot was fired and ran up the corridor, while Cherokee Bill stepped out of his cell and fired at him twice, but missed both times. George Pearce, one of the ringleaders in the plot, jumped from his cell and joined the chase, brandishing a broken table leg for a club. This perhaps saved Eoff's life, as Bill could not shoot squarely at him without endangering Pearce. Eoff took refuge in the doorway of the front cage. But for the prompt appearance of Will Lawson, Bras Parker, and McConnell at the jail door, he would undoubtedly have lost his life. The guards opened fire and drove Cherokee Bill and Pearce back to the south end of the corridor.

With the shooting, perfect bedlam broke out in the prison. Convicts howled and threw their weight against the bars. From some of the cells still unlocked, men made ready for a full-scale prison riot. Above the frenzied yelling of the prisoners, and the shouts of officers ordering them back into their cells, the explosion of firearms rang out again and again, as Cherokee Bill tried to drive the guards from the gate and they replied in like fashion. Smoke so filled the corridor that it was almost impossible to see, which was the reason why more persons were not killed or wounded.

Out of this smoke suddenly appeared a dreadful figure: Lawrence Keating, still carrying his revolver, the blood cascading from his body, his face drawn and pale like the ghost of a man already dead. Dead he really was, except for the effort of will that kept him staggering on, carrying the weapon which the murderer behind might have used, until he collapsed by the gate, gasped, "I'm killed," and died.

Now Heck Bruner, a deputy marshal, came up with a shotgun and blasted with it down the corridor. The "scatter gun" would have done some serious damage, if it could have been brought into play sooner. But when Bruner fired, Cherokee Bill and all the other prisoners had already retreated into their cells, so that the buck shot whined and rattled down the passageway without finding a living target.

The excitement rapidly spread to the city. In an incredibly short time, police and scores of citizens armed themselves with Winchesters, shotguns, and revolvers and hastened to help the guards. Marshal Crump arrived from his home in the suburbs and took personal charge of the situation.

Then began a sniping match. Cherokee Bill, having reloaded his revolver, fired at random from his cell, never putting out his head. Every time he fired, he gobbled. It was an uncanny, though familiar, sound in the territory, half between the bark of a coyote and the throaty cry of a turkey cock — the same cry that the infamous Ned Christie used while under siege. When an Indian "gobbled" it meant sure death to someone within hearing range, as much a threat to kill as if spoken in so many words.

For fifteen minutes Cherokee Bill gobbled and fired at every form and shadow he could see. He fired at Jim Shannon and another citizen as they were carrying Keating's lifeless form outside. The place was fumed with the stench of gunpowder. Only this and the fact that the officers were able to keep Cherokee confined in his cell prevented a dozen men from being slain.

It was always claimed by the officers that just after the first shot, the lever which fastened the cell doors at the top was thrown, thus liberating all the cells which had not been locked with a key. Who was responsible for this act was never settled further than that it was someone near the north end. Henry Starr was suspected of the deed, but none saw him in the act.

Firearms were at every step. The prisoners, for the most part, were badly frightened and had taken refuge beneath their bunks or huddled in the corners of their cells. On the outside of the cell blocks were twenty or more men, all armed to the teeth. Captain Berry vainly tried to induce Cherokee to surrender his weapon. A steady refusal was the only response.

It was at this moment that Henry Starr stepped unforgettably into the picture.

He had been sentenced to hang for the murder of Floyd Wilson, but his lawyer had appealed the case, and he was awaiting a decision on the appeal in his cell in the Fort Smith jail. Now he managed to get

74

the attention of one of the guards, and made this proposal: "If you'll keep the men who are watching the corridor from shooting at me, I'll go into Cherokee Bill's cell and get his gun for you."

He knew the desperado from their association in the Cook Gang. After a consultation was held, the guards agreed not to fire. Released from his cell, young Starr walked steadily down the corridor to the cell occupied by cornered Cherokee Bill.

Starr described what happened next:

> I pledged myself to get Bill's gun if (Crump) would give me his word of honor that he would not shoot him when disarmed, which he did. I went at once to Bill's cell and told him that he could not possibly get out — that he might be able to kill a few more guards, but that would avail nothing, and to take my advice and give his gun to me, which he did, loaded all around. I walked to the end of the corridor and handed the gun to the guards.

It was that simple.

The officers entered the corridor, covering Cherokee with shotguns and Winchesters. A thorough search of his cell turned up a little tobacco sack filled with .38 cartridges. Then he was handcuffed, chained, and locked back inside. George Pearce, found hiding in his cell, was also chained and locked up, and the jail was cleared of spectators.

Cherokee Bill felt remorse at having to shoot Larry Keating. He felt Keating was going to shoot him if he hadn't shot in self-defense. Cherokee went on to say, "Damn a man who won't fight for his liberty!" No less than one hundred shots were fired in the attempted jail break.

The marshals and guards worked until midnight dispersing the crowds and discouraging mob violence. District Attorney James F. Read mingled quietly with the people, assuring them the case would be vigorously prosecuted and the crime would not go unavenged. Nothing else was talked about in public places for a week, while Cherokee became sullen and morose and for several days almost entirely refused food.

At the time of Keating's murder, Judge Parker was in St. Louis. Not in very good health, he knew that very soon his beloved court, in which he had ruled virtually as a personification of fate for so many years, would soon be abolished. The iron-clad case against Cherokee Bill was like a stimulant to him. On Thursday following the crime, the judge left St. Louis and returned to Fort Smith for the purpose of recovering court and calling the grand jury together, that they might return an indictment against Cherokee Bill for the murder of Keating.

The autumn term of court began on August 5. The trial docket, seldom taken up until October, was so heavy that Judge Parker canceled his vacation, which he usually took at that time of year. For the first time in the court's history, the petit and grand juries were empaneled on the opening day. There were twenty-four murder cases scheduled, and the grand jury added twenty more. The first case taken up was the killing of Keating.

(For his courage in the jail, the death penalty against Henry Starr was lifted, and he was permitted to plead guilty to a charge of manslaughter, for which he was sentenced to fifteen years in prison. He was pardoned by the president after five years.)

In Bill's case, the judge's charge to the grand jury was very forceful. Within half an hour, they returned an indictment against Cherokee Bill, and at 1:00 in the afternoon, escorted by a dozen armed deputies and a court bailiff with a heavy billy club, he was arraigned before Parker. He entered a plea of not guilty, and Parker set his trial for August 8.

On Thursday, August 8, Cherokee Bill was again brought into court in chains and under heavy guard. Never had the courtroom been jammed with so many visitors. His defense attorney, J. W. Reed, fought the case with every "hook and crook" from the beginning. He made a motion for continuance on grounds that public sentiment and prejudices of the people of Fort Smith would not allow his client to get a fair and impartial trial at that time, and filed a demurrer alleging that the court did not have jurisdiction because the killing had occurred in jail. Judge Parker ruled that "there is no question as to the jurisdiction of the court in this case"; he became "highly indignant" that a fair and impartial trial could not be had in his court, and stated that "the allegations in the demurrer are wholly false and without foundation." He ordered the panel of jurors called. Twelve men who lived no closer than forty miles to Fort Smith were chosen. He questioned each man closely and, satisfied that they were not prejudiced and could render a verdict in accordance with the law and the evidence, pronounced them "qualified jurors."

The trial lasted three days, the prosecution being handled by District Attorney Read's able assistant, J. B. McDonough. After closing arguments and the verdict of the jury (guilty), Judge Parker sentenced

Cherokee Bill to be hanged September 10.

Again his case was appealed to the Supreme Court, and Parker granted another stay of execution. But, on December 2, the Supreme Court affirmed the decision of the Fort Smith court in the Ernest Melton case. For the third and last time, Judge Parker sentenced Cherokee Bill to die on the gallows and fixed the date as St. Patrick's Day, March 17. There was "no avenue of escape left except executive clemency by the President, who was appealed to in vain."

After his sentencing, Cherokee Bill was placed in solitary confinement. He did not seem to mind it, but he complained bitterly at his inability to obtain his mail. Under the rules, felons were not allowed to either receive or send mail when in solitary confinement, and letters addressed to Cherokee Bill were, of course, opened by Jailer Berry and carefully read. One of the most persistent correspondents was a young mulatto girl, who lived in Indianapolis, Indiana, and claimed to be a relative. She had corresponded with Bill for some months and sent him her photograph. She wrote frequently after he was sentenced and at last her letters showed that she was greatly worried at receiving no replies, fearing she had written something to incur his displeasure. She finally wrote him a sad and last farewell, expressing the deepest sympathy and begging him, if he ever became free, to be certain to visit.

The day Cherokee Bill was informed that his last chance of clemency was gone was an eventful day. He was given a new cell, his games of poker were ended, and no prisoner was allowed to come in front of his door or to converse with him. A guard was appointed to sit in front of his cell constantly. He was allowed a deck of cards with which to play "solitaire." He appeared to be in a fairly happy state of mind and talked freely about his upcoming execution, saying that the worst consideration was how his mother was going to take it. He paid much tribute to his attorney, J. W. Reed, who he said had worked with the same zeal as if he had been certain to receive a large fee. To the last, Cherokee Bill maintained his innocence of the majority of the crimes charged to him, and even refused to admit that he killed Lawrence Keating. He said, "I don't know whether I killed him or not. I don't know whether my shots struck him. He may have been shot by the guard."

On the day before his execution, Cherokee's mother arrived in the city and for the first time she was allowed to talk with him in his cell. She was with him for several hours. During the afternoon he made his will, drawn up by his attorney, which gave his claim in the Cherokee

77

nation to his mother. Just before the close of the interview, the old black Aunty who nursed him in infancy arrived at the jail and had a few words with him. His brother, Clarence Goldsby, also visited the jail and viewed the scaffold and rope and other gruesome preparations.

The *Fort Smith Elevator* carried the following account of Cherokee Bill's execution:

> [Cherokee Bill awakened] this morning at six, singing and whistling. He partook of a light breakfast about eight o'clock, which was sent to him by his mother from the hotel. At 9:20, Cherokee Bill's mother and the old negress who raised him were admitted to his cell, and shortly after Father Pius, his spiritual advisor, was also admitted. The usual noise and hubbub that is always heard within the big iron cage that surrounds the cells was noticeably lacking this morning.
>
> Cherokee Bill's fellow prisoners, many of them under sentence of death seemed to be impressed with the solemnity of the occasion, and an air of subdued quiet pervaded the jail. Many of the men who are already standing within the shadow of the gallows gathered in a group near the cell occupied by the condemned man and conversed in low tones. To his most intimate associates since his confinement, Cherokee distributed his small effects . . .
>
> By 10:30, the corridor in front of Cherokee's cell was crowded with newspaper representatives, deputy marshals, and other privileged individuals, all taking note of every passing incident. Occasionally the condemned man would throw aside the curtain which concealed the interior of his cell and make his appearance at the grated door in order to give some instructions or to make some request of the officer who stood guard.
>
> About eleven o'clock Marshal Crump, after a short conversation with Cherokee, announced that the execution would be postponed until two o'clock, in order to give his sister an opportunity to see him before the death sentence was carried out. She was coming in on the east-bound Valley train, and would not arrive until one o'clock. The 2,000 or 3,000 sight-seers surrounding the big stone wall and within the enclosure dispersed.
>
> It was a struggling mass of humanity that had gathered on and around the steps and walls and when the time came there was a scramble even among those who were provided with passes. There was a crush and a jam for a few minutes but order was at last restored in a measure and all awaited the moment when the door should open for the coming of the condemned man. On the inside there was a repetition of the scenes of the morning. Bill's mother had packed up

several belongings of her son and was ready when called upon to take final leave. Her parting was an affectionate one but she strove as much as lay in her power to restrain her emotion.

Bill was affected by it, but following the example of his mother, gave little or no indication that he was other than perfectly composed.

"Well, I am ready to go now most anytime," said he addressing the guards.

He was taken at his word and the jail was cleared. The crowd outside had swelled to increased numbers, all the available buildings and sheds being occupied. A pathway was cleared through the crowd, and very shortly after the clock struck two the door opened and the doomed man was brought forth, a guard on either side. The march to the gallows was taken up, and at Col. Crump's suggestion, Cherokee's suggestion, Cherokee's mother and the old colored Aunty walked alongside Bill. Father Pius came next, the newspaper men following and the crowd bringing up the rear.

"This is about as good a day to die as any," remarked Cherokee as he glanced around. Arriving at the south end of the jail, he looked around at the crowd and said, "It looks like a regiment of soldiers."

He continued to look around at the crowd, eyeing them curiously.

At the door of the enclosure there was a jam. Everybody crowded up and there was a stop for a few moments. It took several minutes for everyone holding tickets to gain admittance, and by this time the condemned man and guards had mounted the scaffold. Bill walked with a firm step and, taking up a position near the west wall of the gallows, waited for the end.

Turning slightly and seeing his mother standing near, he said, "Mother, you ought not to have come here." Her reply was: "I can go wherever you go."

Colonel Crump suggested to him that he take a seat until all was in readiness, but he replied, "No, I don't want to sit down."

The death warrant was then read, during which Bill gazed about as if a little impatient to have the thing over with. He was asked at its conclusion if he had anything to say, and replied, "No Sir, without he (meaning Father Pius) wants to say a prayer."

The priest here offered a short prayer, the condemned man listening attentively the meanwhile, and then as if knowing what was to come next, he walked forward till he stood upon the trap. Deputy Lawson and others arranged the ropes, binding his arms and legs, and it was while this was being done that Bill spoke to different ones in the crowd below.

"Good-bye, all you chums down that way," said he, with a

79

smile. Just then he caught sight of a young man in the act of taking a snap shot with a Kodak and pulling it sharply back. There was a creaking sound as the trap was sprung and the body shot downward. The fall was scarcely six feet, but the rope had been adjusted carefully by Lawson and the neck was broken. The muscles twisted once or twice, but that was all . . . Twelve minutes from the time the trap was sprung, the ropes that bound his limbs were removed, also the handcuffs and shackles, and the body was lowered into a coffin and borne away and the crowd dispersed. At Birnie's, the coffin was placed in a box and then taken to the Missouri Pacific depot and put aboard the train. His mother and sister took it back with them to Fort Gibson.

The colorful but crime-filled career of Crawford Goldsby came to an end. But the saga of Cherokee Bill was not yet finished.

Crawford Goldsby, alias Cherokee Bill, had been a friend to Ike Rogers while he was making a reputation as the worst desperado in the Indian Territory. Reportedly it was Cherokee Bill to whom, much of the time, Ike Rogers looked for sustenance for his family. At the latter's house Bill often made his home, when he chose to rest quietly for a few days or weeks. And after a raid or holdup, Bill would retire to the home of his supposed friend to remain in hiding until he could once more go forth in comparative safety. Rogers was not a good provider; had it not been for the supplies often brought to his family by the reckless Cherokee Bill, when returning from his raids, they would often have suffered for the bare necessities. More than that, it is claimed that it was not infrequently that Rogers looked out for opportunities and planned burglaries of the country stores or other places containing the articles most needed by his family. After divulging his plans to Bill, Ike would await his return, well laden with the fruits of his crime, in the shape of food, clothing, or money. This is the reason why Cherokee was so easily lured into the trap laid by Rogers, for he trusted the man as a friend.

Even though Ike Rogers had served in the employ of the United States marshal's office, his character was not the best to be found. Many people felt Ike was an opportunist of the worst kind. It is said that he did not work for the marshal's office very long due to his character. Among the citizens of the territory, his reputation was very low.

Clarence Goldsby, Crawford's younger brother, had always been a quiet and well-mannered youth, and he had the respect and confidence of all good citizens of Fort Gibson, his home. A certain animosity naturally grew into his heart against Ike Rogers on account of the latter's betrayal of his brother, but was never manifested in any overt act. Then, in the town of Hayden, Cherokee Nation, in the winter of 1897, the paths of Clarence and Ike crossed, nearly a year after Cherokee's execution.

At Hayden, for a month or more, were located the officials in charge of the payment to the black citizens of the Cherokee Nation. These were individual shares in the money received by the United States government, from the sale of the Cherokee Strip. Clarence Goldsby was entitled to a portion of this money, on account of being the son of a black citizen, and was one of the thousands who traveled to Hayden to receive this money. There he met Ike Rogers, who was present for the same purpose. Rogers attempted to quarrel with Clarence, doubtless from a sense of guilt, at the wrong he had done him, through betraying his brother. For several days he continued to abuse him, addressing him by all manner of vile names and epithets and even threatening his life.

William Lee Starr, a Cherokee Freedman, gave the following account of this encounter:

> I was at the Cherokee Freedmen payment at Hayden. On one of the dancing platforms Clarence and Ike began a dispute about something concerning the arrest of Cherokee Bill. Ike gave Clarence a shove and made some threat. The officials of the payment decided to move the payment to Fort Gibson. Clarence told Ike Rogers that if he put his foot on the soil at Fort Gibson he would be a dead man.
>
> But Ike was not to be bluffed. He notified Clarence that he would be down on the morning train which arrived in Fort Gibson about 10:30 A.M. and that he was ready for him. I was in Fort Gibson when the payment was going on. Clarence had on the hat of my wife's nephew, Will Pack. Clarence went to a room and put on his six-shooter just a few minutes before the train was due. My wife asked him what he was going to do with the gun and he smiled and said, "Nothing." She said to him, "You had better leave it off," but he went straight to the depot. When the train pulled in and Rogers dismounted, having his face toward the train, Clarence shot him through the neck from behind.
>
> After Ike fell on his back, Clarence shot him twice in the face and reached and got Cherokee Bill's gun that Ike had, then passed under a box going east.

Clarence ran toward the forest-covered hills, followed by several deputy United States marshals, firing as they ran but failing to bring him down. One of these deputies was Bill Smith, who had taken advantage of Ike Rogers's duplicity, and aided thereby Cherokee Bill's capture. Smith mounted his horse and followed to a point where he considered it prudent to dismount and run across a field to head off the fleeing man, but Clarence, with exceptionally keen cunning, discovered the situation and ran back, mounted the officer's horse and rode away, much to the officer's surprise and chagrin.

It is reported that Clarence went to St. Louis and enlisted in the army and when discharged he was employed in the Pullman service until he died. His body was shipped from St. Louis to the Indian Territory and he was buried at Fort Gibson, his hometown.

Cherokee Bill's niece, Maud Brown Surrell, in January 1938 gave the following comments about her uncles:

> The fugitive career of my uncle Crawford Goldsby, known as Cherokee Bill, and his brother Clarence, of course, is in the annuals of Indian Territory outlaw history, but I believe if they could have had an opportunity, different environment and proper training during their younger life, they would have been different men.

Glenn Shirley, in his book *Toughest of Them All,* said:

> Take the records of John Wesley Hardin, Bill Longley, Black Jack Ketchum, Sam Bass, or any other Western desperados, and they can be considered "small potatoes" when compared to Cherokee Bill, the most noted renegade to infest the Oklahoma country in the '90s when "there was no Sunday west of St. Louis, no God west of Fort Smith."

CHAPTER 7

Buss Luckey:
Train Robber

While Cherokee Bill was incarcerated at Fort Smith, two tough black outlaws were also imprisoned. Tom Root was brought in during Cherokee Bill's last trial and his cohort, Buss Luckey, was brought in a few months later from Muskogee.

S. W. Harman, author of *Hell on the Border,* describes Tom Root:

> A [N]egro, accused of being a train robber and all-around crook, was brought in from the Verdigris bottoms, in the Cherokee Nation. He is under indictment for the Blackstone train robbery, and was thought to have had a hand in a holdup at Coretta, and was also charged with being implicated in the murder of Deputy Newton Leflore, in the Creek Nation, one year before.

Of the Blackstone train robbery, Tom Root, Buss Luckey, and Will Smith, also black, were members of a gang led by a white man named Nathaniel (Texas Jack) Reed. On the night of November 13, 1894, at 9:57, the Katy's northbound *Katy Flyer,* carrying a shipment of $60,000 in gold bullion and silver, was stopped by this gang at Blackstone switch, near Wybark, eight miles north of Muskogee, Creek Nation. The outlaws opened the switch, and instead of going down the mainline, the northbound *Katy No. 2* shot down the side track. The engineer set his brakes, opened the sand valves, and brought the train to a grinding, screeching halt.

The plan was to stop the train on the siding and blast open the express car with dynamite. What Reed hadn't been told was that American Express Company officials had just instituted a new policy of placing armed guards on all shipments running through the Indian Territory. This was due to the frequency of holdups on the M.K. & T. and the Iron Mountain (Missouri Pacific) railroads. Two of the guards, Bud Ledbetter and Paden Tolbert, would later gain quite a reputation as deputy marshals.

Reed undertook to blow open the express car. He approached the car with his dynamite and ordered the express messenger to open the door or he would blow it off. The answer was a fusillade from the guard's gun. Reed and his gang took positions behind trees on each side of the train. For more than an hour they fired into the wooden coaches, allowing no one to leave, and after numerous threats finally hurled a charge of dynamite that blew off the end of the express car. But Bud and his man stuck to their posts and kept firing their rifles.

During the battle, Texas Jack slipped under cover of some cross-ties stacked along the tracks and entered the front of the first passenger coach, wearing false whiskers and carrying a gunnysack. While the firing was still hot outside, he passed through the entire train. As he entered each coach he shouted, "Everybody drop his valuables in this sack or be killed!" He collected $460, eight watches and three pistols, even forcing one young passenger to go with him and hold one side of the sack.

Things went well until he was leaving the last coach. Ledbetter, through the ragged aperture of splintered boards of the express car, caught a glimpse of him. It was all Bud needed. His Winchester roared. Jack fell, badly wounded; the bullet struck him in the front part of the left hip, cutting down through his bladder and lower bowels, emerging from the outside of his right thigh, at the back. He managed to drag himself to the shelter of the crossties. Buss Luckey, a big, strong man, picked him up and carried him to his horse. Texas Jack had enough, and he gave the order to retreat. After a few more shots, Smith and Root rushed to their horses, and fled into the night.

On December 5, 1894, at Broken Arrow Settlement, Creek Nation, fifteen miles from Tulsa, Deputy Marshal Newton LaForce, Deputy Birchfield and six other men, most of whom were deputy marshals, were in pursuit of Buss Luckey and Tom Root. They were wanted at

Fort Smith for participating in both the Blackstone and Coretta train robberies.

The morning was heavy with fog, and very early six of the posse surrounded the house where Luckey and Root were supposed to be. LaForce and Birchfield proceeded about 200 yards to several haystacks, where they thought the outlaws might be lying, in the event they were not in the house. Dogs at the house discovered the officers and set up a loud barking, which awoke Luckey, Root, and Root's wife, all of whom were sleeping at the haystack. By this time the two officers who had started in the direction of the stacks had separated about 100 yards, leaving the stacks between them.

The dense fog prevented objects from being clearly visible more than a few yards distant. As Luckey and Root rose from their beds in the hay they caught a glimpse of the law officers through the fog and opened fire. The law officers commanded the outlaws to surrender, but to no avail, and a very intense gun battle ensued. The officers at the house, hearing the shots, ran toward the haystacks, firing at objects barely discernible as they ran. Root and Luckey managed to escape, and as the battle ceased, Deputy LaForce was found on the ground with a serious wound. The bullet entered his back and passed through his body. The deputy died the next day.

For these crimes, Root and Luckey were arrested by U.S. deputy marshals in the territory. Luckey hired lawyer J. Warren Reed to defend him. He was soon indicted, charged with the murder of LaForce. Tom Root was induced to surrender to Deputy Jim Pettigrew of Muskogee, and on the thirteenth day of August, he was brought to Fort Smith.

Root had turned state's evidence against Luckey. When the trial began, Luckey had no witnesses in his behalf, while on the part of the government were eight deputy marshals and Root arraying against him. It was a very interesting and hard-fought case, but Luckey was convicted and sentenced to hang. When Luckey was brought out for sentencing, he exhibited very little interest in the remarks of the court, made prior to naming the date for execution. When asked whether he had anything to say, he answered, "I have nothing to say, only I never did it."

In passing sentence, Judge Parker replied:

> Twelve true and tried men of your country have said that you did, and it becomes my duty to sentence. You have been convicted of the murder of Newton LaForce, a United States deputy marshal of the court, in the Indian country. He is one of more than three score

marshals, who, in the last twenty years, have given up their lives in the Indian country while in the discharge of duty to their country, these brave men representing the government and the law in a bloody struggle with outlaw and banditti. They represented peace and order. The banditti represented lawlessness, bloodshed and crime. The killing of Marshal LaForce was but an act in the great war of civilization against savagism which has been waged against the men of crime by this court and its officers for twenty years. The history of this court in its efforts to overcome bloody violence and murder is unequalled in the history of jurisprudence of this country.

You, by the evidence, are a man of blood. You belong to the banditti, to the bands of men who robbed and plundered peaceable citizens, express cars and passengers on railroad trains. The officers were seeking your arrest for robbery, and the crime of obstructing a railroad train. You evaded the officers who were lawfully and properly seeking your arrest. There seems to be a great misconception in the minds of lawless men, as well as many others, in regard to the rights of officers. The idea prevails that they, while in the interest of the law and of peace and order, are entitled to no protection. The truth is, while in the right, in the performance of the responsible duties that devolve upon them in this jurisdiction, they are entitled to all protection. The officers in your case were clearly in the right. You did not permit them to make your mission known before you fired on them and killed Marshal LaForce. Your act can be nothing but murder. It was clearly proven. The action of the jury in finding you guilty is entirely justified by the law. Your conviction but emphasizes a life of crime. You are now about to be sentenced to death for this wicked murder. This is the punishment the law says shall follow the conviction of this crime, and the court when it pronounces sentence but voices the law of the land.

My advice to you is to make an honest effort to obtain forgiveness of your God for this terrible crime, as well as for the other crimes you have committed. The highest duty you owe is to your God. The duty to him demands that you implore him for that mercy you now so much need. Your past life has been such that you specially need the assistance of your Maker to enable you to get away from the condition in which your crimes and wickedness have placed you. For your own sake, I request that you honestly and sincerely seek the assistance of your God.

The sentence in Luckey's case, however, was never carried out. Attorney J. Warren Reed took a writ of error to the Supreme Court in Washington and reversed Judge Parker's decision, securing a new trial, which occurred about two years later. Meanwhile, Mr. Reed lost no time in securing additional evidence and more fully developing his client's case.

At the new trial, he produced a large map, some three feet square, which he used before the jury to indicate the position of the haystacks, the field, the fences, house, and all the premises about where the killing of LaForce took place. The map also showed the course which the marshals ran when firing in the direction of the haystacks, through the fog. By shrewd skill and application of the facts in the case to this map, Mr. Reed made the point and contended before the jury that, notwithstanding, Luckey and Root were firing at the marshals as they fled from the stack, and that a fight ensued. But in fact, neither Luckey nor Root had shot LaForce, or he would have been struck from the front. LaForce, being shot in the back, must have been shot unintentionally by one of his companions as they came from the house firing their weapons toward the stacks. Mr. Reed presented a most ingenious defense, and it was so logically presented that Luckey was acquitted. He was subsequently convicted of participation in the Blackstone train robbery, in which case he could make no defense, and was sentenced to the penitentiary at Columbus, Ohio, for fifteen years.

It is reported that Tom Root was later shot and killed near Cohcharty; Will Smith left the country and was never seen again, and Texas Jack surrendered to federal officers in Arkansas. He was given a five-year sentence, but paroled by Judge Isaac C. Parker a year later. He became an evangelist, traveling in Wild West acts and lecturing on crime-does-not-pay until his death from old age at Tulsa, January 7, 1950.

It is interesting to note that some historians have credited the Coretta train robbery to the Cook Gang with Luckey and Root participating. The following information comes from the *Vinita Indian Chieftain* of June 18, 1896:

> The participants in the Coretta Train robbery . . . were made public for the first time during the trial of Bob Elzey. Henry and Frank Smith, who pleaded guilty to the charge, went on the stand and testified that Buz Luckey organized the band and that it was composed of Luckey, Will White, Elzey, Frank, Henry, and Will Smith.

This newspaper report from the Fort Smith court gives evidence that Luckey possessed leadership abilities. By this account, Root is vindicated of participating in this particular train robbery.

CHAPTER 8

Rufus Buck Gang: Terror Unleashed

In a very short period of time, the Rufus Buck Gang gained instant notoriety with murder, plunder, and rape in the territory. Some historians have reported that Buck was a full-blooded Euchee Indian. The Euchee clan are considered allies to the Seminole or even part of the Seminole family. In 1937, W. F. Jones, a former deputy U.S. marshal who helped arrest the gang, stated that Rufus was part black.

Alec Berryhill, a resident of the Creek Nation, gave the following account of the infamous gang:

> The Creek Indian Tribe did not have many outlaws, but there were a few. Among these was a band known as the Buck Gang, which was headed by a mulatto named Rufus Buck. [It was common in the territory for African-Indians to be called, erroneously, mulatto.] The other members were: Meome [Maoma] July, a full-blood Creek Indian; Louis Davis, a full-blood Creek; Sam Samson, a full-blood Creek; and Lucky Davis, a Negro. These men began by robbing ranches of cows, horses, or anything of value. After a few months they started robbing grocery stores in and around Okmulgee. John Buck, the father of Rufus, lived near the old Indian Mission of Wealaka Boarding School, and the gang used his home as a hide-out.
>
> Mr. Berryhill said he and another man were standing in the

drug store, which is now the First National Bank, when they heard a shot and a loud whoop. They stepped out of the drug store to see what had happened, when a man came up and called for Dr. Bell, the proprietor, saying for him to hurry to the grocery store, as the town marshal, John Gar[r]ett, the freedman, had been shot through the chest and needed attention. The grocery store was located on Seventh and Morton Street. When Dr. Bell got to the wounded man, he told him he had been shot by Rufus Buck; then he went into a coma until he died. The Gang was just starting to rob the grocery store when Gar[r]ett saw them and commanded them to raise their hands. Instead, Rufus Buck drew his gun and shot him.

Garrett was one of many black, white, and Indian deputy U.S. marshals who would lose their lives trying to bring law and order to the "nations."

Carrie Pitman, a resident of the Seminole Nation, stated that Lucky Davis was her nephew and the Buck Gang was composed of three blacks and two Indians.

Riding from Okmulgee, four of them met a Mrs. Wilson, who was moving from one farm to another with two wagons. Her fourteen-year-old son and a young man who was with her were ordered to drive on with the wagons, while they kept the woman. Then each member of the band brutally assaulted her, releasing her afterward and firing at her feet as she fled from their abuse half dead with fright.

Two days later, the whole gang appeared at the home of Henry Hassan between Duck and Snake creeks, and after forcing his wife to prepare dinner for them and gorging themselves like ravenous wolves, they seized and tied her down with a rope, and each took his turn assaulting her while the others held her husband at bay with Winchesters. They then amused themselves by making Hassan and his hired man, who also was present, fight each other and dance, shooting at their heels to make the affair more lively.

The gang met a white man named Shafey on Berryhill Creek, eight miles from Okmulgee, and robbed him of his horse, saddle and bridle, fifty dollars in cash, and a gold watch. Then they discussed the advisability of killing him and took a vote on it. Three of them voted to let him go, and he was allowed to go on foot.

They rode in the night to the home of Gus Chambers on Duck Creek, ten miles from Sapulpa, to steal some horses. Chambers put up a fight, and they filled his house with lead, but no one was harmed. The gang was able to secure one horse.

They robbed a stockman named Bent Callahan and a black farm hand, Sam Houston, who was accompanying him. They took Callahan's clothing and boots, and fired at him as he fled naked. Houston was shot and later died of his wounds.

On August 9, they robbed Norberg's store near McDermott and Orcutt's store in the same locality. Alec Berryhill stated in an interview:

> The gang had an oath to commit any crime that one of the gang committed and if one backed out, the penalty was death by his own men. After they had killed and escaped, they left a trail of plundering as they went. After being at the home of the leader's father for while, they came back to Okmulgee, Oklahoma. As they were roaming around near the little town of Natura, they came upon a white woman who had a baby recently and wasn't well. They took her down and attacked her, one by one, as was the agreement. From there they went west of Okmulgee and came to a grocery store, operated by a man named Knobble. There they went in and were looting the store of food, clothing, and ammunition, when an Indian came to buy coffee. The gang waited on him; they got two gunny sacks and stuffed it with coffee, meat, canned goods, and anything they could think of, loaded his horse, and sent him home. After they had looted the store of its ammunition, they put it in boots and slung them across the back of the horses. From there they went to the northwest of Okmulgee and camped in the hills, about a mile and a half southwest of Preston.

The next day after the Norberg robbery (Saturday, August 10), Capt. Edmund Harry, of the Creek Lighthorse, with Lighthorsemen Tom Grayson, George Brown, and Skansey, accompanied by Deputy U.S. Marshals Sam Haynes and N. B. Irwin and over 100 citizens of the Creek Nation, discovered the outlaws while they were dividing their plunder. Just outside the village, and after a fight in which hundreds of shots were fired, all the outlaws surrendered except Lewis Davis, who escaped during the fight but was captured later. Deputy Marshals Ledbetter, Tolbert, Jones, and Wilson were hot on the trail of the outlaws, and they arrived at the scene of the fight a few minutes after the surrender.

For seven hours the battle raged, while the "brave and desperate" Indian police, deputy marshals, and Creek citizens sought to ascend the hill, and the outlaws, shooting down from their vantage ground, drove them back.

At Fort Smith, shortly after court had convened at 1:00, the first dispatch reached the city that the big posse had made contact with the Buck Gang and "a furious battle" was in progress.

Everyone in Fort Smith had heard of the Buck Gang, and the report of those daring crimes had spread over the entire country. Coming so soon after the Keating murder, their acts had filled the people of the city and country with horror, and women and children feared to step out of doors after dark. The news of the "round up" spread like wildfire; "The Buck Gang" was upon everybody's lips. The news soon reached the courthouse. There were, in the yard and corridors, over 400 persons who had been summoned before the court as witnesses. The courtroom was crowded with people who listened idly to the numerous petty cases that were invariably called up after the disposal of a noted murder trial. Word was passed from lip to lip, to the effect that officers had corralled the "Buck Gang"; almost instantly, all was in a bustle. A bailiff whispered the news to Judge Parker; he nodded, pleasantly, called for order in the court, and proceeded with the regular business. Soon another dispatch came. It read: "Deputy marshals and Indians are engaged in a hand to hand conflict with the Buck gang."

Like a flash, this second dispatch found its way to every nook and cranny in the city. In the courtroom, the bustle increased; attorneys for once forgot to ask questions, and witnesses to answer them, and again and again and again Judge Parker called for the bailiffs to preserve order. His tone was kindly, however, and he seemed to join in with the crowd in secret exultation at the fact that the murderous and unholy gang had been tracked to their lair.

When court finally adjourned, everyone hurried to the streets to learn of any possible late news of the fight, and gathered in little knots to discuss the probable outcome.

Just after dark, there came a dispatch which told of the surrender. The high tension under which the people had been held for half a day was loosened and normal conditions were restored, though many continued about the telegraph and newspaper offices all night, to learn of any possible later developments.

As soon as he heard of the "round up," United States Marshal S. M. Rutherford, of the Northern District, Indian Territory, hurried to the scene, from Muskogee, reaching there while the shooting was in

91

progress. All this time the posse had been lying at full length on the ground, hugging the grass roots, and firing upwards at an angle of probably thirty degrees. The steady weapons fire, with the accompanying flashes, gave the appearance of a constant blaze. A heavy blanket of black powder smoke hid the belligerents from each other. At last, an old Indian, whose misfortune it is that his name was not preserved to history, rose bravely to his feet and said: "Let us stand up and fight like men; I've had enough of this." At the same time he was pushing a dynamite cartridge into his rifle.

This act was even more brave than the other. There was probably not another man in the posse who would have dared to fire a dynamite cartridge from a rifle intended to stand only the force exerted by exploded gunpowder. Quickly, he raised his gun and fired. The terrible explosive struck a tree behind which Buck was standing. A piece of the shell cut his belt and as it dropped to the ground, he threw away his rifle and ran. This demoralized the gang and all ran pell-mell down the opposite side of the hill, and into the arms of newly arrived lawmen. They were captured, with the exception of Lewis Davis, who, twice wounded, had escaped while the fight was in progress. He was captured a few days later. The prisoners were shackled and chained together and returned to McDermott. It was decided to place the outlaws under heavy guard during the night and transfer them to Fort Smith the next day.

Citizens and settlers throughout the Creek Nation swarmed into the little village to get a look at these violent men who had spread such terror among their people in so short a time. At first there were only whispered threats, then lynching was talked openly.

Marshal Rutherford spoke to the assembled throng. He assured them that the bandits would be delivered to Fort Smith and that they would get justice in Judge Parker's court, and the mob quieted down for a while. Then talk began about cases being long-drawn-out affairs that went to the Supreme Court. They talked also of the White House criticism of the tribes in general, and the Creeks in particular, for their laxity in upholding the law and their failure to assist in its enforcement as a cause for much of the crime in their nation. The Creeks had smarted under these accusations, and they saw an opportunity for retribution.

Rutherford realized that if he waited until morning none of the prisoners would leave there alive. The noise of the mob increased; there were more threats, more curses. One large group of Creeks gathered near the marshals' camp and began posting sentries to see that neither the officers nor their prisoners escaped.

Rutherford consulted with his deputies. In the darkness, he believed, they could steal through to safety but for the noise of the heavy chains that bound the bandits together. He told the outlaws that the only way they could remain alive was to cooperate, and if they would pick up their chains and carry them without sound, his officers would try to slip them away. Anxious to save their own lives, although they had little regard for the lives of others, the outlaws picked up their chains and carried them silently for half a mile. From there, the officers whisked them to Muskogee, placed them on the train, and took them to Fort Smith.

W. F. Jones said the shackled gang was slipped down Okmulgee Creek to the Deep Fork River, then to Hichita around midnight, then to Oktaha on the M.K. & T. Railroad. The marshals took them into Muskogee, handcuffed to the horns of the saddle, and on to Fort Smith by train.

They reached the Arkansas city on Sunday morning, August 11. Seven hundred people had gathered at the depot to gaze upon the marauders of the Creek Nation. As the prisoners were escorted off the train with the officers in front of and behind them, the crowd fell back on either side, and the outlaws shot furtive glances, taking in every face, every detail as if at any moment they might attempt a break. One contemporary in describing the situation wrote that "if by some manner or means these men" could have been "unshackled and all provided with Winchesters," what a "scattering" there would have been. Quickly the deputies marched their prisoners up from Garrison Avenue, with the crowd close behind them, following silently, "while the church bells tolled a requiem to the dead victims of this blood thirsty gang." The only other sound was the clanking of their chains upon the sidewalk. Three blocks away the iron gate opened into the old government barracks enclosure. The marshals and their prisoners passed through, and the gate screeched to a close behind as the territory's most savage band of criminals walked within the majesty of Judge Parker's law.

There are some obvious mistakes in names and accounts of what happened. First, they called Louis Davis, Willie Davis. Second, Mrs. Hassan did not die; in the hysteria, rumors were undoubtedly running amuck. Some of the rumors were evidently printed. This story of the

Buck Gang and its capture appeared in the *Muskogee Phoenix*, August 15, 1895:

Rufus Buck and his gang of outlaws, except one, are in limbo at Fort Smith, and are glad to be within its protecting walls. Hundreds of men, whites, Indians and Negroes, in the central portion of the nation turned out to hunt them. Every hill, every bottom and every trail for miles around was being critically searched, and there was hardly a hope for the brutal young men who had suddenly made such a record of fiendish crime. For several days, the officers trailed them before they began raping. A squad of officers was within three miles of them when they raped Mrs. Hassan, their first victim, and did not learn anything of it until some hours later when they approached the place and learned of the crime. The search then became more vigorous. The people became panic-stricken. Women and children were congregated together and put under guard for their protection, and the men went to hunt down the outlaws. Marshals, police, lighthorse and citizens covered the country for miles. The gang was trailed by their week of crime. Women were raped, men shot, stores burglarized, horses stolen, people robbed on the highway. All kinds of crimes and indignities perpetrated against people. The story was worse than we published last week and its details are too revolting to print. Wednesday they robbed Norburg & Co.'s store at Arbekochee of $20 in money and about $300 worth of jewelry and goods. They took two watches, one a solid gold watch, chain and charm worth about $150. They took boots, clothing, guns, cartridges, canned goods and candies. They selected high grade clothing, boots and hats, the best in the house. The boots were tied together for saddle riders and the legs were filled with cartridges. This robbery was about three o'clock in the evening. They were trailed for many miles toward the Concharty mountains. About 3 o'clock in the morning they were heard shooting. The pursuers had lost their trail, and when daylight came Captain Edmond Harry, of the Okmulgee district lighthorse, with a squad of five men, went out to reconnoiter in search of the trail. There were with him Lighthorsemen, Sam Haynes, Tom Grayson, Dave Bruner, Skengar and Sandy Tobler.

A posse of citizens composed of Stanford Berryhill, J. A. McMullen, W. S. Hines, Harry Walker, John Gossett, Thos. Berryhill, William Berryhill and J. H. Minter under the leadership of C. G. Sloan, who had been attracted by the shooting and were upon the outlaws' trail coming from the opposite direction. Captain Harry found the trail and the outlaws at the same time. They were on a little hill where they had stopped to rest, and before beginning their day's work were taking an inventory of what they had stolen and were cleaning up their guns. Goods and ammunition were scattered over the ground and Buck was cleaning his gun when they were discovered. Both sides began shooting at once. The robbers were taken by surprise and were driven from their horses and ammunition. The lighthorse dismounted and a fight on foot lasted fifteen or twenty minutes. The outlaws retreated, running from tree to tree, fighting as they ran. They shot about twenty-five times each. Just as they had unloaded their guns they ran into Sloan's squad of citizens who were coming, meeting them. They surrendered and it was discovered that there was never a poorer score made out of so many shots. Three horses were killed and some others wounded, but not a man was scratched. At the beginning of the fight a bullet passed through Captain Harry's hat, and grazed his head. The force of the shot knocked him from his horse and stunned him, but it brought no blood. Three of the outlaws surrendered to the citizens. Captain Harry says they were going away from the lighthorse and if it had not been for the citizens, they would have escaped. The three who surrendered were Rufus Buck, Neoma [Maoma] and Lucky Davis and Willie [Louis] Davis escaped. It was also thought at the time that Sam Simpson [Sampson] fell down in the grass and was overlooked. Sam was badly scared. They were all young fellows and had never been in a fight before. After the fight, he went home and told his sister that he was afraid they were going to kill him and he wanted to get to the officers and surrender to them for protection. He preferred standing his chance with the law to getting into another like that one. She hitched up a wagon and concealing him in bed at the bottom of the wagon she started to take him to Okmulgee to turn him over to the marshals. On the road, the officers and citizens with the other prisoners overtook them and took charge of frightened Sam. Along the road, the people dropped into line in squads and pled with the officers to give the prisoners to them. Some cried in their rage to find the ravishers so near and yet so far. The strong guard of officers and the temerity of the law-abiding country people at antagonizing the law prevented a raid to mob the prisoners.

When they got to Okmulgee, the town was crowded with people who heard of the fight and came in from miles around to see the criminals. Nearly everyone had suffered in person or through a relative or friend from their crimes, and a mobbing was the cry. The prisoners were put upstairs in the stone capitol building and were strongly guarded, but it looked for a while as if the mob would rescue the prisoners from their stronghold and mob them. The conservative element talked to the crowd and the officers promised them that they would hold the prisoners securely and deliver them to Judge Parker who would execute swift justice unto them. The people of the country have an abiding faith in Judge Parker in such cases, and when handcuffs and shackles were put on the prisoners the mob sentiment began to subside. But it remained so threatening that the officers thought best to steal them away from Okmulgee and bring them to Muskogee that night. Saturday they were landed in jail here. It was visitor's day at the jail, and all people could get in. Scores of people went to see them. They were admitted in little squads by Jailer Rector, and the people pushed and scrambled to get in when the gate was open. The prisoners got tired of the curious gaze and crouched in the corners of their cell to avoid it. Buck was the only one who looked the crowd steadily and sullenly in the face.

It was the common expression during the day that the gang should be lynched, and by night the mob sentiment was fairly developed. About six o'clock, Benton Callahan, Mr. Hassen [Hassan], the husband of one of the outraged women, and the father of the girl who died from the outrages of the gang, together with some others from the west, came into the city. It is probable that they were merely on their way to Fort Smith to appear against the prisoners, but it started rumors of a lynching bee to occur that night, and the presence of the aggrieved parties lent vigor to the local mob advocates. By night, it was very well understood that a mob would be organized. Rumors came that a strong band would come in from the country for the purpose, and that a party would come up from Checotah. People from all over town began to bunch together under the arc light on Main Street, until the street was almost blockaded. When the train came from the south the crowd rushed the train to see who had come from Checotah. It seemed to be disappointed when only Joe Lighdell and Perry Murphy from Checotah, as innocent and meek-looking as country deacons, got off the train, and they were not prepared to do any good at a hanging bee. In the meanwhile, Marshal Rutherford had put a strong guard in the jail stockade, and expressed a determination that the prisoners should be protected.

After the train left, the crowd again gathered in Main Street in expectancy, and directly it began to move to the courthouse. It was a speechmaking from the courthouse steps; it marched back to Main Street and then toward the jail. Just before reaching the jail, it was met by Marshal Rutherford and Chief Deputy McDonald. The mob was halted and then it was the government's time to do speechmaking. Mr. McDonald made an earnest talk which made the mob waiver. Marshal Rutherford followed in an appeal to them to abide the law, and ordered them to disperse. He stated the jail was stationed with guards. The prisoners could not be had without a fight. He appreciated the indignation and the feeling which impelled the people to arise against the prisoners, but the majesty of the law must be preserved at any cost, and the life of one of the citizens or one of the guards was worth the whole coop of prisoners. When he referred to Judge Parker as a certain punisher of crime, the crowd cheered. Before he had finished speaking, the crowd began to break and drift away, and directly all were moving back towards town.

During all of this threatening time, the prisoners lay on the floor of their cells and slept, utterly oblivious of the storm that was waging against them on the outside.

By twelve o'clock most everybody was abed, but some of the boys were out for a hanging, and were determined to have a hanging. So they stuffed a dummy and hung it on an electric light pole in front of the Patterson Mercantile Co. The next morning the prisoners were carried to Fort Smith and lodged in jail without further trouble, and the dummy was laid to rest.

The report comes to town that Willie [Louis] Davis, the member of the Buck gang who escaped in the fight with the officers last Thursday, has been arrested. He went to the home of an Indian on Salt Creek about eight miles west of the fight and the Indian family took charge of him and sent word to the lighthorse to come and get him last Sunday. Tom Grayson and Jim Haynes went out to the home, and it is expected they will bring him in today if he does not die from his wounds and escapes lynching. He was shot through the shoulder and leg in the fight, and the party who carried the information to the officers said the wounds were badly inflamed and were smelling badly. It develops that four women was the number raped by the gang. Mr. Ayers' daughter, the girl who was taken from the wagon outraged, was the first to die. An Indian girl was outraged near Sapulpa and died the latter part of the week and information comes from Okmulgee that Mrs. Hassen [Hassan] has died. [This rumor was not correct; Mrs. Hassan later testified at the trial.] A Mrs. Wilson, an elderly lady, was outraged by only one member of the gang and will recover.

A gentleman from Okmulgee says that it was a sight to see the fury of the crowd at Okmulgee when the prisoners came in. Hundreds of people wanted them, and were yelling to hang them, and shooting their guns in the air at once. The prisoners were scared almost senseless. The mob, shooting and yelling, made a break to get them. The officers ran their team to an open gate in the wall of the capital yard. The prisoners were tied hand and foot and the officers in their hurrying threw them out of the wagon. They were too badly scared to see the open gate, and tried to climb the wall to es-

97

cape the crowd. They were rushed into the capital building and saved. The crowd was from all quarters, of all colors, of all kinds, and continued to come in during the day. It looked like Falstaff's army. They were riding mules, horses and ponies, with saddle, bare-backed, blind bridles, rope halters, and every kind of quick make-shift. They bore rifles, shotguns, pistols and clubs. It was an ominous crowd and had blood in its eye. The mob sentiment subsided somewhat the first day, but the second people came in from the country and quietly planned a mob that Friday night, but the officers got onto it and slipped the prisoners away. It was a determined crowd of fighters who wanted them the second day and the citizens of the town think that they would have taken them Friday night even if a fight had occurred.

Even with the mistakes and misspelled names in the news story, the excitement of the event is conveyed by the item. That the majority of the populace was affected by the gangs is an understatement. The court case was assigned to Assistant District Attorney McDonough, who had prosecuted Cherokee Bill and obtained his second conviction. For a week, McDonough collected evidence surrounding the gang's "most shocking, dastardly crime" — the rape of Rosetta Hassan — which was placed before the grand jury and an indictment returned as follows:

UNITED STATES OF AMERICA, WESTERN DISTRICT OF ARKANSAS. IN THE CIRCUIT COURT, MAY TERM, A.D., 1895
UNITED STATES
vs.
RUFUS BUCK and LEWIS DAVIS and LUCKY DAVIS   RAPE
and SAM SAMPSON and MAOMA JULY.
The grand jurors of the United States of America, duly se-lected, empaneled, sworn and charged to inquire into and for the body of the Western District of Arkansas aforesaid, upon their oath present:
That Rufus Buck and Lewis Davis and Lucky Davis and Sam Sampson and Maoma July, on the 5th day of August, A.D., 1895, at the Creek nation, in the Indian country, within the Western District of Arkansas aforesaid, in and upon Rosetta Hassan, a white woman, and not an Indian, feloniously, forcibly and violently an as-sault did make, and her, the said Rosetta Hassan, then and there, and against her will, forcibly, violently and feloniously, did ravish and carnally know, contrary to the form of the statue in such case

98

made and provided, and the peace and dignity of the United States of America.

E. V. Black, Foreman of Grand Jury.
James F. Read, U.S. District Attorney,
Western District of Arkansas.

An insightful account of what happened during the trial is given in S. W. Harman's *Hell on the Border*:

At 8:30 o'clock on the Tuesday, August 20, the prisoners were taken into open court and arraigned; they entered pleas of not guilty and September 23 was set for a hearing of the case, time being allowed for the assembling of witnesses.

On the day of the trial, court opened at 8:30. Within a short time the courtroom was packed with an eager crowd, of all kinds and classes, and the whole motley throng, unmindful of the suffocating heat, sat through the trial, eagerly drinking in the loathsome details of the horrible crime; some out of pure depravity and for the mere sake of feeding upon a recital of an awful wickedness, others drawn thither by an inborn craving, as the buzzard or the vulture is attracted to the polluted carrion whose odor ascends to the heavens; others that they might gain a knowledge of the minutest details of the frightful crime and so work themselves to a pitch where they could more fully enjoy the punishment, even if inadequate, so certain to be dealt them.

Henry Hassan, the husband of the injured woman, was the first witness examined. He described how, on Monday, the fifth day of August, as he lay sleeping beneath an arbor, his wife sitting nearby preparing fruit for the family larder, the gang rode through the front gate. Awakening, he greeted them pleasantly and asked them if they were hunting. Buck replied in the affirmative and called for water. Sending his wife's little brother for a pail of fresh water he started to meet them and then discovering that one of the number was Lewis Davis, with whom he had previously had some slight difficulty, he knew he was at the mercy of the terrible band of whose depredations he had heard. He hesitated a moment, then started for a corner of the house, hoping to reach cover, then enter a door, inside of which hung his Winchester. He gained the corner safely, then ran towards the door and as he started to enter was stopped by Maoma July, who had entered from an opposite door and securing the coveted rifle now brushed his face with its muzzle, while Sampson at the same time covered him with a six-shooter. Hassan backed away, and the others coming up, Buck, with an air of bravado, said: "I'm Cherokee Bill's brother; we want your money." With vile curses they commanded

99

Hassan to sit in a place designated, then ordered his wife and her mother to prepare dinner. The women hastened to cook a meal, and meanwhile Lewis Davis stayed with Hassan to keep him under control by threats of death, boastfully declaring himself to be Tom Root. While the meal was being made ready, the rest of the gang searched the house and appropriated $5.95 cash, a suit of clothing, some baby's dresses, together with whatever struck their fancy. After having appeased their appetites, they came out and stood guard over Hassan while the negro went in to dinner, after which the assault on Mrs. Hassan was made.

Having satisfied their lusts, they mounted their horses and ordered Hassan to go with them; just then a young man came, unsuspectingly, to the house from a little distance and they held him up, and marched both him and Hassan two miles away and, after dire threats of death, amused themselves by making the men dance while they fired random bullets at their bare feet. Their next amusement was to compel the men to jump into a pool of water, then forced them to wrestle and fight, then commanded Hassan to kill the other. Finally, when their ideas of fun were exhausted, they ordered the men to go home, warning them: "If you ever appear against us, our friends will kill you." Hassan hurried to his home as soon as released, but found his wife was missing. She had been so wrought up over the ordeal through which she had passed, believing it the only means of saving her husband's life, the continued absence of the latter had caused her to believe her sacrifice had been useless and that he had already fallen a victim to their love of crime, and finally, overcome with fear, she had fled to a nearby cornfield and hid. After a continued search, her husband found her, in a paroxysm of fear, nearly dead from apprehension. Hassan's story, as related on the witness stand, was straightforward, and was given with but little interruption on the part of the prosecuting attorney and whatever by the attorneys for defense. Through it all the members of the gang sat unmoved, pretending an inability to understand English. If the testimony of the husband was listened to by the vast assemblage with thrilling interest, then there is no adjective capable of describing the interest shown during the time that the injured wife and mother was giving a recital of her wrongs.

The murmur of indignation that ran through the crowd when Hassan stopped speaking and retired, ceased as Mrs. Hassan was escorted into the courtroom and took position on the stand, and but for the bustle occasioned by the shifting and craning of necks by the members of the crowd to secure a view of the witness, all was silent . . .

Her appearance was most modest and it was evidently with a great effort that she was able to sit there, under so many curious pair of eyes. She still showed the effects of her frightful experience. She spoke slowly and in low but tremulous tones showing the strong nervous tension under which she was still laboring; at times her breath came quick, the hot blood surged to her temples and with her head bowed low she would give way to heartrending sobs, as the questions propounded by the prosecution or the court brought back with awful vividness the horrible scene through which she passed but a few weeks before. She related, much as her husband had done, the coming of the gang to her home, to ask for water, of her fears for the life of her husband, of the hastily prepared meal which she hoped might be the means of saving him. Urged to tell what occurred after they had eaten, she described between sobs, how Lucky Davis, the [N]egro, had told her: "You have to go with me," and how she pleaded with him not to take her away from her babies; how he had replied, "We will throw the G-d — brats in the creek"; how he had commanded her to mount his horse and ride away with him, only desisting when she declared she could not ride; how he then ordered her to go with him a little way, and she hesitated and had finally obeyed, believing if she refused they would kill her and the rest of her family, and marched on, while the black brute held the muzzle of the Winchester close to her head. She told how they continued until they reached the back side of the barn, out of sight of the house and 200 feet away, and of Davis then laying down his rifle and drawing a pistol from his belt — then paused.

Judge Parker said kindly, "Just go on and tell everything that occurred there. The law makes it necessary to tell it. It is a very delicate matter, of course, but you will have to tell about it."

"Did he tell you what to do?" asked Mr. McDonough.

"Yes sir," she answered in a tone barely audible.

"What did he say?"

"He told me to lie down"; and the witness broke down completely, while her frame shook with convulsions and she sobbed like a child, yet as a child could not. The effect on the audience was magnetic. They had listened with sympathetic eagerness, forgetful of their own existence, and the result, when the climax was reached is indescribable; during the several minutes that elapsed before the witness could regain her composure there was the most profound silence, broken only by her sobs; . . . The few women in the crowd gave way to a mighty surge of grief, and even Judge Parker . . . removed his spectacles and while a suspicious moisture twinkled upon his lashes, drew a handkerchief from his pocket, wiped the lenses, then spoke a few words of gentle encouragement to the witness.

Mrs. Hassan, unwillingly, continued to describe what followed, and gave an account of each one of the brutal outlaws taking their turn at the revolting crime, while at all times, three of the gang remained on guard over the husband, ready to send a bullet crashing through his brain, if he attempted to fight or made an outcry.

It required no effort on the part of any member of the jury to arrive at a verdict of guilty. They did not even take time to ballot. One of their number was chosen foreman, his signature was affixed, and the jury was once returned to the court room, where in silence, the verdict was awaited. It read: "We, the jury, find the defendants, Rufus Buck, Lewis Davis, Luckey Davis, Sam Sampson, and Maoma July guilty of rape, as charged in the within indictment. (Signed) John N. Ferguson, Foreman."

A most remarkable fact is here to be related. Immediately after finding of the indictment for the rape of Mrs. Hassan, the grand jury had returned a true bill charging the Buck gang with murder, the victim named being the Negro marshal John Garrett, the killing of whom was the first crime committed by them as they started out on their short and terrible career. As soon as the verdict convicting them of rape was read, Judge Parker excused the jury and at once another panel was drawn, a new jury was selected, and, without being permitted to leave their seats, the prisoners were placed on trial for murder. The case continued until the next day, resulting in a verdict of guilty.

Wednesday, September 25, was a day that the Buck Gang and the massive crowd remembered. They assembled in the courtroom to hear Judge Parker pronounce the sentence. He said:

"Rufus Buck, Lewis Davis, Lucky Davis, Sam Sampson and Maoma July, stand up. You have been convicted by a verdict of the jury, justly rendered, of the terrible crime of rape. It now becomes the duty of this court to pass sentence upon which the law says shall follow a conviction of such crime. Have you anything to say why the sentence of the law should not now be passed in your case?"

"Yes, suh," Lucky Davis replied. "I wants my case to go the Supreme Court."

"I don't blame you," commented Judge Parker, then he continued speaking to all of them. "I want to say in this case that the jury, under the law and the evidence, could come to no other conclusion than that which they arrived at. Their verdict is an entirely just one, and one that must be approved of all lovers of virtue. The offense of which you have been convicted is one which shocks all men who are not brutal. It is known to the law as a crime offensive to decency, and as a brutal attack upon the honor and chastity of the weaker sex. It is a violation of the quick sense of honor and the pride of virtue

102

which nature, to render the sex amiable, has implanted in the female heart, and it has been by the law-makers of the United States deemed equal in enormity and wickedness to murder, because the punishment fixed by the same is that which follows the commission of the crime of murder . . .

"Your crime leaves no ground for the extension of sympathy . . . You can expect no more sympathy than lovers of virtue and haters of vice can extend to men guilty of one of the most brutal, wicked, repulsive and dastardly crimes known in the annals of crime. Your duty now is to make an honest effort to receive from a just God that mercy and forgiveness you so much need. We are taught that His mercy will wipe out even this horrible crime; but He is just, and His justice decrees punishment unless you are able to make atonement for the revolting crime against His law and against human law that you have committed. This horrible crime now rests upon your souls. Remove it if you can so the good God of all will extend to you His forgiveness and His mercy.

"Listen now to the sentence of the law which is, that you, Rufus Buck, for the crimes of rape, committed by you upon Rosetta Hassan, in the Indian country, and within the jurisdiction of this court, of which crime you stand convicted by the verdict of the jury in your case, be deemed, taken and adjudged guilty of rape; and that you be therefore, for the said crime against the laws of the United States, hanged by the neck until you are dead; that the marshal of the Western District of Arkansas, by himself or deputy, or deputies, cause execution to be done in the premises upon you on Thursday, the thirty-first day of October, 1895, between the hours of 9 o'clock in the forenoon and 5 o'clock in the afternoon of the said day; and that you now be taken to the jail from whence you came, to be there closely and securely kept, until the day of execution, and from thence on the day of execution as aforesaid, you are to be taken to the place of execution, there to be hanged by the neck until you are dead.

"May God, whose laws you have broken, and before whose tribunal you must then appear, have mercy on your soul."

He then pronounced the sentence upon each remaining member of the gang, while they "exhibited no sign" and seemed to care nothing of it.

An interesting story concerns Sam Sampson. Supposedly he was persuaded to join the Buck Gang, after they murdered U.S. Deputy Marshal Garrett, as a decoy. In doing so he committed crimes as the others did, therefore not drawing suspicion from the gang on himself.

During his incarceration, Sampson appealed to the man who had persuaded him to serve as a decoy but the man acted ignorant about the agreement. Therefore he was not exonerated by his "friend," and met the same fate as the rest of the gang.

Buck claimed that, given the opportunity, he could prove an alibi, and the case was appealed. Judge Parker issued a stay of execution, but this time the Supreme Court refused to interfere. The decision was affirmed without opinion, and Judge Parker resentenced the gang to hang on July 1, 1896.

The trial was amply covered by the Fort Smith press and newspapers in the Indian Territory, St. Louis, Little Rock, Kansas City, and other cities near and far.

The following report of the execution was in the *Cherokee Advocate,* July 11, 1896:

> Rufus Buck, Louis Davis, Lucky Davis, Maomi [a] July and Sam Sampson comprising what is known as the Buck gang were executed here today. President Cleveland refusing to interfere in the carrying out of the sentence of Judge Parker's court.
>
> The Buck gang, composed of five members, were convicted of murder and rape September 23rd, 1895, in Judge Parker's court, and sentenced to hang on October 31. An appeal to the Supreme Court acted as a stay, but the appeal was in vain, the higher court refusing to interfere.
>
> The condemned men spent a good portion of Tuesday night in devotional exercises, singing and praying until about 3 o'clock when they retired. For several days they had received instructions from Father Pius, pastor of German Catholic Church, and Tuesday that gentleman administered to them the rite of baptism. Wednesday morning they arose at the usual hour and ate their breakfast with the usual degree of relish.
>
> Tuesday morning the prisoners in the lower tier spent a couple of hours with the boys singing hymns, which were interspersed with prayer. The inmates of the upper tiers joined in the exercises and altogether the scene was solemn. When the religious exercises were at an end the jail quieted down. The usual hilarity and boisterous behavior of the inmates ceased. All seemed to feel the solemnity of the occasion.
>
> Tuesday it was decided that the execution should take place at 10 o'clock. There was a division of opinion upon the matter. Lucky Davis, the little negro, wanted to be hanged at 10 o'clock in the morning. He wanted the business done so that his body could be taken home on the Cannon Ball at 11:30 o'clock. The others ob-

104

jected. Rufus Buck said that if he were hanged at an early hour he would be subjected to the inconvenience of several hours' delay before he started, and this would inconvenience him. The four Indian boys sided together. Luckey Davis held out. Finally it was agreed that Col. Crump should set the hour, and he set it at one o'clock. Luckey suggested that he be hanged by himself, but to this Col. Crump objected.

The "gang" was usually well behaved most of the time while they were in prison, and were unusually quiet after Father Pius began to give them instructions. Major Berry, the jailor, says he never has any trouble with malefactors after the Catholic priests have begun to work with them.

It was seven minutes past 1 o'clock when the doors of the jail opened for the egress of the condemned men. As they passed out, many of their fellow-prisoners called out, "Good-bye boys." The poor fellows responded in a rather low tone of voice. Rufus Buck was the first to come from the jail door. He was perfectly calm. The others followed, and were equally cool. All were clad in black suits, and Rufus Buck, Maomi [a] July and Lucky Davis wore large boutonnieres upon the left lapels of their coats. Father Pius, their faithful spiritual adviser, accompanied them, closely following the train toward the gallows were the sisters of Sam Sampson and Lucky Davis.

When the prisoners entered the gallows enclosure they took a glance at its hideous paraphernalia and then ascended the steps without the least sign of emotion. They remained seated upon the bench while Col. Crump read the death warrant. Most of the officers and spectators seemed impressed by this part of the proceedings, and stood with uncovered heads. When this part of the preliminaries had been disposed of, Col. Crump asked the condemned men if they had any remarks to make. All except Lucky said they had not. Lucky simply said he wanted the priest to pray for him.

Father Pius uttered a short prayer in silence during which all present stood with uncovered heads.

This over, the prisoners stepped upon the fatal trap. As they did so they recognized a number of persons among the crowd around the gallows and saluted them. Lucky Davis shouted, "Good-bye Martha," to his sister, who stood in the corner of the yard, and Sam Sampson extended the same salutation to his sister who was also present. Rufus Buck and all the others bade young Dick Berry good-bye. Dick had been about the jail a great deal and has been mighty clever to the boys.

It took but a short time to complete the work after the preliminaries had been arranged. The prisoners stepped forward like Trojans. During the time Col. Crump was reading the warrants none of

105

the condemned men except Lucky Davis showed any signs of trepidation. Lucky was nervous, and showed his nervousness by restless movements and twitching of his face. Beyond this he showed no signs of fear. When he stood upon the scaffold he was perfectly cool. He kept repeating prayers even after the black cap was placed over his head.

The trap dropped with its horrible "chug" at 1:28 o'clock. Louie Davis died in three minutes, his neck being broken. The necks of Sam Sampson, and Maomi [a] July were also broken and they died easily. Rufus Buck and Lucky Davis were strangled to death.

After the attending physician had pronounced life extinct, the bodies were cut down and placed in coffins. Three of them were taken to Birnie's Undertaking Establishment, and from there shipped to their former homes.

Davis's body drew up several times before it straightened out. Rufus Buck did not suffer, of course, unconsciousness coming over him as soon as the rope tightened around his neck and shut off his breath; but it was several minutes before the contortions of his body ceased.

The father of Rufus Buck, a big, heavy old man, got into the jail enclosure and attempted to come up the steps to the platform where his son stood; but he was stupidly drunk and for that reason was escorted below.

The sisters of Sam Sampson and Lucky Davis entered the gallows-yard and stood until the black caps were placed in position. Then they left, returning however as soon as the trap fell.

The execution was conducted in a quiet and orderly manner. There were very few inside of the jail-yard, Col. Crump having issued an order that only physicians and reporters would be admitted, and the order was rigidly applied.

The Buck gang was executed for the crime of rape. The case murder, with which they were charged, never came to trial, neither were any of the other offenses against them.

This, we believe, is the first time in history of this country that five men have been sentenced by one court and executed by one gallows for this hideous crime.

The executions Wednesday swell to eighty-five the number of those who have been charged at this place for violating the laws of the country.

Little sympathy has been felt for the men executed Wednesday, owing to the fiendishness of the crimes committed by them. For downright dare deviltry and complete abandon they stand at the head of all the dissolute characters who have swung into eternity on the gallows at the federal jail.

In Rufus Buck's cell, after his execution, was found a photograph of his mother. On its back, he sketched a strange farewell poem, decorated with a cross and a drawing of the Savior. It read:

My, dream, — 1896
I, dreamp't, I was, in, heaven,
Among, the, angels, fair;
i'd, near, seen, non, so handsome,
that, twine, in, golden, hair;
they, looked, so, neat, and, sang, so, sweet
and, play'd, the, the, golden harp,
i, was, about, to pick, an angel, out,
and, take, her, to my, heart;
but, the, moment, i, began, to plea,
i, thought, of, you, my love,
there, was none, i'd, seen, so, beautifull,
on, earth, or heaven, above,
good, bye, my, dear, wife, and. mother

all.so.my.sisters

RUFUS, BUCK

Youse. Truley

I Day. of. July
Tu, the, Yeore
off
1896

H
O
L
Y
Father   Son
G
H
O
S
T

virtue & resurresur.rection.

Remember, Me, Rock, Of, Ages

107

CHAPTER 9

Others Who Rode the Trail of Crime

One of the first tasks Heck Thomas took on after receiving his commission as a U.S. deputy marshal in 1886 was to search out the black outlaw Della Humby, who had been a confederate of Jim and Pink Lee. Jim and Pink had stolen cattle in Texas and found refuge in the Chickasaw Nation until Heck and Jim Taylor, a U.S. deputy marshal, killed them.

Della Humby was charged with murdering his wife; he also shot and killed Sgt. James Guy of the Chickasaw Indian police while hiding out at the Lees. Humby had a $400 bounty on him and was the last of the Lee gang riding the territory.

In the process of tracking down Humby, Heck arrested three black outlaws with outstanding warrants. The first was Tom Ike, wanted for larceny, whiskey selling, and assault with intent to kill. The next two were John Davis, who had murdered a young white man in Texas, and Emmanuel Patterson, who had killed Willard Ayers, a U.S. deputy marshal, six years before. All three were caught in the Chickasaw Nation.

Humby had been with the three but had left for the Seminole Nation where he had friends. On December 29, 1886, Heck and his posse reached Sasakwa, where Seminole Chief John Brown had his mansion and operated a trading post and store. Brown summoned a Seminole

Lighthorseman (police) to assist them in their search for Humby. Just before dark, they located Humby in the abandoned cabin of an old trader named Manuel Buenes. Humby was arrested without a fight after being surprised and caught off-guard.

Emmanuel Patterson got a life sentence for killing Deputy Ayers, and died in prison. Davis was prosecuted in Texas. Tom Ike received a stiff sentence for his crime. Humby was ably defended by Fort Smith attorneys, who fought his case through two terms of court. In the first trial, he was found guilty; in the second, acquitted. And when Heck Thomas went to collect the $400 reward, he learned that it had been withdrawn.

Backing the Boomer cause for their own self-interest, railroads, banks, and other commercial developers lobbied Congress for the opening of Indian lands to settlement. Congress succumbed and, in 1887, passed the General Allotment Act (or the Dawes Severalty Act), which broke certain tribal landholdings into tracts and allotted them to individual Indians who sold them to whites. By 1889, two million acres had been bought from the Indians, usually at ridiculously low prices, and thrown open to white settlement in the land run.

On May 2, 1890, President Harrison signed the Organic Act, which created six counties and six county seats and extended the territory to include all of the former Indian Territory except the tribal reservations of the Quapaw Agency northeast of them, and the unoccupied portions of the Cherokee Outlet, but including the Public Land Strip and Greer County.

Now there were two territories — one called Oklahoma and one called Indian, which was basically where the Five Civilized Tribes resided in Eastern Oklahoma. Black outlaws were active also in this new territory called Oklahoma. This new territory was located in the center of the present state; Guthrie was chosen as the legislative capital of the territory.

Chris Madsen, another well-known U.S. deputy marshal, worked out of the El Reno and Guthrie marshals' office. There is a story concerning Madsen traveling into the Arbuckle Mountains, west of Ardmore, to arrest a notorious black known as Jo-Jo. This Jo-Jo was distinguished by being tall and fierce-looking and wearing huge brass earrings. Madsen was able to arrest him and bring him in without incidence.

On another occasion, Madsen had a warrant for a black man who resided on Walnut Creek, east of Chickasha. Madsen found out the

109

suspect had smallpox and told him to report to Chickasha as soon as he got better. The wanted black man gave his word and kept it.

Madsen said the court in El Reno was filled with a wide assortment of characters including outlaws, cowboys, blacks, Freedmen, ranchers, horse thieves, and Indians. He also told of a black justice of the peace in El Reno named Judge McCarver.

One of the most popular U.S. deputy marshals to work in Oklahoma Territory was George Thornton. Deputy Thornton was stationed in Oklahoma City and occasionally worked with Chris Madsen. Thornton was killed in a gun duel in the Seminole Nation by an outlaw named Captain Wiley, who was of African-Creek blood. Wiley was so badly hurt by Thornton's fire that he died in the Fort Smith jail soon afterward.

In the early 1890s, Tom Smith, captain of the Texas gunmen who had been hired for the Johnson County War of Wyoming, was saved from death by the timely intervention of African-American cavalry; he was saved only to be killed a few months later by a black desperado (name unknown) on the Santa Fe passenger train between Gainesville, Texas, and Guthrie, Oklahoma Territory.

Following are three different territorial newspaper articles giving three different versions concerning the death of Tom Smith. The first is from *The Langston City Herald* of November 17, 1892:

A DUAL DEATH
Two Men Empty Their Revolvers
and Fall Dead in Their Tracks

AN ALL-AROUND FIGHT
A Bloody Tragedy Over the Compartments
of the Texas Railroad Cars Between a
White and Colored Man In Which
Both Men Lose their Lives

State Capital. The Santa Fe railroad trainmen brought news this morning of a bloody tragedy that took place last night on the south bound train just this side of Gainesville, Texas, inside of the Chickasaw nation.

A deputy marshal named Smith went into the Negro compartment of the car that the law of Texas provides. An old colored man jocosely objected to such an infringement on the negro's rights by white men, when a colored man from Guthrie, whose name is unknown, took the matter up in earnest, and with an oath declared that the white man had no business there.

Nothing serious, took place in the cars, but when the train

stopped the two men with many others stepped off and the quarrel being resumed both men jerked out their revolvers and began shooting at each other. Emptying their revolvers, they both fell dead in their tracks. It seems that no one else was hurt.

The bodies of the two men were brought up to Ardmore where they now lie. Two other colored men were arrested as there seems to have been an all around fight, and now lay in jail at Ardmore.

The second article is from the *Muskogee Phoenix* which was printed a day earlier, on November 16:

Tom Smith, a deputy of the Paris court, was killed last Thursday night on the Santa Fe train near Thackerville, by a negro who was immediately after killed by deputy marshal Tucker. The deputies were passing through the compartment of the car reserved for the colored people, when the negro began abusing them, saying that if negroes could not ride with white folks the white folks should not ride with the negroes. Smith replied very angrily to the abuse, when the negro drew a revolver and fired, killing Smith instantly. Tucker then shot the negro through the neck, from which he died in a short time. Smith's body was put off at Ardmore, where it was prepared for burial.

The last article came from the *Lexington Leader* on November 12, 1892, and was printed even earlier and was located closer to the scene of the crime:

KILLED ON A TRAIN
A Deputy Marshal Murdered —
His Assassin in Turn Killed

Ardmore, I.T., November 7. — A bloody tragedy occurred early yesterday morning on the Santa Fe passenger train between here and Gainesville, Texas, in which one deputy marshal and a negro, passengers on the train, were killed. The tragedy took place in the half of the combination smoking car which is reserved for negroes. In that compartment of the car there were traveling four negroes and three United States deputy marshals named Smith, Armstrong and Booker. One of the negroes remarked in an offensive manner, that that portion of the car was reserved for negroes and he would like to know what business white men had in it. Deputy Marshal Smith replied that white men could ride where they pleased, and supplemented his remarks with an oath which angered the negroes. Smith was riding in front of the negroes and he rose to go back to the other compartment of the car. The negro who had started the quarrel evidently thought the deputy was about to attack him, and drawing his revolver shot him through the heart, killing him instantly. Immediately a general fight between the whites and blacks ensued, in which a large number of shots were fired on both sides.

When the melee came to an end it was found that the negro who shot Deputy Smith had himself been shot and killed. When the train arrived here all those concerned in the affair were arrested.

Oklahoma/Indian Territory was tough on legendary gunfighters. The infamous Bill Longley of Texas crossed the Red River into Indian Territory looking for a sanctuary. He had a fight with some tough Indians and received a bad gunshot wound. A half-breed Cherokee girl nursed him until he could make his way to the house of a friend in Arkansas. You could say he got his fill of the "Nations."

On June 30, 1895, the Christian brothers made a daring escape from the Oklahoma County jail in Oklahoma City. The jail was situated at the juncture of an alley running north from Grand Avenue and an alley connecting Broadway and Robinson. Bill and Bob Christian had been incarcerated for killing Deputy Sheriff Will Turner of Pottawatomie County in a grove near Violet Springs. On that Sunday afternoon, the Christian brothers made good their escape from the county jail and murdered Oklahoma City Police Chief Milt Jones in the process. One of the local newspapers stated, ". . . it is known that they now have four followers who are among the worst of the Indian Territory desperados — John Fessenden, John Reeves, Doc Williams and Ben Brown, a powerful negro and notorious thief and bad man."

On Sunday, July 5, 1896, Bill Doolin, one of Oklahoma Territory's most famous outlaws, escaped from the Guthrie jail along with thirteen prisoners. The ringleader of the jailbreak was a black outlaw of African-Cherokee descent named George Lane. The following is an account describing Lane's capture by U.S. Deputy Marshal Heck Thomas from *West of Hell's Fringe*:

> Thomas had learned from a letter observed by a friendly postmistress that George Lane, whose daring had effected the wholesale jail delivery for Doolin, was stopping with friends near Greenwood, a small town thirty miles east of Kansas City. At Kansas City, Heck contacted Chris Madsen. Being outside his jurisdiction, he asked Madsen to accompany him. On the afternoon of November 19, the two deputy marshals took the train to Greenwood, passing through the settlement so they would not be seen getting off the train, then hired a livery rig and drove to the cabin where Lane was staying a

112

half-mile from town. It had been Lane's boast that he: ". . . would never be taken alive," and the marshals took no chances. About dusk they left their team in the vicinity of the cabin. Thomas went to the rear door and Madsen to the front. As they rapped, an old colored woman stepped to the rear door, opened it, while Lane, who had been sitting before the fire whittling, stepped to the front door, the knife still in his hand. He was covered by the pistols of the two deputies so quickly that he offered no resistance, and his hands went obediently into the air.

Lane was brought to the city last night and the necessary papers for his return to Guthrie were granted.

"I regard him as the real 'bad man' in the territory," said Marshal Thomas to a *Times* reporter. "His escape proved it . . . Doolin, Dynamite Dick, and all of them were afraid to make the break, except Lane."

Lane once served a penitentiary sentence in Texas for horsestealing . . . but during his youth went to school at Lincoln Institute, Jefferson City. He talks well and readily, and expressed no chagrin at his arrest.

"After I broke jail," he said, "they hunted me night and day. Many times I could have reached out and touched them . . . once I swam the Cimarron River with shots whistling around my head. Another time I stepped over the sleeping bodies of the Osage chief of police and two assistants, secured a gun, and walked away. I could have killed them all as they slept.

"I knew the country better than my pursuers . . . but it was a dog's life I led. Green corn was ripe then, thank God, or I would have starved to death. Once I didn't even have that for three days."

On December 20, 1937, William J. Layne, justice of the peace at Hartshorne, Oklahoma, gave the following account of an African-American outlaw:

I was the first elected marshal of this town when it first got a charter in the days when this was Gaines County, Indian Territory.

The first city marshal was appointed; they appointed Jim Brasell. He didn't particularly want the job, but kept it until we could have an election. I was elected in 1903 and served two years . . .

I never captured any famous law breakers, but I can tell you about one case that happened before I became marshal. It was the capture of the famous, or maybe I should say, "noted," outlaw named Step Ody. I didn't help capture him, but I know all the details; I saw Ody before and after the capture.

Ody was considered quite a bad man and had a big reputation

in this part of the Choctaw Nation. He was a Negro; lots of the early day outlaws were.

In 1900 I was working at old Number 2 mine, now abandoned. You can see the remains of the dump yet, a mile east of "Slate Ford" on Brushy Creek.

One day after lunch — I was working "on top" — I went for a walk through the woods; you know how a man likes to do that sometimes. I walked along the side of a hill and sat down to rest awhile before going back to work. I noticed a cabin down in the bottom below.

A man came riding up to the cabin. He tied his horse out of sight in a shed and knocked on the door; a Negro woman opened the door for him. The man looked up at me and I got a good view of his face; he was, as I found out later, Step Ody, the outlaw, I heard him say, "Who's that man up there on the hill?" The woman answered, "It's all right, he's just one of the miners."

I never thought any more about the incident until after Ody was captured, and then I remembered seeing him that day . . .

Ellis, Fortune, and some others cornered Step Ody in an abandoned log cabin in the Brush bottoms. He shot it out with them until he ran out of shells, then he called out that he was giving himself up, and walked out with his hands in the air.

I saw him when they brought him to town. They put him in jail here overnight, then took him to Fort Smith to stand trial there. He was a horse thief and a killer, and general all around bad man.

The first execution in the Indian Territory under the laws of the United States occurred at Muskogee, on July 1, 1898, when Henry Whitefield and K. B. Brooks, two African-Americans, suffered the death penalty for murders and rape committed in the Northern Judicial District of the Indian Territory after the removal of the jurisdiction of the Indian Territory from the United States District and Circuit Courts for the Western District of Arkansas.

According to the *Muskogee Daily Phoenix,* the most famous gunfight ever staged in the streets of Muskogee occurred between a band of black socialist and city police with U.S. deputy marshals led by Bud Ledbetter. This gun battle took place on March 26, 1907.

In 1905, at Wagoner, I.T., a black former preacher named William Wright organized a society he called the Tenth Cavalry. He called himself General Grant and had circulars printed which proclaimed him to be an agent of the president of the United States. President Roosevelt sent the Secret Service to Wagoner to investigate Wright's Society.

114

The Tenth Cavalry suddenly went out of business and Wright left town.

Wright next showed up in Muskogee, where he organized a society called the Money Diggers. He claimed to have received Divine revelation as to where treasure was buried. The men were charged $5.00 and the women $1.50 to join. He usually salted the digging site ahead of time. As soon as the coins were dug up, he talked his followers into giving them to him for safekeeping. Wright got too greedy to salt the diggings and the diggers soon lost interest.

Wright's next venture was the organization of the United Socialist Club. It cost ten cents to join and the new member got a badge of authority from the Private Detective Agency in Cincinnati, Ohio. There was also the promise of 160 acres of land which would be deeded over as soon as authorization was received from the president. Wright claimed to be in constant touch with the president, and the authorization to deed the land was expected momentarily.

According to Wright he taught the scriptures. He also taught anarchy and peculiar teaching of the supernatural. His followers were taught that they had the right to occupy any property they pleased without paying the owner anything. He also taught that the wearing of a conjure bag would render the wearer immune to death.

A black woman by the name of Lucy Curtis occupied a house in the south part of town which was owned by A. A. Trumbo. Trumbo was unable to get any rent from the woman or to get her to move. He hit upon the idea of moving the house to North Fifteenth Street. The black woman was unperturbed, building a fire and cooking her meals in the house while en route to the new location.

Another black woman by the name of Carrie Foreman took over a house belonging to Rowsey and Young, on Fon Du Lac Street between Second and Third streets. Being unable to collect any rent from the woman, the owners sold the house to a Mr. Sitz. When Sitz went to collect his rent, he was referred to the woman's lodge. There he was informed that she was a member of the United Socialist Club and had the right to take any property she chose and keep it as long as she pleased. Sitz promptly went to the city marshal's office and swore out a warrant for Carrie Foreman.

Two constables, John Cofield and Guy Fisher, were dispatched to serve the eviction warrant. When they arrived at the house and stated their purpose, they were seized by two male members of the Club who were both armed, one with a revolver and the other with a shotgun.

The two officers struggled with their assailants, finally managing to break away. Fisher escaped toward town but Cofield was shot through the chest, near the heart. Fisher was slightly wounded in the shoulder.

The *Muskogee Daily Phoenix* on March 26, 1922, gave the following description of the gun battle:

> About 2 o'clock in the afternoon March 26, 1907, the quiet of the town was shattered when Charlie Kimsey, chief of police, dashed down the muddy, unpaved street in his buggy, down by a spirited sorrel horse, and drew up in front of the old federal courthouse at Second and Court Streets.
>
> There he repeated the report that had come to him that Policeman John Cofield had been shot down by negroes barricaded in a big two-story building in the north end of town.
>
> "Uncle Bud" (Ledbetter) was on the front steps. He grabbed two rifles and jumped into the buggy besides Kimsey. As they dashed away, a Phoenix reporter who was also at the courthouse, scrambled into the back of the buggy and clung to the seat for his life.
>
> The other officers at the courthouse, among them Chief Deputy Marshal Ernest Hubbard and Deputy Marshal Paul C. Williams, were galvanized into action and they arrived at the scene close behind Ledbetter and Kimsey.
>
> As the chief of police drew in his horse in front of the building a rifle was fired and the zip of a bullet overhead caused "Uncle Bud" to leap out of the buggy, rifle in hand.
>
> The shot was followed by another, and Chief Kimsey's horse was panic stricken and it ran away. The reporter was thrown out of the back end of the buggy, but lost no time getting to cover. The horse dashed away with Kimsey, but as quickly as possible he regained control of the animal and hurried back.
>
> Two negroes were standing on the front porch of the building as "Uncle Bud" jumped out of the buggy. He started toward them, and as he did so they opened fire on him, one with a rifle and the other with a revolver.
>
> Almost as quickly "Uncle Bud" fired back, and one of the negroes flinched as the bullet struck him. "Uncle Bud" sought shelter behind a telephone pole and emptied his rifle at the two negroes, hitting them both several times but escaping unscathed himself.
>
> Before he had fired his last shot from his rifle and thrown it down for his pistol, Paul Williams had reached his side and together they continued the fire. Other officers surrounded the house and opened fire.

When the first of the two negroes finally fell, the other stooped to take aim at Ledbetter, but was instantly shot through the head.

As "Uncle Bud" fired this shot, another negro on the second floor poked a rifle through the window and took deliberate aim at him. Paul Smith, a negro policeman there with the other officers saw him and shot the negro through the head, killing him instantly and saving "Uncle Bud's" life.

Another negro leaned far out of a window to take aim at an officer and "Uncle Bud" shot him through the stomach.

"Uncle Bud" was known to have killed at least two of the negroes and Smith another. Later two others were found at some distance from the house, lying dead. They had been wounded and had dragged themselves away to die.

Two other negroes were wounded and four others were taken prisoner. Cofield and Guy Fisher, another officer, were shot, but both recovered . . .

Following the fight, feelings were at fever heat throughout the town, but at no time was a race war threatened because negroes were as bitter in their condemnation of the socialist outlaws as were the white people.

Two thousand or more white people and negroes gathered together about the federal jail and for a time it was feared that together they might lynch the negroes who had been taken prisoner, but a heavy guard was maintained until the excitement died down.

Negroes who had been eyewitnesses to the fight made public statements commending the officers and declaring that nothing else could have been done under the circumstances . . .

Ed Jefferson, a prominent black citizen, witnessed the initial shooting and called the police. A short time later, he noticed several men had congregated at the house on Fourth Street and he telephoned the United States marshal's office to inform them the police would need reinforcements.

Of the leaders of the Socialist fanatics, Tom Jackson was shot through the neck and J. T. Terrill was shot in the groin. The latter escaped and was found the following morning in a shack in the Dean settlement, near an old brickyard in the south part of town. William Wright, Milo Wilson, Richard Gootch, and Allen Andrews surrendered to the officers. Tom Jackson and James Brown were dragged out and taken to the hospital where Brown's arm was amputated. The house was spattered with gore where the wounded men had dragged themselves around.

Marvin D. Tipton, an eyewitness to the battle, credited Ledbetter with killing two of the blacks; he also credited African-American policeman Paul Smith with saving Ledbetter's life. Frank Reed, another African-American policeman, also handled himself in an exemplary manner by taking the arrested men to jail and by his handling of the crowd which gathered at the jail.

Of the ten leaders of the United Socialist Club, three were killed, three more wounded, and four others lodged in jail. William Wright denied any responsibility for what had occurred, claiming he just happened to live where men took refuge after the first shooting of the two constables.

A political meeting was held at Jones Hall, in the Third Ward, the night following the battle. Leaders of the African-Americans strongly denounced an afternoon newspaper for publication of a story that a race riot was on in Muskogee. They endorsed the actions of the officers in doing their sworn duty.

The African-American and Native American outlaws of Indian/Oklahoma Territories were as bold and brazen as any outlaws found anywhere in the Wild West. Names such as Cherokee Bill, Ned Christie, and Dick Glass caused many sleepless nights for lawmen and peace officers. As dangerous as these desperadoes were, there were men just as brave and bold who were ever at the ready to uphold the law and preserve the peace.

Part II

LAWMEN

Indian Police and Lighthorse

CHAPTER 10

Cherokee Lighthorse:
Tahlequah Justice

The term "lighthorse" is a familiar one in connection with "Light-Horse Harry," a nickname conferred upon Gen. Henry Lee, because of the great rapidity of his cavalry movements during the Revolutionary War. This expression was a common one in the Indian Territory where the Five Civilized Tribes were equipped with a body of men known as the "lighthorse," who served as a mounted police force. The name appears frequently in the law books of the different nations as acts were passed directing the organization of such bodies of men to carry out the laws, the length of terms they were to serve, the funds appropriated to pay for their services, the number of men in each body, and the captains who commanded them. The lighthorsemen were given considerable latitude in enforcing the judgments of the court as much reliance was placed upon their discretion.

In 1808 the chiefs and warriors of the Cherokees passed an act appointing "regulators, who were authorized to suppress horse stealing and robbery," to "protect the widows and orphans," and kill any accused person resisting their authority. These regulators were evidently the forerunners of the lighthorsemen.

The *Cherokee Advocate* reported November 13, 1844, that the National Council had passed a bill authorizing a Lighthorse Company, which was to be composed of a captain, lieutenant, and twenty-four horsemen. Their duty was "to pursue and arrest all fugitives from justice."

The Cherokee Lighthorse were imitated by the other Civilized Tribes where they also performed the function of police. Criminals apprehended by them were turned over to the tribal courts for trial and punishment.

The Cherokees tried several court systems, and their laws appear harsh and severe by modern standards. Rapists for the first offense were punished with fifty lashes upon the bare back and the left ear cropped off close to the head; for the second offense, one hundred lashes and the other ear cut off; for the third offense, death.

For a period of about twenty years before the Civil War, no lighthorse operated among the Cherokees; sheriffs and their deputies exercised the police power. Revived after the war, the lighthorse operated until the dissolution of the Cherokee government. Although on paper the Cherokee political institutions were quite sophisticated and differentiated, in practice the available lighthorse frequently had to serve as policemen, judges, and jurors. Their job was eased in 1874 by the construction of a substantial prison at Tahlequah presided over by a high sheriff.

But more than a sturdy prison and a handful of lighthorse were necessary to maintain law and order in eastern Oklahoma in the 1870s. Thirsty Indians and the Trade and Intercourse Act of 1834, which banned introduction of intoxicating liquors into the Indian country, created a tremendous bootlegging problem. Occasionally a jug was smashed or a barrel stove in, but profits as high as $4 a gallon on bootleg liquor kept the flow constant. Where enforcement was attempted, jurisdictional squabbles between Indian and United States' courts diluted its effectiveness. In the 1870s, treaties existed which granted Cherokee courts jurisdiction over all tribal members, including adopted whites. But cases of murder, robbery, assault and battery with intent to kill, and simple assault, unless the parties involved were all Indian, fell within the jurisdiction of the district court sitting at Van Buren until 1871 and after that at Fort Smith.

Even before the Civil War, the Cherokees had resented the activities of federal marshals in their nation. These law officers arrested Cherokees and hauled them off to courts as much as a hundred miles distant from their fellow tribesmen. Occasionally, the Indian was unable to speak enough English to understand the court procedures or summon witnesses to testify in his defense. Sometimes Cherokee courts

121

held that they should have cognizance of the case, and they disputed the authority of overzealous marshals. One such disagreement in 1872 led to the death of eleven men in a violent gun battle in a Cherokee courtroom.

This story revolves around one of the most colorful and legendary Cherokee lawmen, Ezekiel Proctor. Proctor was born July 4, 1831, in the Cherokee Nation of the state of Georgia, seven years before his family was forced to leave their homeland. Once relocated, the Proctor lands were in the Going Snake District of the Cherokee Nation. The district received its name from a full-blooded Cherokee chief who was an eloquent speaker of the old Indian style.

When the Civil War broke out, most of the Cherokees were sympathizers with the South since many of them had been slaveowners in their native Georgia. Proctor, however, joined the northern cause. His war record indicates he enlisted on July 7, 1862, at a point near the present Baxter Springs, Kansas, and served three years as a private in Company L, Third Regiment of the Indian Home Guard, under the command of Colonel Riley. He was wounded in the shoulder during a battle along the Arkansas border. The reason Proctor chose to serve in the Federal army, when most of his friends fought for the Confederacy, is not known. It is conjectural that Proctor didn't believe in slavery because of his lifelong love of freedom.

Proctor was one of the leaders in the Keetoowa Society, which was started by conservative Cherokees. The society, which exists today, originally began as a religious resistance movement. As American citizens began crowding into the Cherokee Nation, the Keetoowa Society was formed with the purpose of preserving the nation's right of independence, tribal customs, and traditions.

The Keetoowa Society was often referred to as the Pin Indian Organization. The name derived from the pin made from two crossed feathers that the members wore on their clothing or saddle blankets. The pin signified that through their Keetoowa Society membership they were strong supporters of the Cherokee national government, principle, and treaty rights of independence from America. Also, the pin warned that strong reprisals would be taken against anyone who harmed a member of the religious order.

Proctor's standing was such that he was a delegate to the General Council of Indian Territory held in Okmulgee, September 29, 1870.

Problems originated in a charge of murder filed against Ezekiel Proctor by a Cherokee court and a charge of assault with intent to kill

122

filed against him by the Fort Smith authorities (Proctor killed Lucy Beck while attempting to kill her husband, James Kesterson). Proctor was actually undergoing trial in the Going Snake court of Judge B. H. Sixkiller, one of eight Cherokee district court judges, when a posse led by two deputy marshals from Fort Smith attempted to seize the prisoner. Included in the posse were Cherokees of a faction (named Beck) bitterly hostile to Proctor and intent on either capturing or killing him, so what resulted was in large part a byproduct of Cherokee feuding.

The best account of the fight, which took place April 15, 1872, is found in *The Last Cherokee Warriors* by Steele:

> The small schoolhouse was jammed full of spectators, and hundreds of others who could not get in the courtroom surrounded the building outside. Four guards were posted outside the door to prevent anyone from forcibly interrupting the trial. These guards were Lincoln England, John Looney, John Walkingstick, and Jesse Shill. While the prosecuting attorney, Johnson Spake, was arguing a motion before the court, Deputy Marshals Peavy and Owens arrived with a posse that had accompanied them from Fort Smith. Marshal Owens had instructed the posse not to try to enter the courtroom and remain peaceably outside until the court's decision was made. The posse consisted of Kesterson, White Sut Beck, several others of the Beck family and their friends. As the posse approached the school, White Sut Beck appeared to take over command of the group and was joined by other members of the Beck family and their friends who were all heavily armed and waiting outside the school building. Sut Beck leveled his double-barreled shotgun at the guards by the door and demanded they step aside. The group then burst into the courtroom, guns in hand. Sut Beck immediately aimed his shotgun at Zeke. Johnson Proctor, Zeke's brother, grabbed the gun's barrel just as it fired and received the full charge in the breast. The second shot struck Zeke in the knee. Pandemonium then broke out as the Beck and Proctor factions fired wildly. For a while it seemed a duel to the death. What was left of the posse was forced to run as they were overpowered by the guns on the Proctor side, the Indian police, and the spectators around the building. When the smoke cleared the dead and the wounded covered the ground in front of the little log schoolhouse. Nine men had been killed in the battle and two were mortally wounded. An undetermined number of others received minor wounds. Those killed on the Proctor side were Johnson Proctor and Mose Alberty, Zeke's attorney.
>
> Alberty had been sitting on the judge's desk when he was

struck by a bullet. On the Beck side those killed were Sam Beck, Black Sut Beck, William Hicks, Riley Woods, George Selvage, and James Ward. Deputy U.S. Marshal Owens and Bill Beck were mortally wounded in the battle and died a short time afterwards. Marshal Owens stated, as he lay dying, that he tried to stop the battle but could not. Those wounded on the Proctor side were the presiding judge, B. H. (Cornick) Sixkiller, Zeke Proctor, Ellis Foreman (a juror), Joseph Churver (a juror), Deputy Sheriffs John Proctor, Isaac Vann and Palone.

The United States court refused to prosecute Proctor because of the treaty between the U.S. government and the Cherokee Nation. It was ordered that Proctor be arrested and brought before the court where a "treaty" was made with Proctor that he would be released if he agreed to become a law abiding citizen. Thus, Ezekiel Proctor had the distinction of being the only individual with which the U.S. government made a treaty.

Proctor did finish his life as a law abiding citizen. He had already been elected sheriff of the district in 1867, and was senator of the Going Snake District in 1877. The Fort Smith federal court records state that Proctor served as a deputy U.S. marshal and took the office on November 20, 1891. Proctor was appointed sheriff of the Going Snake District May 4, 1894, and again on February 12, 1895, received a commission as a deputy U.S. marshal. Proctor's knowledge of Indian Territory and its many hideouts provided an invaluable service to the Fort Smith court in bringing many criminals to justice.

CHAPTER 11

Choctaw Lighthorse: Tuskahoma Justice

Lighthorsemen were organized in each district of the Choctaw Nation soon after the missionaries went to Mississippi and established mission schools in 1818. In the Indian Territory, it was their duty to ride over the country to settle all difficulties that arose among parties or individuals and to arrest all violators of the law. The old tribal custom of allowing a murderer to be disposed of by relatives of the dead man was set aside and "the right of trial by the lighthorse who acted in a three fold capacity — sheriff, judge and jury — was awarded to all offenders." The lighthorse were brave and vigilant men and "nothing escaped their eagle eyes; and they soon became a terror to white whiskey peddlers who invaded the Choctaw territories at that time." When apprehended, the peddlers were informed that their room was preferable to their company and the liquor was poured upon the ground.

It is a proud boast of the Choctaws that a prisoner never tried to evade punishment. On the day appointed, he would appear for a whipping administered by the lighthorse. People of the neighborhood would assemble around the church where they engaged in smoking and visiting while the culprit chatted and smoked with the various groups. As soon as the lighthorse appeared, the crowd adjourned to the church and spent the time singing hymns until the whipping or shooting was over. The prisoner was reinstated to his previous position in the tribe and the matter was closed, never to be mentioned again.

When a murder was committed the lighthorse took the affair into consideration and, after listening to all of the testimony, pronounced the verdict. When the accused person was declared guilty, without delay the time and place of his execution was designated. The Choctaws, like the Creeks, punished murderers with death by shooting.

Choctaw Freedmen were allowed minor political offices in the Nation, but did serve as county deputies, constables, and lighthorsemen.

The annals of Judge Parker's court are filled with violence occurring in the Choctaw country. The last man hanged at Van Buren, before the court's removal to Fort Smith, was a Choctaw who had murdered and robbed a peddler and his black servant. Another case in 1874 involved a Texas bandit who had killed a posseman near Little Blue River in the southwest corner of the Nation. This outlaw boasted that the posseman was the "eighth I've killed — niggers and Indians don't count." While this was a typical attitude of Southwestern desperadoes, it added great bitterness to the natural resentment the Choctaws had toward white intruders.

A Choctaw lighthorseman and a deputy sheriff of Kimachi County found it "necessary to take the life" of Alexander Shield, a noncitizen, when he resisted arrest for violation of the pistol law. Five hundred dollars was appropriated for attorney's fees at the Fort Smith trial, because "it is the duty of the Nation to defend her officers when they become involved in difficulties while engaged in the legitimate discharge of their duties."

One of the better known Choctaw Lighthorsemen was Peter Conser. Peter was born Peter Coinson in 1852, near Eagletown in present McCurtain County, Oklahoma. His father was a white trader of French descent, and his mother, Adeline, was a Choctaw Indian. Peter probably adopted the surname of Conser because of the difficulty Choctaws had in pronouncing the French name Coinson.

When Peter was still a child his parents separated and his mother soon died of smallpox, leaving him alone. Little is known about this part of Peter's life, but he probably worked as a farm hand. In 1862, with the Civil War in progress, Federal forces invaded Indian Territory from the north. Peter, along with other members of the tribe, followed the retreating Confederates to relative safety in the south. Peter eventually settled on a Red River plantation of the wealthy Choctaw, Robert M. Jones. This plantation, with its bountiful crops, far from the

Federal soldiers, provided Peter with a haven during the remainder of the Civil War.

After the war, Peter returned north and arrived at the Hodgens area. With a small amount of seed corn he had brought with him, Peter began farming. Gradually, through hard work and careful planning, he began to accumulate considerable wealth. Affluence brought social recognition and in 1877, at age twenty-five, he became deputy sheriff in Sugar Loaf County. He was later a captain of the Choctaw Lighthorse in the Moshulatubbee District.

By the 1870s, the Choctaw Lighthorse had been stripped of its judicial powers but remained an effective peace-keeping force. As captain, Peter Conser was responsible for preserving order and discipline among the men and seeing that each man was properly armed, equipped, and mounted. Peter also had many public duties as captain of the lighthorse. He served as a representative and then a senator to the Choctaw Council. In addition, Peter ran a large farm, a blacksmith shop, grist mill, and a saw mill. He also kept a general store with a post office. Peter Conser died in 1934, but his home remained in the Conser family. In 1967 the house was donated to the Oklahoma Historical Society.

The *Dallas Herald,* March 1, 1873, copied an article from the Fort Smith *Independent* of February 6, which related:

> Dr. Fanin of Skullyville tells us that two companies of Choctaws, one from Sugar Loaf county and one from Skullyville headed by light horse captured 16 horse thieves; after a council they took six of the gang and shot them. They made a confession implicating others and the company is in pursuit of them. The thieves were Choctaws, part full blood and part half bloods.

In 1877, at the age of sixteen, Samuel Robert Wilson moved from Arkansas to Sugar Loaf County, Choctaw Nation, where he learned to speak the Choctaw language so fluently that he served as interpreter many years. When twenty-two years of age, Wilson married Julia Hickman of the Nation, and as an intermarried citizen he was called upon to join the National Lighthorsemen under the leadership of Peter Conser. Later he held special commissions as deputy sheriff under every sheriff in LeFlore County until his age prevented active service.

In a feature story that appeared in the Texarkana (Texas) *Gazette,* August 28, 1949, Mrs. James H. Crook of McCurtain County related some of her pioneer experiences. She and her husband moved to the

Choctaw Nation in 1898, and they lived near a spring of white sulphur water which the Indians called Alikchi Oka (meaning literally "Doctor Water"):

Alikchi was a Choctaw court ground and sessions were held there twice a year. The tribal court and whipping ground were adjacent to the store kept by Crook. When a murderer was convicted and condemned to be shot, he was placed on the edge of his coffin in a sitting position with a small piece of paper pinned over his heart, and the "sheriff" or "lighthorseman" as he was more commonly called, shot the convicted man . . .

John Tonihka, about 82, a full blooded Choctaw Indian, recalls that the last execution at Alikchi occurred the year after the Crooks moved there.

William Goings, a youthful Indian who had been convicted of murder, had run away after his conviction . . . During this time the jurisdiction of the Indian courts in murder cases had been taken away and placed with the federal courts which had been established in the territory.

When Goings was recaptured, the federal court decided he should be executed by the Indian authorities because he had been legally convicted while their courts were still in authority. He was resentenced to be shot on July 13, 1899 . . .

When the time for the execution came, Sheriff Thomas Watson, a tall rangy Choctaw, formed his "light horse" as guards and possemen were called, into lines with each man armed. The sheriff kneeled at a small bench, and fired one bullet through the body of Goings . . .

The *Tulsa World,* July 17, 1950, contained a story of the "Last Choctaw Execution" under the Choctaw laws:

The condemned man was Silan Lewis and he was sentenced to death for the murder of Joe Haklotubbee; the scene of the execution was in the yard of an Indian courthouse on the western edge of Brown's Prairie, about fourteen miles southwest of the present Red Oak; the date was November 4, 1894 and an immense crowd of Choctaws and white men had gathered to watch the execution.

The trial of Lewis had been held in December, 1892, before Judge H. J. Holson, circuit judge of the Choctaw Nation. It appears that it was because of political differences between the Progressive party to which Haklotubee belonged, and the Nationalists of which Lewis was a member, that the murder was committed by a party of men who charged down on the Indian's cabin, south of Hartshorne.

128

Lewis was charged with the crime and he appeared to receive his punishment as was the universal custom among the full blood Indians.

In the assembled crowd of Indians, many carried Winchesters and officers of the Light Horse were present to keep order. Two of them carried out a coffin from the brush near the courthouse and presently two other policemen brought Lewis from near the creek where he and his family were camped.

Lewis was seated upon a blanket on the ground, his chest was bared and an officer made a spot on it with a white powder. Two Indians held his hands when a deputy sheriff stepped about twenty feet from the condemned man, took aim and fired; Lewis fell back and the mournful wailing of a woman arose from the creek bank.

The last vignette concerning the Choctaw Lighthorse concerns the most common and typical conflict that occurred between lawmen and outlaws in the Nation. It is excerpted from an article on the Indian lighthorse police in *Great West* magazine.

On the bluff above Colbert's Ferry on the Red River, the two Choctaw Lighthorsemen watched the six riders board the ferry on the Texas side. Even from their lookout point, the Indian watchdogs could tell the six were full of "Texas Lightning," as well as the crock jugs slung over their mounts. They had been over to Maupins' Store, a mile south of the Big Red, trading ponies for whiskey and tobacco. Now they were on the return trip with a bootleg load, for it was strictly illegal to have booze in the Indian Nations.

Captain Jim Hillhouse warned Chickasaw Ben Colbert: "Clear the trail and keep under cover. They're comin'!"

As soon as the ferry hit the bank and the end gate dropped, the six Indians lashed their mounts and started up the stage road incline at a gallop. With shirt-tails flying and black braids swinging beneath floppy, high-crowned hats, the six tried to make it to the safety of timbered hills before they were spotted by Indian lawmen.

But they were too late —

Hurtling down the slope toward them were the two Lighthorsemen, Winchesters and six-shooters ready for action. The two factions met head-on in a gun-blazing shootout. When the thick gunsmoke and swirling dust subsided, five of the Indian bootleggers and two horses lay dead. The two members of the Lighthorse were wounded, but still upright and able to continue carrying their duties.

CHAPTER 12

Creek Lighthorse: Okmulgee Justice

The laws of the Upper and Lower Creeks were collected into a uniform code for the nation and adopted by the General Council in 1840. The simple laws were enforced by a body of men known as lighthorsemen. Most of the civil cases, particularly probate matters, were decided by town councils, and the execution of their judgments were entrusted to the lighthorse.

Agent William Garrett advised Elias Rector at Fort Smith in 1860 that some important changes had been made in the Creek government, one of which was that more ample authority had been conferred upon the police, termed "lighthorse." Their duty was to destroy all spiritous liquors brought into the Nation and to levy a fine or inflict a penalty upon all persons found guilty of introducing it, or of the commission of other offenses.

Article IV of the *Constitution and Civil and Criminal Code of the Muskogee Nation,* approved at the Council Ground Muskogee Nation, October 12, 1867, contains the provision that "the Muskogee Nation shall be divided into six districts, and each district shall be furnished with one company of lighthorsemen, whose compensation shall be provided by law."

Each company consisted of one officer and four privates who were elected for two years by the vote of their respective districts. One judge was selected by the National Council for two years in each district and the lighthorsemen were subservient to his orders.

Each lighthorse captain received an annual salary of $200 while the privates were paid $100 per year. The officers who approved these laws were Samuel Checote, Oktars-sars-har-jo, Micco Hutkey, and Pink Hawkins. G. W. Grayson was the secretary.

In order to put a stop to horse stealing, Chief Checote during the latter part of August and first of September, 1871, called out about 900 assistant lighthorsemen. Part of them were retained in their home districts as home guards, but a large body was assembled at Okmulgee. Lochar Harjo had collected a large number of his followers in the neighborhood of the Creek Agency and a battle seemed imminent when the constitutional party advanced to meet them, but Col. Benjamin H. Grierson, 10th Cavalry, called the leaders of both parties to Fort Gibson, where a truce was arranged. Creek Agent Franklin S. Lyon estimated that this armed demonstration cost the Nation $30,000.

Trouble resulted between Oktars-sars-har-jo (or Sands) and Samuel Checote over disbursement of money from the U.S. government to the Creeks. Oktars-sars-har-jo insisted that the funds be equally divided between the Upper and Lower Creeks. Checote, choosing to ignore the Civil War split in the tribe, made the distribution on the per capita basis among members of the whole tribe. Angered at his defeat as Checote's opponent in the election of 1871, Sands led a band of 300 men into Okmulgee and ousted the council then in session. Gen. Pleasant Porter, captain of the lighthorse, with the aid of his men and the Federal agents, quickly put an end to the disturbance.

While living with one wife, Timothy Barnett, the court clerk of Wewoka District in the Creek Nation, was maintaining a second wife in the Greenleaf settlement. One day he was informed of another Indian paying her visits on the sly, and he promptly killed his competitor. Judge Nocus Yahola called in twenty-one special lighthorsemen to bring in his court clerk. After a blazing gun battle, Barnett surrendered to the lighthorse when they promised a fair trial. But on the way back to the court, they riddled his body with lead. For some reason there was never an investigation, and the lighthorsemen were paid their regular wages.

The Creek Freedmen settlement at Marshalltown on the "Point" between the Arkansas and Verdigris rivers was a turbulent spot for many years, especially between 1878 and 1885. Cattle theft was common in the region, and occasionally some of the Cherokee cattlemen attempted to take the law into their own hands to recover their cattle and punish the thieves. Generally, lighthorse police in the Muskogee District were blacks, and racial antipathy was added to the bad relations between the young Cherokee and the African-Creek law officers. In Muskogee on Christmas of 1878, serious trouble broke out when some African-Creek lighthorsemen disarmed John and Dick Vann, two young Cherokees from a prominent family. A lawless Texan passing through the town attempted to put the black officers in their place. He led the Cherokees in the gunfight that eventually cost the life of one of the lighthorsemen and wounded three of the other officers. In August 1879 another gunfight took place in Muskogee; John Vann was killed and the lighthorse captain was wounded. Chief Coachman, upon advice of leading Creeks, decided to place a lighthorseman on guard in Muskogee, and it is reported that:

> . . . he ordered Richard Beryhill, the reliable and efficient captain of the Eufaula District, to undertake the work. But Berryhill protested that the assignment "Seems to me to be a severe one. If the town of Muscogee was really an Indian town I would not wait a moment, but as it is there are but few Indians there. I am more than willing to serve my people but the way things are I don't see how I am to risk my life for non citizens."

One of the most stubborn Creek horse thieves was Jim Grayson, who was caught, tried, convicted, and scourged so many times his back was a solid mass of scar tissue. Exasperated, the Creek tribal court ordered the lighthorse to execute Grayson by shooting him. At the last moment, Chief Checote pardoned him.

During the Green Peach War (so called because it began when the peaches were green), Chief Checote authorized each district judge in the Nation to call out fifty assistant lighthorsemen to disarm the warriors and restore order in his district. By August the insurrection was crushed but the lighthorsemen remained under arms for thirty to sixty days. On October 19, 1882, the council appropriated $19,700 to pay 1,150 assistant lighthorsemen called out to enforce the laws for eight days during the Green Peach War.

Daniel "Goob" Childers, an ardent mixed-blood supporter of Isparecher, was captain of the lighthouse in the area around Welaka Mission. He operated a pole ferry on the Arkansas River near Wealaka Mission. His name appears frequently in the annals of the Creek Nation where he lived a violent life and came to a violent death.

One of the most notorious of the Creek bootleggers was Wesley Barnett; his gang in 1887–88 carried on a campaign of robbery, murder, and liquor running. Barnett was a vicious young man, with not the slightest qualms at killing his fellowman. On a bright sunny day in Tulsa, I.T., the principal Creek chief, L. C. Perryman, and a Creek official named Muddaloke were standing on a street corner striving at some solutions to a great many problems confronting their tribal government. Glancing up, they both saw the beligerent Barnett rushing down on them, waving his pistol in the air. He began firing before they could dive for cover, and Muddaloke fell dead in the street. As the outlaw sped past, Chief Perryman felt the wind of death as bullets knocked his hat off. Shaken over his own brush with death and the sorrow of losing a friend, Chief Perryman demanded that his lighthorse let nothing stand in their way of running Barnett and his gang to extinction. Joining their efforts with the deputy United States marshals from Fort Smith, the ruthless gang was broken up and its members killed or sent to the federal penitentiary.

What follows are two newspaper articles from the *Fort Smith Elevator* concerning the exploits and demise of Wesley Barnett:

October 26, 1888;
Wesley Barnett, the murderer of Deputy Marshal John Phillips is reported by the *Indian Journal* as having stormed the Creek capital with a crowd and shot twenty-six bullet holes through the cupola of the building. Armed men guarded the town afterwards to prevent similar raids. Wesley is worth $500 to anyone who will lodge him in the U.S. jail here.

January 18, 1889;
News reached the Marshals office Tuesday that Wesley Barnett, for whom there was a reward of $500 was killed. The following letter to Marshal Carroll explains how it was done:

Eufaula, C.N., Jan. 15, 1889
Hon. John Carroll, U.S. Mar.
We killed Wesley Barnett Saturday night about 10 o'clock, near Okmulgee. The circumstances of the killing are about as follows; I sent Salmon north of the Arkansas river with three men, then I went up North Fork with three more, sending my posse, William Sevier, up Deep Fork, accompanied by John Barnell and Wallace McNack. They stopped at John Porters to stay over night. About the hour mentioned above Wesley Barnett and Wiley Bear came in on them and commenced shooting. In the fight Wesley was killed. We

133

turned his body over to friends. Will be in as soon as we can. The waters are very high.

Yours, etc.
D. V. Rusk,
U.S. Dep. Mar.

We would infer from the above that Wiley Bear escaped . . . but it is only a question of time when all will be arrested or killed off.

The Creek Lighthorsemen, assisted by deputy U.S. marshals, were successful also in capturing the dreaded Buck Gang (see Chapter 8) which flourished only a few weeks in the northwestern part of the Creek Nation.

One of the most outstanding citizens and notable Creek Lighthorsemen, who later became a minister, was Samuel Jonathan Haynes. He was born on January 8, 1857, at what was known as Longtown, about two miles southwest of Okmulgee. A short time later he became a special deputy in the lighthorse and that fall was elected to membership in the troop.

Sam Haynes carried on his work in the lighthorse, becoming a captain of the troop. He took part in two skirmishes in the Esparhecher War, at Pecan and Pole Cat creeks. Along with captain in the lighthorse, he was also appointed a deputy U.S. marshal by the federal court at Fort Smith. As such, he worked with Capt. Edmund Harry of the Creek Lighthorse and Deputy U.S. Marshal N. B. Irwin to capture the brutal hardcases comprising the Buck Gang. Haynes went on to become interpreter for the House of Warriors; as a delegate representing the Creek Nation, he made sixteen trips to Washington on various missions for his people. He passed away at Newtown, Oklahoma, northwest of Okmulgee, on April 4, 1948.

CHAPTER 13

Seminole Lighthorse: Wewoka Justice

The Seminole Council, which is represented by the various tribal bands, typically selected two of its members as candidates for chief. Upon the day of election, the two candidates would take their place in the main street of Wewoka, the Seminole capital, and the legal voters would line up behind their choice of candidates. The one who had the most in his line was elected chief for four years.

The council served as the court, with the chief acting as judge. The laws were enforced by the lighthorsemen, who were the appointed law enforcement officers. The respected officials of the Seminole Lighthorse comprised a captain, lieutenant, and eight privates. The law contained specific provisions protecting the officer in the performance of his duties: "If, notwithstanding the orderly deportment of the officer, the person to be arrested shall make resistance by force of arms, then the arresting officer shall have the right to kill." It was the strongly executive character of the Seminole law, and the trend toward prompt enforcement, that was resented by Creeks and other Indians who sometimes came in contact with the lighthorse police of the small Nation; the effectiveness of the police was discouraging to criminals who were non-Indians also. When a criminal was apprehended, he was brought before the court. If found guilty of a minor crime, he was sentenced to twenty-five licks across the bare back with a six-foot hickory switch. If the prisoner was tried for a second offense, the punishment was doubled. There were no jails, so a prisoner waiting for his trial or punishment was handcuffed to a tree. If it was a major crime such as murder, the punishment was death by the firing squad. In such a case, the offender was allowed to go free on his word that he would return in time for his punishment. At no time did a Seminole convicted for murder fail to return to face his executioners.

The Seminole, of all the so'called Five Civilized Tribes, kept many of their traditional beliefs and customs intact in the Indian Territory. Carrie Cyrus, daughter of a Seminole Freedman, told of the laws and lighthorse:

> The Indians had many laws, many of which were like the ones we have now, and they were strict that their laws were not broken; and, if they were broken, the culprits were taken to the old whipping post tree and tied hand and foot and whipped with a hickory switch. For the first crime committed he was given fifty lashes with the switch and for the second, 150; and for the third crime, 250 lashes were administered and if a murder was committed, death was the penalty. When an Indian committed such a crime, he would be tried and the date set for his execution. The Light Horsemen would take the accused home with them and tie him till the day of punishment. If the crime was not too bad he would be turned loose and told to come back on a certain day for his punishment, and he would always be there even he had to swim a river to get there. On that day he would be shot by two men firing at the same time.
>
> The Indian peace officers were called Light Horsemen and all of the people feared them.
>
> If a bad outlaw came in the Territory that they wanted to catch, the Light Horseman would gather with what they called the Snake Doctor, who would mix a quantity of herbs together; such as, Devil Shoe String, Conquer John and others not known. He would put these into a big kettle and put a fire under it and boil this all together until it looked like tea. Then the Horsemen would gather around the fire and spit till they put the fire out. But during this time the Snake Doctor was spitting in their faces with the medicine that was in the pot. This was supposed to carry them through battle without getting shot.

Robert Johnson, a Seminole Nation resident, told of the last Indian man executed at Wewoka under the tribal government in 1896:

> He (Robert) saw this man, Pul-muskey, executed. Pul-musky and

136

John Factor got drunk and got into a fight and John Factor was killed. Pul-muskey was given the death sentence. When he was sentenced under the Indian law, he was turned loose to be free until the day of the execution and when the time, day and hour came, the prisoner was there among the crowd and he walked forward. He was blindfolded, and he sat on a rock by a tree; a white paper heart was cut and placed over his heart and then two Lighthorsemen were selected to shoot him. Cumsey Bruner and Ceaser Payne were the ones and they were Negroes.

Carrie Cyrus-Pitman also told of a gang that operated in the Seminole Nation under the leadership of Bob Dossay. She said that Dossay was killed by African-Seminole Lighthorseman Ceasar Payne.

Mrs. Pitman's first husband, Cyrus Dennis, was an African-Seminole Lighthorseman for twenty-five years. During five of those years he held a commission as a deputy United States marshal under Marshal John Carroll. Mrs. Pitman said that Dennis served under the tribal laws and he helped to apply the sentence of whipping to several prisoners. Dennis died on December 24 of the year 1912.

Other African-Seminole Lighthorsemen included Thomas Bruner, John Dennis, and Tom Payne.

In 1897 a study was done on the Five Civilized Tribes by the *Kansas City Star* newspaper, and attention was given to African-Indian Lighthorsemen:

> The Indian constabulary of the Creek and Cherokee nations are called "Light Horse police." In the Creek country many of them are citizen negroes, and they are a fine, dashing lot of men, fearless riders and, if need be, savage fighters. One seen in Muscogee last week would have delighted the eye of Remington. He seemed to have dropped out of a Remington picture. He was coal black and sat on his white horse like a Prussian grenadier. He wore a reefer jacket buttoned to the chin; the large pearl buttons on it glinted in the sun. His head was covered by a wide brimmed black hat. His trim legs were encased in tight fighting breeches and riding boots, and his coat was bulged on the hips by the big cavalry revolvers strapped to his side. He was the type of officer who brings back his prisoner when he goes after him.

One of the better known African-Indian Lighthorsemen in the Creek Nation was Robert Marshall. The Muskogee *Indian Journal* on June 10, 1886, carried the following story concerning Marshall's police work:

Friday, June 4th, Policeman Foreman and Robert Marshall captured the Indians who signed the statement and confession made below. They had five horses. The men are lodged in jail here and the horses in Turner's pasture:
The gray horse belongs to an Indian named Armister (young man), who lives on Deep Fork near Tuskeketown. We took the horses the second of June in the morning. The bay mare and the colts belong to a negro named Jim Anderson, our neighbors. We live at Tuskeketown, near Judge R. R. Bruner's.
Signed,

Ma-Pa-ye-cher
(Tommy Fixico)

I corroborate the statement made above.

Sam. Bosey

On June 1, 1893, the *Muskogee Weekly Phoenix* carried an interesting story concerning police officer Robert Marshall:

Last week Robert Marshal {*sic*} a colored Indian police, well known over the Indian Territory, was arrested by Bos Reves [Bass Reeves] and then taken to Fort Smith on a requisition from Texas for one Robert Marshal Thompson charged with murder. Robert Marshal was not the man wanted and was released. Some years ago Robert Marshal was rather wild and wooly and several men it is said have died from getting troubled with him, but of late years he has been very orderly and law-abiding and an efficient officer.

Marshall's life came to a tragic end in Muskogee, a too common occurrence in the Indian nations for lawmen. A description of his killer and the killing is given in *Hell on the Border*:

Charles Smith killed John Welch and Robert Marshal {*sic*}, at Muscogee, on the morning of September 10, 1894. Smith was a negro, as black as night. He had once before been tried in Judge Parker's court, for killing a man, and sentenced to ten years imprisonment for manslaughter. He was of a particularly vicious nature and while engaged in cutting the harness from some horses, the property of one Newlin, he was discovered by Welch, who was running a booth in the vicinity, because of the latter remonstrating with him, he became angered and killed him, with a bullet. Robert Marshal was an Indian policeman and in attempting to arrest Smith, he in turn was killed. At the trial, Smith set up the claim that he killed Marshal in self defense, Marshal having shot at him first. The jury was out only two hours. On reversal by the Supreme Court, Smith

138

was given a new trial and he was sentenced to ten years imprisonment for manslaughter.

Outside of the nations of the Five Civilized Tribes, the Indian police were also diligent in bringing in lawbreakers. The Plains Indians were headquartered in the western portion of the Indian Territory, which would later become Oklahoma Territory. One example of their police work took place at the Kiowa Agency at Anadarko, whose police force patrolled east to the now Oklahoma City area. On this particular occasion a black man, Monroe Barrett, rode from an Anadarko store with a new saddle and boots without the formality of paying for them. He was trailed by Police Chief Frank Farrell and Pewo, one of his privates. Overtaking Barrett when he stopped for water, Pewo grappled with him; the black man grabbed Pewo's revolver and got one shot off at Farrell while using Pewo as a shield. But Farrell was a good man with a gun, and he managed to kill the thief. The stolen goods were then returned, but the summer heat made disposal of the corpse a real emergency. The agent met it by a telegram to Barrett's relatives at Chickasha:

> Monroe Barrett was just killed by my Chief of Police while resisting arrest; you are instructed to immediately notify me what disposition to make of the body, and it should be taken care of at the earliest possible moment, owing to the weather conditions.

CHAPTER 14

Sam Sixkiller: Indian Policeman Bar None

In 1871 the United States agents for the Five Civilized Tribes were headquartered individually with their tribes. The Cherokee agent had his offices in Tahlequah; the Choctaw and Chickasaw agent was located at Boggy Depot; the Creek agent was at Okmulgee; and the Seminole agent was at Wewoka. On July 1, 1874, the government ordered the consolidation of these agencies, and thereafter the United States Agency for the Five Civilized Tribes was known as Union Agency.

After two years of negotiation, the consolidated agency was finally located at Muskogee, and on or about January 1, 1876, the agent for the Five Civilized Tribes moved into a brand new Union Agency building. The choice of Muskogee as headquarters for these land-wealthy Native Americans was probably the decisive factor in Muskogee's survival. (Currently the Five Civilized Tribes Museum is housed in the former Union Agency building in Muskogee.)

In February of 1880, Col. John Q. Tufts, United States agent for the Union Agency at Muskogee, I.T., organized a unit of Indian police to operate throughout the Five Civilized Nations. The authorization for the creation of these police forces at the various agencies within the United States was brought about by Congress in May 1878. The experiment was well under way by November 1878, with about one-third of the Indian agencies participating, and by 1880 there were Indian police forces at two-thirds of the agencies.

The biggest obstacle and the touchiest point was salary — eight dollars per month for officers and five for privates. However, Agent Tufts helped his recruits overcome this inadequacy by providing duty schedules which permitted his men to serve as guards for various coal mine companies and as special agents for the railroads. They also could draw expense money for removing "boomers" — or white intruders — on Indian lands.

In regard to the funding of the Union Agency police, Agent Leo E. Bennett, who would later become a federal marshal, made the following statement:

> An Indian policeman, to perform his duty acceptably, must not only be a moral man and be courageous and faithful, but he must be a man of considerable discretion. This character of man is far from being a rarity among the Indians of this agency, yet it is not always possible to find in every locality one of this high character who is willing, or can afford to make the personal sacrifice of time and business interests necessary to the discharge of the duties of an Indian policeman at the pay allowed, $10 a month. Deputy United States marshals and all other peace officers are much better paid and their standard of morality and efficiency is not, as a rule, up to that of the Indian police . . . Besides, they should be properly armed with the best grade of Winchester rifles and Colts revolvers.

Agent Tufts's organization of Indian policemen consisted of thirty members, one-third of which were Cherokees. Their duties were to preserve order, arrest thieves and violators of U.S. law, suppress the whiskey traffic, and execute the orders of the Indian agents. They were stationed at different points within the jurisdiction of the Union Agency, and were on duty wherever found.

The first chief of the Union Agency police force and the most famous Indian policeman in the history of the Indian Territory was Capt. Sam Sixkiller.

Samuel Sixkiller was born in the Going Snake District of the Cherokee Nation, son of Redbird and Pamelia Whaley Sixkiller. His two maternal grandparents were white, one paternal grandparent a full-blood Cherokee, while the other was a half-breed. Sam was educated at a Baptist mission and it was apparent by his demeanor that his teachers had been thorough.

Sam was nineteen years old when the Civil War broke out. The conflict enveloped the Indian Nations in the nationwide blood bath. It

141

was decided by his father that Sam would stay behind and look after the farm while he journeyed north with other loyal Indians and joined the Union army in Kansas. However, when some of Sam's young friends in the area left to join the Confederate army, Sam dropped the plow and reins and went with them. Later, he regretted this impulsive action and deserted, working his way to Fort Gibson on the bank of the Grand River, which had been taken by Federal forces. There he found his father in charge of an artillery company as 1st Lt. Redbird Sixkiller and enlisted in the company for the remainder of the war.

After the war ended, Sam married and moved with Fannie, his new bride, to Tahlequah, the small beautiful capital of the Cherokee Nation. It lay in a fertile valley surrounded by protective hills and undulating meadows. Sam worked at oddjobs and farmed until he was appointed high sheriff in 1875 of the Cherokee Nation and warden of the National Penitentiary.

The prison at Tahlequah was a very solid building of massive stone, surrounded by a jail-yard. It was the headquarters of the high sheriff. Each district in the Nation had its sheriff, which corresponded with the sheriff of a county in the states, and the high sheriff was the head of all the district officers in the Cherokee Nation.

The prisoners in the penitentiary had been incarcerated for various felonies, from murder to larceny. They were worked regularly on the government farm and at the national brick yard. As the high sheriff and warden, Sam Sixkiller maintained a thorough discipline and the prisoners were always well fed, clothed, and healthy.

Like his father, Redbird Sixkiller, then serving as a justice of the Cherokee Supreme Court, the son was well known and respected. A rather short, stocky man, whose dark skin suggested his Indian forebears, Sam Sixkiller discharged his routine duties as warden and sheriff in an exemplary manner. Sixkiller was planning on the capital being the permanent home of his family, which now numbered seven, for he bought several lots on May 27, 1878.

But fate played him a different hand, and his zeal for curbing riotous activity on the Tahlequah streets proved his downfall. On a quiet day in November 1878, the capital was suddenly jarred by a band of young Cherokee ruffians galloping through town as they whooped, fired their pistols, and tried to run down anyone who happened to get in their way. The high sheriff and some of his deputies chased them out of town, trying to get them to halt. Ignoring the stern command of the officers, the rowdies continued to ride toward

142

the hills, even turning in their saddles and firing at their pursuers. The lead whistling over their heads was the last straw. Sixkiller ordered his men to return the fire and they laid down a volley at the young Cherokees.

Hit hard, Jeter L. Thompson dropped off his mount and rolled in the dust. The dying youth accused Sixkiller of firing to kill because of a grudge the sheriff had been holding against him.

The *Tahlequah Cherokee Advocate,* June 11, 1879, carried this item concerning the shooting:

> Sam'l Sixkiller, High Sheriff, Evarts Thorne, Richard Robinson, and John Boston, guards of the National Prison and town policeman, have been arrested upon a preliminary warrant sworn out before the Clerk by the Solicitor of this district charging them with the murder of Jeter L. Thompson, during last council. There seems to be considerable interest in the case. The preliminary examination will be held on Thursday the 12th inst.

In the June 18, 1879, issue of the *Cherokee Advocate* was a follow-up report:

> The preliminary trial of Sam Sixkiller, R. Roberson, Evarts Thorn and John Boston, charged with the murder of Jeter Thompson, was held last Thursday. The Solicitor and Clerk found an indictment against them. The trial will be on the 30th inst. . . .

The trial ended with a hung jury and the charges were transmitted to the Council Branch of the National Council of the Cherokee Nation for investigation by the members.

In Cherokee Volume 270 (page 166) at the archives of the Oklahoma Historical Society, the following information is found from a letter dated November 14, 1879, to D. W. Bushyhead, principal chief, Cherokee Nation, from Ose Hair, speaker of the National Council. It advises that charges which were transmitted to the Council Branch against Samuel Sixkiller, high sheriff, charged with malpractice in office and suspended from office upon such charges by ex-Chief Charles Thompson, had been carefully investigated by the Council Branch of the National Council. They found no proof that Sam Sixkiller was guilty of malpractice in office as charged; therefore, the charges were ignored by a majority vote of the body.

After missing so much time from the job, family coffers were very meager. Sixkiller asked for five and one-third months' back pay and attorney fees which accrued, or he felt should have, during his suspension from the police force. This amounted to $355.50 in lost wages and $975 in attorney fees. But the council apparently did not agree. Sam was suspended again in June 1879 as high sheriff, this time over the monetary dispute. On June 7, 1879, S. H. Downing was appointed acting high sheriff. Downing got little cooperation from Sixkiller, however. He accused Sixkiller of refusing to turn over the prison books and claimed Sixkiller was interfering his inventory of prison property.

After being cleared of the murder charges, Sixkiller felt that the affair had stigmatized him in the community. He believed it would be impossible to carry on his duties as high sheriff or even to live in Tahlequah for a while. So the Sixkiller family moved to the Creek Nation and took up residence in the typical sprawling frontier town of Muskogee, a cattle shipping and supply center for the ranchers and farmers of the area. There was a population of 500 souls in the Katy Railroad town, with the houses scattered about on the bald prairie unbroken by either shrubs or trees. A few false-front business buildings lined the railroad tracks and carried on a more active business than one would first suspect.

On February 12, 1880, Sam received a better position than the one in Tahlequah. He was appointed captain of Indian police at Union Agency. Tufts, the Indian agent, picked Sam to be chief of his new police force. The *Indian Journal* of February 12, 1880, made the following announcement:

> Sam Sixkiller received here last Friday his commission from the United States with the great seal attached as captain of the Indian Police. There are seven on the force at Muskogee and there is a very noticeable improvement. We are all quiet now and we hope to remain so.

As top man of the Union Agency police force, Captain Sixkiller had thirty men, and later as many as forty men under his command. This was a position of considerable influence since the U.S. Indian Police had jurisdiction over the lands of all Five Civilized Tribes. Naturally, Muskogee itself was the foremost responsibility of Captain Sixkiller, since the Union Agency was headquartered there. Agent Tufts was also authorized to build a United States jail at Muskogee and the money for the project was in his hands before construction had ever begun on the solid two-story building. When completed, it too was

144

placed in the charge of Captain Sixkiller, with more or less the same duties as his former occupation as high sheriff in Tahlequah.

During his service with the Indian police, Captain Sixkiller also held a commission as a deputy United States marshal, under the Fort Smith court of Judge Isaac C. Parker, and was paid about $1,200 a year as a special agent for the Missouri Pacific Railroad. However, none of these side obligations ever interfered with his performance of Indian police duties; he always served faithfully and in a very competent manner.

As William T. Hagen states in his book, *Indian Police and Judges*. ". . . Sam Sixkiller's duties more nearly corresponded to one of the fabled city marshals of frontier days — a Wyatt Earp or a Wild Bill Hickock."

Sixkiller's problems centered around bootleggers, cattle thieves, murderers, rapists, timber thieves, land "boomers" (white men trying to illegally move onto Indian land), train robbers, card sharks, prostitutes following the railroad towns, etc., and it seemed the Indian nations were overrun with some of these characters. It was an arduous and always potentially dangerous task, as most of these would not hesitate an eyelash to shoot to kill.

Four years after Sixkiller took office, a newspaper in a neighboring town referred to him as "highly respected," a man who "may be safely relied on at all times, whether at the festive board or in a rough-and-tumble, when coolness and decisions are desirable qualities."

Sixkiller's duties in Muskogee and throughout the Union Agency brought him into contact with the most dangerous characters in a society which proliferated them. Although involved in many shootings, in six years' duty with the Indian police he is known definitely to have killed only two men. A target himself on many occasions, he was hit just once prior to his last fatal encounter.

One responsibility of the Indian police was to stop the flow of liquor into the territory. Because it was a federal violation to sell liquor to Indians, many found the illicit trade a profitable business. A large number of jugs and barrels were destroyed, but with profits as high as four dollars a gallon, it seemed an overwhelming task. In one month, Captain Sixkiller and his police destroyed over 5,000 gallons of whiskey, but still the overflow of illegal liquor continued to saturate the Indian Territory. This illicit trade in alcohol can be likened to the illegal drug trade in the more current era of our country.

The first man Sam Sixkiller had to kill was involved in the illegal liquor business. Solomon Copple of Missouri made a good living selling whiskey in the territory. Sixkiller was tipped off that Copple was bringing in a load of "moonshine" to peddle in Muskogee. Sixkiller met Copple on the trail outside of town. The bootlegger had his head down when Captain Sixkiller stepped out of the brush in front of his team of horses. Frightened, the team jerked back and stopped. Copple saw the shield badge with the stars along the top flash on the dark blue shirt of the stocky young Indian police chief, and he made a grab for the shotgun beside him on the wagon seat.

"Hold it, Copple! You're under arrest!" the captain shouted. When he saw Copple reach for the shotgun, the six-shooter in his holster seemed to leap into his hand, leveling out in a blurring motion. Copple never had a chance. He was dead as the shotgun was raised off the seat. The unwise bootlegger pitched forward into the trace chains and wagon tongue, causing the team of horses to snort and paw at the air in terror.

In the 1880s the prostitutes in Muskogee were an irritation to Agent Tufts, for the places where they plied their trade soon became rendezvous points for ruffians and riff-raff from all over the area. Entire neighborhoods were often terrorized by their fighting and the reckless firing of their guns.

After being notified of six or eight new "nymphs du pave" arriving in town and taking up residence at the Hotel de Adams, Agent Tufts called in Captain Sixkiller and ordered a round-up of the known prostitutes — including the new arrivals. It was time to crack down; evidently they thought that Muskogee was an open town. By the time the "calico queens" were locked up in the new bastille, Captain Sixkiller and his men decided they would rather have gone up against a band of desperate outlaws. After a short term in the agency jail, the "soiled doves" decided to accept Captain Sixkiller's invitation to depart to more congenial climates.

Sixkiller developed a quick mind when it came to outsmarting and catching criminals. He learned various tricks of the trade that outlaws utilized to escape the law. Sixkiller's most spectacular and sensational conquest against the criminal element was the shootout with the Indian Territory's worst outlaw, Creek Freedman Dick Glass. The killing of Dick Glass by Sixkiller was covered earlier in the book. What follows is yet another territorial newspaper story concerning the demise

146

of Glass and gang by Sixkiller and his posse. This article is from the *Muskogee Indian Journal*, June 11, 1885:

DICK GLASS GONE
He and a Companion Now Are
Now Slowly Roasting

On Thursday night Capt. Sixkiller received a telegram from Policeman Robert Murry, of Colbert, stating that Dick Glass and three companions has passed that place bound for Denison with several ponies to exchange for a load of whiskey and that he would return the next day. Friday morning Capt. Sixkiller was on hand and and Policemen Robert Murry, Frank Gooden; Leflore and C. M. McClellan, a well known cattle man of the Cherokee Nation started out to Past Oak Grove to intercept them. They arrived there about ten o'clock at night and by means of a colored man located the parties about five miles south of Emit and thirty miles from Colbert. When the moon rose about three o'clock Saturday morning they saddled up and getting near Glass' camp hid their horses and laid in the brush for them to appear. About seven o'clock the outfit was discovered coming along the road. Richmond Carolina was driving and Jim Johnson, Dick Glass and Sam Carolina were walking behind the wagon, the forty gallons of whiskey they had proving as much as their tender shouldered ponies cared to pull. When within a few feet of them the officers stepped into the road, Sam Sixkiller in the lead, and ordered the negroes to surrender. Instead of doing this they attempted to escape. Dick pulled his pistol and turned to shoot when a charge from Capt. Sixkiller's shotgun went into his breast and another into his head, killing him instantly. Jim Johnson also attempted to shoot but a dose of lead settled him. In the meantime the driver had whipped up and as he was going by Leflore and McClellan ordered him to halt. As he did not they fired and he fell into the wagon apparently dead. Then they pursued Sam Carolina and after a half mile chase succeeded in capturing him. Returning they found Richmond Carolina had only been slightly wounded and had unhitched and taken the horses and Dick's Winchester and escaped. Laflore and Gooden started after him but the latter's horse soon gave out and after a chase of five miles Laflore alone came up with him. The darky made for a tree with the intention of resisting but was headed off and compelled to surrender. The prisoners and the two bodies were brought to Colbert where Dick was identified without a doubt. He and Johnson were buried there and the prisoners were brought here and put in the cooler preparatory to being taken to Ft. Smith. The reward of $500 for Glass was "dead or alive" and Capt. Sixkiller will apply for it in a few days.

147

The same newspaper carried another story on January 28, 1886, concerning Captain Sixkiller's police work:

A GOOD CAPTURE

Capt. Sixkiller made a slick capture last week at Weber's Falls. He was after Alf. Rushing, alias Ed. Brown, wanted for the killing of Jackson Barfield in 1877. Also for the murder of the city marshal of Wortham, Freestone County, Texas. He received information that Brown was working near the Falls and had been for several years. As the Captain and Bill Drew came near the place where Brown was staying, they gathered up a bunch of cattle, and, driving them up, asked permission to put them in a yard there for the night. The request was granted, and Brown was called from the crib where he was at work to help pen them. While driving them Sam worked around to where Brown was, and throwing down on him, took him completely by surprise, and he could offer no resistance. The cattle were then turned loose. Brown denies he is the man wanted by the officers, but they are certain they have the right party, and he is being held here awaiting the Texas officers.

A subsequent encounter with lawbreakers was highlighted in the article "Captain Sam Sixkiller — Indian Policeman" in *Golden West* magazine:

The next severe gun battle was on the streets of Muskogee and described by the editor of the *Vinita Chieftain* as "a lively little scrimmage." This incident occurred in September, 1886, and set the stage for later events.

Stepping high on "Muskogee water," mixed-blood Cherokee Black Hoyt, and a white man named Jess Nicholson started shooting up the town and trying to "hurrah" the townspeople. There was to be a music concert that evening, but it was cancelled because people were afraid to leave their homes. Captain Sam and another outstanding Indian policeman Charley Leflore, moved in on them and ordered them to hand over their guns.

"Men, you are under arrest!" Captain Sam cautioned the two wild drunks as they hesitated, a belligerent look on their darkly flushed features. "Give us your guns now, before someone gets hurt."

"Go to hell!" Nicholson screeched, firing at Sixkiller, creasing his arm.

For a few seconds, shots rang out thick and fast. When it was over, Captain Sam had a slight injury in the arm and Jes Nicholson had a bad wound in his foot, but still managed to escape capture.

148

Black Hoyt was taken prisoner and locked up in the calaboose. The next morning, Hoyt's father appeared and began acting hostile to the officers, threatening to kill Captain Sam, so he too was locked up.

Information was passed to Captain Sam that Nicholson had ridden out in the country to a close friend of his, another mixed-blood Cherokee, Dick Vann; therefore, Captain Sam sent one of his men out to bring him in to Muskogee and place him under custody. Since he knew Nicholson was wounded, he anticipated no trouble. Nevertheless, there was another factor — hot headed Dick Vann. When the officer arrived, he was met at the door by Vann.

Easily, trying to avoid trouble, the Indian policeman said, "We understand that Jes Nicholson is here. I'm here to take him to Muskogee . . . I have a warrant here for his arrest."

"He'll get medical attention as soon as I get him into town." As he spoke, the police officer took a step forward.

Instantly, Dick Vann drew his gun and cocked the hammer back.

"Get out of here or I'll kill you!"

The policeman stood his ground for awhile, arguing: "You're foolish, Vann. We will be back after Nicholson and you!" When he saw he was getting nowhere, he mounted his horse and reined back toward town. He would be back, with reinforcements and a warrant for Vann as well as for Nicholson.

Back in town, he informed his chief about Vann standing him off.

Captain Sam shook his head as he said, "Vann is pushing his good fortune. Not too many months ago, he was sentenced to prison for three years for assaulting that army captain at Fort Gibson, then was paroled by the President. I'd think he'd be so thankful over that, he wouldn't want any more trouble with the law. But if that is what he wants, we'll have a warrant for him made out for obstructing an officer in the performance of duty."

In the meantime, Nicholson died from his wound. This did not deter the policeman from arresting Vann, and he was locked up along with Black Hoyt. Simmering down after a few days in jail, Milo Hoyt was released.

Vann also was not held very long in the Muskogee jail. The explanation that Black Hoyt offered for their conduct was indicative of the temper of the times and the precarious position occupied by the Indian police in the territory of the Five Civilized Tribes. The men were charged with having fired on deputy marshals, both the policemen

149

holding federal commissions. But Hoyt protested that they were "just shooting at police." The agent for the Five Civilized Tribes requested legislation to outlaw this frivolous pastime. He also complained of the presence in the community of:

> Women of the "baser sort," plying their vocation, and their houses are often the rendezvous of reckless men, who carry deadly weapons, and who become involved in broils, and shoot off their pistols, and terrorize the neighborhoods.

Jim Hannon, a resident of the Creek Nation, stated that he witnessed a confrontation between Vann and Sixkiller, at which time Vann swore revenge:

> It started during the fair. The fair grounds then were about where the city hospital now stands. Sixkiller was keeping the gate at the fair grounds and Vann started to ride in. He was drinking a little and Sixkiller stopped him and says, "Vann, you will have to behave if you go in there." Vann replied very nicely, "Well I'm going to behave." Sixkiller said, "Well I am just telling you that if you don't I'll put you in the calaboose." From that they started arguing and Sixkiller did throw him in but when he pushed him in at the door he kicked him. Vann said, "Sixkiller, that kick will cost you your life."

Another Creek Nation resident described Sixkiller as overbearing and very mean. Burl Taylor, a Freedman, stated that every time a group of half-breed Indians from Goose Neck Bend came to Muskogee, they would get drunk and Sam would beat them with his gun.

As today, it is not very hard for policemen to be labeled abusive. Then as now, tough measures were necessary for tough characters. If nothing else, the views of the above citizen show there was a difference of opinion in the territory on Sixkiller's character.

Sixkiller was to have an unscheduled meeting with Vann that would cost him his life. The previous mentioned incidents undoubtedly helped Vann build up a hatred for the peace officer.

Sixkiller had planned to take his family to the Methodist Church on Christmas Eve, 1886, to see the huge holiday tree and participate in the communal sing-along part of the program. Feeling slightly ill, Captain Sixkiller first took a stroll to the business district, hoping Dr. M. F. Williams could give him some medicine from his drugstore that would bring some relief. Since he was off duty, he was unarmed.

A horse race had been held in Muskogee for the past two days and

150

had attracted huge crowds to the Creek capital; among them were many hoodlums and desperadoes. Dick Vann, out of jail again, drifted into town with his brother-in-law, Alf Cunningham; dividing their time between the races and trying to drink all the bootleg whiskey in town. Both of them were mean-natured and were much alike in their hatred for any kind of a lawman.

Cunningham, separated from Vann, was loitering in Muskogee after the race. Alf pulled his pistol on Creek Freedman Tom Kennard, a lighthorseman, who happened to be standing in the door of the Commercial Hotel. Kennard was saved by someone who grabbed Cunningham's gun, giving the officer an opportunity to draw his own weapon, bash it against his assailant's skull, and disarm him.

Unfortunately, Kennard failed to jail Cunningham, and Alf continued to prowl the streets later that evening. Many good citizens refused to venture out, but Cunningham joined forces with his brother-in-law. Together they attempted to buy a pistol and were refused. Then they swaggered into the Mitchell House, where Cunningham seized a shotgun belonging to Ray Farmer, one of the proprietors. Now armed, the two jumped the city marshal, Shelly Keys, who happened to come along unsuspectingly. As a crowd gathered they contented themselves with taking his pistol. Emboldened by the pistol and shotgun, they looked around for Kennard, the lighthorseman. By chance, they ran into Captain Sixkiller first.

Sixkiller was stepping up on the platform on the north side of the Patterson Mercantile Store. The platform was made of wood and had a long set of steps on the east end. Sixkiller was just to the top of the steps when Dick Vann and Alf Cunningham rode up and Vann called to Sixkiller: ". . . you'll never do that to me again." Just as Sixkiller turned around, Vann shot at him with the double-barreled shotgun, the buckshot only riddling his clothing. Sixkiller fell off the platform, and as he hit the ground he tried to elude the gunfire. Cunningham started shooting at him with his pistol and Sixkiller was hit three times, once in the head. Sixkiller managed to get up and run around in a circle a few times, then dropped dead.

The murderers rode out of town as quickly as possible. They might have walked, or even remained in Muskogee, for no pursuit materialized. Other law officers chose discretion and remained out of sight. Marshal Keys "changed his coat and hat that he might conceal his identity and looked as though he might like to contract for a cast iron suit of clothes," a reporter observed sardonically.

Sam Sixkiller's death was a severe loss to the community, testified to by doleful and outraged editorial comment, and up to that time he had the most impressive funeral accorded in Indian Territory. Two thousand turned out to mourn the law officer described as fearless, conscientious, and devoted to his duty. "That a man with so little thought of danger should fall by violence seemed in no way strange," one editor lamented. Indian Agent Robert L. Owen, himself a Cherokee citizen, praised the dead man to the commissioner of Indian affairs:

> Saml. Sixkiller died a martyr to the cause of law and order and had the respect and confidence of all the decent people in the country particularly of Hon. I. C. Parker, U.S. Judge of the District, M. H. Iandels, Pros. Atty., John Carroll, U.S. Marshal. Every newspaper in the territory had the most respectful and complimentary notices of him.

A resolution passed by the Muskogee council had this to say about the man:

> . . . Samuel Sixkiller, captain of the U.S. Indian Police and Deputy U.S. Marshal . . . was a willful and cowardly assasination. For seven years he had been captain of the U.S. Indian Police . . . and as such [was] a vigilant, honest and courageous officer, an acknowledged leader in all perilous enterprises and we regard his unfortunate death as being directly due to his honorable and faithful services against the lawless elements that afflict this country.

Richard Vann and Alfred Cunningham were never brought to trial for the murder of Sam Sixkiller. The labyrinth of conflicting jurisdictions in Indian Territory proved to be a staunch ally of the killers. Both were indicted by a Creek court, but the fugitives were in the Cherokee Nation, and that required extradition. Creek Chief J. M. Perryman formally requested custody of the two men from Cherokee Chief D. W. Bushyhead, but before the requisition could be honored, Dick Vann was killed in another gunfight in the streets of Fort Gibson. Alf Cunningham's case was complicated by the fact that some time after the killing in Muskogee, marshals of Judge Parker's court had taken him to Fort Smith on a larceny charge. This led to extensive correspondence between the federal judge and the two chiefs, since Parker would release Cunningham to Bushyhead only if the Cherokee chief would agree to return him if he were acquitted of the murder charge. And this, of course, required agreement between Bushyhead and Perryman. Parker finally waived this requirement in view of the gravity of the matter: "This case is one of the most important which has been presented to your Courts. The murder was a brutal, barbarous assasination . . . It has attracted the attention of the whole country. It has been alluded to in debate in the Congress of the nation."

But Cunningham was not yet in the courtroom. Delivered to Creek authorities, he made his escape back to the Cherokee Nation, and the extradition process had to be repeated. It was prolonged when a new Cherokee chief took over and some of the legal steps had to be started over again. Finally returned to Creek custody, he managed to escape again and, as public interest in the case went, Cunningham faded into obscurity, a free man.

The murder of the Cherokee peace officer did focus attention on the need for a change in the law. Not until 1965 did it become a federal offense to kill a president of the United States, but Indian policemen have been protected for years under an act which is testimony to the stature of Capt. Sam Sixkiller and may be considered his memorial. An appropriation act, passed in March 1887, carried a section extending the protection of federal law to the Native American. On March 2, 1887, a bill was signed into law by the president of the United States which reads in part,

> any Indians committing against the person of any Indian policeman appointed under the laws of the United States, or any Indian United States Deputy Marshal, any of the following crimes, namely, murder, manslaughter or assault with intent to kill, within the Indian Territory, shall be subject to the laws of the United States relating to such crimes and shall be tried by the District Court of the United States.

While legislators debated ways to protect them, being an Indian policeman continued to be a risky business. Sixkiller's successor as captain of Union Agency police lasted only three months before he was shot to death. Indian juries in the Union Agency seemed to reflect a bias against policemen. A lieutenant on the force killed a thug in self-defense and was convicted of manslaughter. In another case, Chickasaw jurors condemned an Indian member of a posse as an accessory in the killing of a tribesman, while a federal court freed a white man who was the principal in the case. As their agent once remarked: "They do their work, not for the small salary, but in a public spirit, pro bono publico."

153

Over the years, many deeds and actions performed by the Indian police and lighthorse members have been forgotten. In many instances, credit has been given to the federal deputies operating out of Fort Smith. But they served their purpose, bravely and intelligently. The legacy of the lighthorse police will always occupy a special niche in the history of frontier Oklahoma.

After January 1, 1898, the U.S. courts in the Indian Territory had exclusive jurisdiction over all civil and criminal cases and persons, irrespective of origin or race. With this being the case, the lighthorse police were disbanded and ceased to exist. The deputy U.S. marshals, along with municipal and county lawmen, would continue to uphold law and order until statehoood in 1907; major crimes were investigated by the federal officers. The Seminole Lighthorse lasted until a few years after the turn of the century, thus becoming the last of the lighthorse to exist.

Part III

LAWMEN

Deputy U.S. Marshals

CHAPTER 15

Men Who Rode for Parker

One of Judge Isaac Parker's early moves after being appointed in 1875 to the Fort Smith court was to order his marshal to hire 200 deputy marshals to enforce the law in the Indian Territory. Parker reopened investigations into many old, unsolved murders and other felonies, issued warrants for the arrests of the most notorious outlaws and their gangs, and told the deputy marshals: "Bring them in alive — or dead!"

The task was a large order. Two hundred deputies were a mere handful to cover an area of 74,000 square miles, where the outlaws knew every trail and hideout and the deputies had little protection other than their own discretion and skill in serving these processes of law. A year's imprisonment was the only penalty for resisting a federal officer. "To a man who will risk his life to avoid arrest," commented the attorney general, "a year's confinement is a small matter."

In recruiting his force of deputy marshals, Parker looked reality square in the eye. He hated gunfighters, but he knew it took one to catch one. He also knew that some of the men who applied for the job were attracted less by its fees and capture rewards (no salaries were initially paid) than by the opportunities their badge would provide for graft and corruption. Parker tried to screen out the crooks, but if a man was good with a gun, the judge was willing to overlook blank spots in his background. He hired some deputies who later turned to crime, among them two of the Dalton brothers. He also took on some suspicious characters who remained honest and died in combat for the law. Altogether, sixty-five of his deputies would die in this manner during Parker's two decades at Fort Smith. By statehood in 1907, at least 130 deputies and deputized possemen would be victims of criminal action in Indian and Oklahoma Territory.

In 1875, Parker's men fanned out through Indian Territory on the greatest mass manhunt in history. Usually in the early tenure of Parker's reign the deputies rode in teams of four or five for self-protection, and a team brought with it a movable headquarters — a van or wagon equipped to serve as office, arsenal, dormitory, kitchen, and jail. While some teams were sent out as posses on special missions, most were not assigned a definite destination. They were "on the scout," in a lawman's sense of the term — poking and prying, searching shacks for stills or contraband whiskey, prowling in canyons and ravines for stolen horses, investigating suspicious wayfarers, trying to flush criminals of any kind.

The deputies' prison wagon was often called a "tumbleweed wagon." Tumbleweeds would break off in the fall and roll endlessly across the prairie country until they lodged in a brush patch or a fence corner. Sometimes the weeds would pile up like snowdrifts. One of the sights of the territory was to see a tumbleweed bumping along, stopping, going on again. These wagons were so named because, like the weed, they traveled, first in one direction, then rolled off in another.

The prison wagon had a driver and an escort of deputies. The driver sat on a spring-seat, unarmed, while the deputies rode horseback, armed to the teeth. The idea of having the driver unarmed was to prevent prisoners in the wagon from getting any foolish ideas in their heads. Sometimes the wagons carried a cook, usually African-American. If he rode in the wagon he was unarmed. Sometimes he rode horseback; in that case he would be armed. At night the cook helped serve as camp guard.

Frank (Becky) Polk, a tall black man, was selected by Deputy U.S. Marshal Paden Tolbert to serve as a cook with the posse that killed Cherokee Ned Christie. Polk had served with Tolbert on many such missions and was not only an excellent cook but also could handle a pistol and rifle as well as any man.

The prisoners wore leg irons; at night in camp, they had to make themselves useful. They had to peel the potatoes, chop firewood, and wash the tin dishes. If they muttered, they didn't get so much to eat.

157

Going to bed was a ceremony. A chain was fastened to a tree, then the prisoners were secured to the chain, like fish on a line. If there were no trees, as was often the case on the prairie, the chain was snubbed to a wheel of the wagon.

When people saw a "tumbleweed wagon" rolling across the prairie, they veered their course to see who might be inside. Sometimes mounted men would ride along with the deputies, exchanging news. The deputies enjoyed this attention, and often would ask where a certain man was, or what a certain man was doing. That was one of the ways they kept track of the "artful dodgers." The arrival of a prison wagon in town was a social event. In no time at all, word was around and people would gather, wanting to see who the deputies had captured. Sometimes it was somebody in that particular town or village who was wanted.

The deputies never shot to kill if they could possibly avoid it; every man they brought back to stand trial was worth an arrest fee of two dollars, and they got nothing at all for a corpse unless, by a rare stroke of luck, a dead-or-alive reward for the victim had been posted by the railroads or stage companies or some civil authority. A wounded prisoner was permitted to ride in the wagon, chained to its sideboards; the healthy ones quite often would be marched alongside at the point of a gun.

The deputies from Fort Smith worked west to Fort Reno, then south to Anadarko Indian Agency and Fort Sill, for a distance of 400 miles from their origin. In those days the Missouri, Kansas & Texas Railroad, running north and south across the territory, marked the western fringe of civilization. Eighty miles west of Fort Smith was known as the "dead line," and whenever a deputy marshal from Fort Smith or later Paris, Texas, crossed the M.K.&T. track, he took his own life in his hands and knew it. On nearly every trail would be found, posted by outlaws, a small card warning certain deputies that if they ever crossed the dead line, they would be killed. Many outlaws bit the dust, trying to ambush a deputy, and more than a few deputies were "bushwacked" by unknown parties.

The two principal trails that led up from Denison, Texas, into the Indian country were frequented by horse thieves, bootleggers, and others of the criminal type. They were known as the Seminole trail and the Pottawatomie trail. The former led up via old Sasakwa and on toward the Sacred Heart Mission near present-day Shawnee, Oklahoma. The Seminoles hated the Pottawatomies. The two trails, though they were practically parallel, were never used by the same Indians. It was along these two trails, which also led to Fort Sill, Anadarko and Fort Reno, that most of the encounters between deputies and outlaws took place.

The government allowed seventy-five cents a day to feed the prisoners captured and mileage for the distance they traveled at ten cents a mile. A deputy going west was not allowed to arrest a man east of the M.K.&T. Railroad tracks; these warrants were served on the return trip to Fort Smith. If a deputy caught a man a mile west of the M.K.&T. Railroad tracks, however, he was entitled to pay, both for feeding and mileage expense, both ways, if he carried the prisoner 300 miles west to Fort Sill and back to Fort Smith. A deputy was allowed thirty days' time to make a trip as far west as Fort Sill and to return. If he had to stop for high water he was paid for the delay. It was a very hazardous business, but some deputies made big money.

As the haul of captives mounted, a team frequently exceeded its allowance for daily feeding of prisoners, and the deputies were forced to make up the difference. However, they did have a steady source of funds: they were authorized to collect fines for minor offenses and to keep the money as extra income. This incentive plan inevitably encouraged some deputies to become lawbreakers themselves. Dipping into their collection of evidence, they would plant confiscated whiskey or stolen goods in someone's wagon or property, then fine the owner for all of the contrived violations.

The felonious practices of some deputies made a hard job more difficult for all of them. Almost everywhere they were met with suspicion, since the territory now held plenty of people with reason to be leery of them. Besides those shady characters hanging around railroad depots and other legitimate installations, there were thousands of others who had circumvented the law prohibiting white men from purchasing Indian land; they had married Indian women or signed long leases with Indian landowners, and settled down to farming and ranching. All together, Indian Territory by 1878 had about 20,000 white inhabitants, and many of them translated their distaste of outside authority into hostility toward Parker's deputies. Some even went so far as to aid and comfort lawbreakers.

The problem was made even more difficult by the practice of some of the settlements to furnish known criminals "a sort of asylum in exchange for immunity." Often whole gangs of outlaws "bore themselves so quietly among the citizens of the town while their lurid escapades filled the border press." Decent citizens were afraid to let a deputy marshal stay overnight or otherwise accommodate him for fear of reprisals the next day.

Hardened outlaws fled to the Indian Territory for the protection and opportunity it afforded to further engorge their keen appetites. Marshals were "intruders" in their criminal empire, and they connived and banded together to prevent the lawmen from performing their duty. From the prairies in the wild country to the west rose high knobs or hills, which they used as lookout posts. Lights at night or flashing signals in the daytime, relayed from one hill to another, often warned fugitives miles away that officers were in a certain locality. The messages also told the size of the force, and even gave their identity.

After the 1870s it was common for deputies to travel in smaller units, sometimes in pairs or solo with a cook and a posseman, depending on what outlaws were being sought. Sometimes the deputies didn't want to draw a lot of attention to their movements and worked undercover.

A deputy served under the most hazardous conditions imaginable. Bad weather, ranging from stifling heat to razor sharp cold, was only a minor irritation to a deputy when he was on a manhunt compared to what faced him when he located his man. In the first place, practically everyone carried a weapon, and as stated earlier, laws pertaining to the charge of resisting arrest would only bring a maximum punishment of a year in jail, therefore resisting arrest was a standard practice. Because of this, a deputy could usually expect a violent reaction whenever he tried to serve a warrant. Whether this was gun-play or a fist fight depended largely on the criminal charge of the warrant. If the charge was a major one, punishable by death, what did a man have to lose by resisting arrest? If he resisted arrest and either escaped or killed the deputy, he was that much ahead of the game, because word had spread to the effect that if a man was convicted of a hanging offense in Judge Parker's court, he was as good as hanged. So, why not shoot it out with the deputy? The odds of beating the deputy were much higher than beating the hand Judge Parker dealt out.

The deputy's posseman or cook was under no obligation to aid the deputy in the capture of criminals if he didn't feel like it, and most didn't. They just guarded the prisoners or cooked the meal. For this, it is apparent that a deputy was constantly under pressure from the time he left Fort Smith, until he returned. If he served all his warrants and made all his arrests without getting killed or beaten up, he still had to wet-nurse a wagonload of chained, surly prisoners thinking only of escape. The deputies couldn't relax until they were back in Fort Smith with their load of prisoners. No matter how capable a man was with his fist or guns, the sheer mass of numbers in a wagonload of prisoners could overwhelm the best deputy in an instant if he was careless and did relax. Also of concern was a bullet from ambush somewhere along the long haul back to jail; this was a constant threat.

The deputy marshals had to also contend with the fact that there were more bandits, horse thieves, counterfeiters, whiskey peddlers, and train robbers per square mile in this territory, which later became the state of Oklahoma, than any other place in the United States at that time. It wasn't uncommon, as discussed earlier, for travelers to disappear and never be heard from again. A good example of the dangerous environment the deputy marshals were thrust into at the time centered around a country store near Caddo, in the Choctaw Nation. The store looked as innocent as a Sunday school room. Inside, it was a bit different, for there was what was called the "Shelf of Skulls." On the shelf behind the counter were five skulls the proprietor had picked up in the woods near the back of the store. He said he took only the skulls that hadn't been crushed, all victims of foul play.

Judge Parker had the highest respect for his deputies. "Without these men," Parker said time and again, "I could not hold court a single day." And in his later years, when he talked much of his record on the bench, he gave a great deal of credit to the deputy marshals, particularly the sixty-five who gave their lives in the field to the cause of peace and decency during his term at Fort Smith.

In 1889 the Fort Smith court's jurisdictional land area was broken up. Muskogee was selected as the first court in Indian Territory. Paris, Texas, and Wichita, Kansas, also had federal courts for segments of Indian Territory. Later, in 1890, Guthrie, a Santa Fe Railroad town, would become the federal court seat for the newly opened Oklahoma Territory. In the early '90s the deputy marshals continued to work on the fee system, but the business was not as lucrative because of the shorter distances they had to travel. On the other hand, their work was made easier by the nearness of the court. The deputies remained on the fee system until the Curtis Act of 1898 opened the way for Oklahoma statehood. At that time courts were created for Northern, Central, and Southern districts of the Indian Territory, and the deputy marshals were put on salary at $900 a year. The principal courts were Muskogee-Northern District, McAlester-Central District, and Ardmore-Southern District.

The deputy marshals for the most part were brave men, picked for their ability to handle tough assignments. They had a good record of getting their man, but did not make a corps' boast of it as did the Northwest Mounted Police and the Texas Rangers. The test was not always being able to bring in the criminal dead or alive. The prosecution needed evidence to convict, and often a man-sized share of courage was needed to collect it. Deputies such as Heck Thomas, Bill Tilghman, and Chris Madsen have received recognition for their efficient police work in the territories.

One of the little known aspects about the federal police force in the Indian Territory was that besides the inclusion of Native Americans, there were a number of African-Americans commissioned as deputy U.S. marshals. The blacks were recruited after Judge Parker was sworn in as the chief judge in Fort Smith. It should be noted that the black deputies performed all the usual duties, often with outstanding valor and distinction. While many were themselves former slaves with virtually no educational background, they successfully carried on the functions of office and initially had relatively little attention paid to color. They were a remarkably able group since none of those whose names are recognized were ever known to be reprimanded for misconduct, as many others were and then discharged. It is not possible to know how many African-Americans served as deputy U.S. marshals; the federal records did not show a man's race. Therefore racial recognition was made only through newspaper accounts and oral history preserved by settlers.

By the 1890s the following African-American deputies were identified with the corresponding towns: Bass Reeves, Muskogee; Grant Johnson, Eufaula; Zeke Miller, Alderson; Bill Colbert, Atoka; Neely Factor, Carbon; John Garrett, Okmulgee; Jim Ruth, Durant; Charles Pettit, Pawhuska; Robert Fortune, Wilburton; and Rufus Cannon, Fort Smith.

The above deputies were the most well known. Other black deputies included Isaac Rogers, Crowder Nicks, Edward D. Jefferson, Robert Love, John Joss, Dick Roebuck, Morgan Tucker, Eugene Walker, Ed Robinson, Wiley Escoe, and Dick Shaver. Some were Indian Freedmen, like Cyrus Dennis, and held dual commissions with the Indian and Federal Police in the territory. Some of these black lawmen could have been commissioned in the field of operation, depending on the circumstances and whether the manpower warranted more deputies. After reviewing evidence, not many were bonded and held regular commissions, therefore many of them held auxiliary positions.

Native Americans living within the borders of the Indian Territory during this era had mixed opinions about deputy U.S. marshals. Those Indians living on the immediate periphery of the Indian Nations, adjoining Kansas, Arkansas, and Texas, had long enjoyed a close association with white men; mutual trade and cultural intercourse were natural and spontaneous. If these Indians did not trust and respect white men in general, it was so well concealed in their relationship that it was not readily apparent and it created no problems. White men with federal authority were generally accepted at face value and were not hindered in their work.

However, deep in the interior of the Indian Territory, a great many Native Americans had nothing but trouble from their contact with white men, for this was the illegal range of the outlaw element. The white outlaw, completely free of any legal responsibility in this area, ran wild. He abused the Indian women, he stole the Indians' cattle and horses, he commandeered the Indians' food and homes, and he killed any Indian foolish enough to question his right to do these things. Even an organized attempt by a group of Indians to retaliate against the white outlaw was generally doomed to failure because the white outlaw ran in packs, carried generally superior weapons, and was completely ruthless and without pity in a pitched battle. He had nothing to lose by fighting to the death. If an outlaw was captured and expelled from the Indian nations into one of the adjoining states, he was usually arrested for previous crimes committed there, tried, and either promptly hung or sent to prison with a long sentence.

These conditions led the white outlaws to effect a brutal, rough attitude even worse than their own natural, nasty disposition in the belief that fear and intimidation would keep the Indians under their thumb, and thus insure their position as lord and master of this outlaw paradise.

As a direct result of the white outlaw activities and sometimes unscrupulous white deputies, the Indians in the interior developed a deep distrust of all white men. They reasoned that all white men were exactly like the outlaws, so all white men were not to be trusted. It should be pointed out that a large percentage of the white deputies who went into the interior of Indian Territory — that is, into the Creek and Seminole Nations — never returned to Fort Smith.

The scenario for Indian and black outlaws was a little different than that for the white outlaws. The Indian and black outlaws would prey on the white settlements along the border and whites traveling through the Indian nations. The Indian and black outlaws would then hide in their communities deep in the interior of the territory, where they would be among family and friends.

In 1875, when Judge Parker began to organize his force of deputies, many people who knew the situation in the interior of the territory advised against the idea of sending a white deputy into this area. A hostile, uncooperative Indian population would cause a white deputy to be almost completely useless. The problem was especially apparent in the Creek and Seminole Nation, where deputies were desperately needed.

The full-blood Indians found something in common with blacks. Perhaps they felt that the African's history of slavery was akin to their own past history of mistreatment and abuse by the white man. Many blacks had lived their lives among the Indians and therefore understood and appreciated Indian customs. It is also likely that blacks made a greater effort to understand the Native American languages. Irregardless of the reasons involved, the two races were very compatible. Intermarriage and mixing had taken place between the blacks and Choctaws, Cherokees, and especially the Creek and Seminole. This bond tended to strengthen the relationship.

These factors indicated that an African-American would be accepted as a deputy marshal by the Indians. Also, since the Indians respected courage and a straight tongue above all other qualities, it was felt that if black men could be found with all these characteristics, the problem of finding an acceptable deputy for the interior would be solved. Judge Parker was able to find some black men to fit the description needed for the job.

One of the interesting facts regarding black deputy U.S. marshals was that in the Indian Territory they had the authority to arrest whites and defend their lives in doing so. In other words, they had the authority to kill whites or anyone else if the situation called for it. This aspect of law enforcement in the Indian Territory was unique for the United States at the time. However, during post-Reconstruction, in the Southern states, blacks were being politically disenfranchised, murdered, and lynched on a fairly regular basis. While there were other black peace officers in the West after 1875, most were found in urban areas. The highest concentration was found in the territory later to become the state of Oklahoma. Conditions for blacks, irregardless of occupation and status, changed drastically as Oklahoma moved toward statehood in 1907.

CHAPTER 16

Bass Reeves:
The Invincible Marshal

C. W. "Dub" West, an Oklahoma historian, says the newspaper obituary tribute given to a black peace officer by the *Muskogee Phoenix* on
January 13, 1910, was unusual for the time. It was as follows:

BASS REEVES DEAD;
UNIQUE CHARACTER
Man of the "Old Days" Gone
Deputy Marshal Thirty-Two Years.

Bass Reeves is dead. He passed away yesterday afternoon about
three o'clock and in a short time news of his death had reached the
federal court house where the announcement was received in the various offices with comments of regret and where it recalled to the officers and clerks many incidents in the early days of the United States
court here in which the old [N]egro deputy figured heroically.

Bass Reeves had completed thirty-five years service as deputy
marshal when, with the coming of statehood at the age of sixty-nine
he gave up his position. For about two years then he served on the
Muskogee police force, which position he gave up about a year ago
on account of sickness, from which he never fully recovered. Bright's
disease and a complication of ailments together with old age, were
the cause of his death.

The deceased is survived by his wife and several children, only
one of whom, a daughter, Mrs. Alice Spahn, lives in Muskogee. His

165

mother, who is eighty-seven years old, lives at Van Buren, Arkansas, where a sister of his also is living.

The funeral will be held at noon friday from the Reeves home at 816 North Howard street. Arrangements for the funeral had not been completed last evening.

BASS REEVES' CAREER.

In the history of the early days of Eastern Oklahoma the name of Bass Reeves has a place in the front rank among those who cleansed out the old Indian Territory of outlaws and desperadoes. No story of the conflict of government's officers with those outlaws which ended only a few years ago with the rapid filling up of the territory with people, can be complete without mention of the [N]egro who died yesterday.

For thirty-two years, beginning way back in the seventies and ending in 1907, Bass Reeves was a deputy United States marshal. During that time he was sent to arrest some of the most desperate characters that ever infested Indian Territory and endangered life and peace in its borders. And he got his man as often as any of the deputies. At times he was unable to get them alive and so in the course of his long service he killed fourteen men. But Bass Reeves always said that he never shot a man when it was not necessary for him to do so in the discharge of his duty to save his own life. He was tried for murder on one occasion but was acquitted upon proving that he had killed the man in the discharge of his duty and was forced to do it.

Reeves was an Arkansan and in his early days was a slave. He entered the federal service as a deputy marshal long before a court was established in Indian Territory and served under the marshal at Fort Smith. Then when people started to come into Indian Territory and a marshal was appointed with headquarters in Muskogee, he was sent over here.

Reeves served under seven United States marshals and all of them were more than satisfied with his services. Everybody who came in contact with the negro deputy in an official capacity had a great deal of respect for him, and at the court house in Muskogee one can hear stories of his devotion to duty, his unflinching courage and his many thrilling experiences, and although he could not write or read he always took receipts and had his accounts in good shape.

Undoubtedly the act which best typifies the man and which at least shows his devotion to duty, was the arrest of his own son. A warrant for the arrest of the younger Reeves, who was charged with the murder of his wife, had been issued. Marshal Bennett said that perhaps another deputy had better be sent to arrest him. The old negro was in the room at the time, and with a devotion of duty

166

equalling that of the old Roman, Brutus, whose greatest claim on fame has been that the love for his son could not sway him from justice, he said, "Give me the writ," and went out and arrested his son, brought him into court and upon trial and conviction he was sentenced to imprisonment and is still serving the sentence.

Reeves had many narrow escapes. At different times his belt was shot in two, a button shot off his coat, his hatbrim shot off and the bridle reins which he held in his hand cut by a bullet. However, in spite of all these narrow escapes and the many conflicts in which he was engaged, Reeves was never wounded. And this notwithstanding the fact that he said he never fired a shot until the desperado he was trying to arrest had started the shooting.

In 1901 there was a comprehensive book published about the Indian Territory that was descriptive, biographical, and genealogical. It was written by D. C. Gideon, who made the following statements about Reeves:

> Among the numerous deputy marshals that have ridden for the Paris (Texas), Fort Smith (Arkansas) and Indian Territory courts none have met with more hair-breath escapes or have more hazardous arrests than Bass Reeves, of Muskogee. Bass is a stalwart [N]egro, fifty years of age, weighs one hundred and eighty pounds, stands six feet and two inches in his stockings, and fears nothing that moves and breathes. His long muscular arms have attached to them a pair of hands that would do credit to a giant and they handle a revolver with ease and grace acquired only after years of practice. Several "bad" men have gone to their long home for refusing to halt when commanded to by Bass.

This inclusion of Reeves by Gideon was the first time Reeves was discussed in a book and would remain the only reference on him for another seventy years. Western historians wrote about Reeves's peers in the territories, but he was unfortunately overlooked.

In 1971, seventy years after Gideon's book, the Oklahoma City Public Schools published a book, edited by Kay M. Teall and entitled *Black History in Oklahoma — A Resource Book.* In the book, Teall stated: "Bass Reeves had a reputation as a lawman second to none in the territory."

In more recent years, other historians have taken a look at the career and life of Bass Reeves.

Nudie Williams, history professor at the University of Arkansas, wrote: "The mark of this man was not that he died with his boots on, but what he did with them while he wore them. He was a man who did a big job that had to be done and his contribution is a record without parallel in early law enforcement history."

Jimmie Lewis Franklin, history professor at Vanderbilt University, wrote: "Reeves carried an enviable and well-deserved reputation as a courageous officer who 'got his man.' As legend would have it, both blacks and whites feared 'the sudden pop of his unerring gun' and many of the men for whom he had warrants were carried back to . . . court . . . feet foremost because they made the mistake of matching their pistols with Reeves."

It is believed that Reeves was born near Paris, Lamar County, Texas. Bass was born a slave; unfortunately, slave records did not record names and are very sketchy if they can be found. One source gives his year of birth as 1824, but his obituary notice stated his mother was living when he expired and that she was eighty-seven. This would mean that Reeves's mother was born in 1823. The same obituary notice stated Reeves was sixty-nine when he retired from the U.S. marshal's service. This would mean that Reeves was born in 1838. This date becomes consistent when considering the interview of Reeves in the *Oklahoma City Weekly-Times Journal* of March 8, 1907, which gives his age as sixty-eight. Also, D. C. Gideon interviewed Reeves at the turn of the century, at which time he said Reeves was fifty years of age. The 1900 census gave his birthdate as July 1840, Texas. This information could have been given by his wife, who would have known his approximate date of birth and place of origin. Given the available data, this author believes that Reeves was born in Paris, Lamar County, Texas, in July of 1838.

In a newspaper interview in 1901, Reeves stated that as a slave he belonged to Col. George Reeves of Grayson County, Texas. Reeves worked alongside his parents as a youngster, first as a water boy and later as a field hand after gaining physical maturity. But young Reeves's spirit and pride had already marked him for something in life other than being a common field hand. As a youngster working in the fields as a water boy, Reeves caused concern for his mother because he spent so much time singing about guns, rifles, butcher knives, robberies, or killings. She felt he might turn out to be a desperado, since he spent so much time in the field singing about them.

The slave owner, Col. George R. Reeves, was an interesting figure in his own right. George R. Reeves was born January 3, 1826, in Hickman, Tennessee, and died September 5, 1882, at Pottsboro,

Texas, from hydrophobia after being bitten by his dog. Colonel Reeves is buried at Georgetown Cemetery in Grayson County, Texas. He was a farmer, Grayson County sheriff, tax collector, state legislator, before and after the Civil War, and colonel in the Confederate Army. He organized the Texas 11th Cavalry Unit for Grayson County, was Speaker of the House of Representatives for the State of Texas, and master of the George R. Reeves Masonic Lodge of Pottsboro, named in his honor. Reeves County in West Texas is also named for him.

Col. George R. Reeves did not own a large plantation before the Civil War but operated a modest-sized farm. He owned a total of seven slaves, of whom Bass was one. The slaves lived in the same house as did Reeves and his family, but in a different location.

Oral history recorded by the Bass Reeves family stated that Reeves was picked to be his master's companion or body servant. Reeves had the qualifications; he was big, strong, handy with firearms, ambitious, and held the respect of all who knew him. He also had a quick mind, was good-natured, and had a zest for life that made him good company under any conditions. Reeves could evaluate people immediately, which was an indispensable talent in the days before the Civil War. It also would come in handy during his law enforcement career.

Family history goes on to state that there may or may not have been a sequence of events that led up to the mysterious parting of Reeves and his owner. The straw-that-broke-the-camel's-back supposedly occurred while Reeves and his master were playing cards, alone. There was a heated argument about something, and young Reeves gave his master a beating; he "laid him out cold with his fist and then made a run for the Indian Territory north across Red River, with the hue and cry of 'run away nigger' hounding him up until the Emancipation." It is said that everyone who knew anything or might have been involved refused to talk about the incident or events leading to it.

Reeves gave the press and one of his fellow deputies a different story of his time spent during the war. He stated that as being a body servant, he accompanied his master, Col. George R. Reeves, into battle. Reeves told the press that he was at the battles of Chickamauga and Missionary Ridge. He said that he had seen the renowned General McCulloch, of Texas Ranger fame, get killed at the battle of Pea Ridge.

The story given by Reeves cannot be verified because records were not kept concerning body servants of Confederate officers, and Col.

169

George R. Reeves does not mention Bass in his known war memoirs. There is the possibility that Reeves left his master during the war, which would give some plausibility to oral history kept by family members. Reeves may have felt that the truth wouldn't sit well with the many Confederate veterans he worked with and who lived in the territory. At this point, much about his life will have to be left to conjecture.

One thing is certain: During the war years Reeves perfected his complete mastery of firearms. He also became very familiar with the Indian nations. It is well known that Reeves learned to speak several Indian dialects during this time. He was fluent in Creek and could converse reasonably well in the languages of the other Five Civilized Tribes as well as several lesser tribal tongues.

One old-timer reported that Reeves had held a sergeant's rank in the Union army during the Civil War. After the war, Reeves settled down and bought a farm outside of Van Buren, Arkansas. He married a very pretty light-skinned black girl named Jennie; she was from Texas. They proceeded to raise ten children — five boys and five girls. Reeves was an excellent farmer and stockman; his prosperous farm was proof of his industrious skills.

Sometime during 1875, Bass Reeves was approached and asked to serve as a deputy U.S. marshal. He accepted the offer and became one of the first men who "rode for Parker." Reeves is considered to be one of the first, if not the first, African-Americans to be commissioned a deputy U.S. marshal west of the Mississippi River. The first African-American to become a marshal was Frederick Douglass, appointed on March 17, 1877, by President Rutherford B. Hayes. None of the black deputies that ever worked the Indian or Oklahoma Territories reached the highly political office of marshal.

Reeves was a big man for the time in which he lived. He stood over six feet and his weight during his law career was always somewhere between 180 and 200 pounds. His weight was spread over a large frame, large muscular arms, and long powerful legs, with the characteristic small waist and hips of a man who spends most of his time in the saddle. His hands were very large; he could practically cup a Colt revolver in his palm the way lesser men would hold a derringer. His knuckles were large and knotty, and they were scarred and battered as proof of his prowess as a "rough-and-tumble" fighter. It was said that Reeves could "whip most any two men with his fist."

An early pioneer of Indian Territory said that Bass Reeves was "boastful and lusty, full of life and wore a large black hat." His smile came easily and often, for Reeves saw much in the simple joys of life to make him smile. His voice was deep and resonant, with the drawling smoothness of his Southern background, and his laugh was thunderous and booming in extreme. He moved with the easy grace of a man used to the open spaces of the Great Plains, with all the stealth and sureness of the natural hunter, and with the confidence and poise of a strong man whose strength has been tested and proven many times.

The first story heard by this author concerning Reeves was from an old-timer who remembered an incident which occurred in the Creek Nation. Rev. Haskell James Shoeboot was a Cherokee Freedman, born in Fort Gibson and reared in Muskogee. As a young man he drove a hack for Bud Ledbetter and occasionally for Bass Reeves. Rev. Shoeboot related the following story concerning an incident which would have occurred late in Reeves's career:

> Bud Ledbetter was in pursuit of a white outlaw near Gibson Station, I.T. Ledbetter and his posse were able to pin down the outlaw early in the day with gunfire. As the day progressed, Ledbetter and his posse did not make any gain in subduing the outlaw and by late afternoon had expended a large amount of ammunition. Ledbetter became very frustrated and requested the assistance of Bass Reeves. Reeves was brought to the scene of the shootout. At this time the posse was still shooting at the outlaw; one of the deputies in the posse was W. B. Depue. The desperado decided to make a run for it on foot as daylight was fading. Posse members fired at the running target but missed. Ledbetter hollered, "Get 'em Bass." Bass replied, "I'll break his neck." At a distance of a quarter-mile, Bass with one shot from his Winchester rifle broke the outlaw's neck.

This particular story has not been substantiated, but Bass Reeves did have unusual capabilities with both pistol and rifle. His ability with firearms is legendary, so much so that he was barred regularly from competition in turkey shoots that were common to the local fairs and picnics of the territory. His speed with a pistol has been likened to that of a "Methodist preacher reaching for a platter of fried chicken during Sunday dinner at the deacon's house." It was fast and sure, with no wasted or unnecessary motion. Reeves could draw and shoot from the hip with great speed and accuracy if necessary, but he favored the slower, even more accurate method of taking his time, planting himself solidly, and drawing "a bead as fine as a spider's web on a frosty morning." When he shot this way, "he could shoot the left hind leg off

171

of a contented fly sitting on a mule's ear at a hundred yards and never ruffle a hair." Reeves was an expert with the old cap and ball guns, but favored the Colt .45 and .38-.40 pistols with his Winchester rifle chambered for the same cartridge. Reeves was also known to sometimes carry a double-barreled shotgun in his arsenal. He wore two pistols, handle butts forward for a quick draw.

With a rifle, Reeves claimed to be "only fair." This characteristic modesty belies the truth, for Reeves was truly an expert with a rifle. For example, he once rode over the crest of a rise, way out on the fringes of the Kiowa-Comanche country, and interrupted six wolves as they were in the process of pulling down a steer. Shooting from the back of his horse at the wolves, which scattered in all directions, he killed all six with only eight shots. True, he broke one wolf's leg and "gut-shot" another to miss a clean, one-shot kill. But he did stop them both, only using a second shot to end their suffering. Eight shots for any six kills with moving targets is fine shooting in any man's language.

It is said that Reeves would always sing softly to himself before he went into a gunfight. Whenever those within earshot of Reeves heard him break into song, they knew he meant business and lead might fly at any time.

Reeves's physical strength was also legendary in the territory. Once, while riding in the southern portion of the Chickasaw Nation, Reeves came upon some cowboys attempting to extract a full-grown steer from one of the bogs along Mud Creek, which emptied into the Red River. The cowboys had roped the steer and were attempting to bodily drag it back to solid ground with their horses. Several ropes had broken under the strain. The steer was big and was buried so deep in the bog that only its head and upper back were visible. Its eyes were rolled back into its head; its neck had been pulled and stretched until its tongue lolled out of its mouth into the mud and slime of the bog; its windpipe was so restricted by the ropes that its breath was only an occasional labored, rasping wheeze. In fact, the cowboys were almost ready to give him up as lost. They were seriously considering riding off and leaving the steer where they found him, with a bullet in his brain to soothe their consciences and mark their defeat.

Bass rode up, watched for a few minutes, grunted his dissatisfaction, and, stepping down from his horse, began to strip off his clothes. Without saying a word, he stepped into the bog and began to work his way out to the trapped steer.

First, he removed all the ropes so that the steer could breathe again. Then, grabbing the steer by the horns, he began to lift and pull, all the while talking low and steady to the steer. He pulled and heaved and lifted and grunted under the strain until he sank into the mud almost to his waist before the cowboys could detect the first progress in moving the steer. Stopping to catch his breath, he wiped his sweating, muddy hands dry on the back of the steer, and stooped to lift and pull again.

Ever so slowly, the steer was lifted until the lethal suction of the bog holding the forequarters of the steer was broken. Reeves then moved to the steer's flank and began the torturous process again. By this time, the steer had regained its breath and began its first attempts to help. These attempts were feeble at first, but grew stronger with each great sucking breath.

Reeves repeated this process of lifting and pulling, first at the steer's head and then at its flank, until the steer, with great convulsive twists and turns, was able to lunge toward solid ground under its own power. Upon reaching solid ground, the steer, without so much as a glance at its savior, wobbled off into the brush and disappeared, bawling its triumph for all the Chickasaw Nation to hear.

Reeves waded out of the mud, scraped himself as clean as he could with the flat of his hands, stuffed his clothes into his saddlebags, mounted his horse, and rode off stark naked while mumbling something about "damn dumb cowboys." He rode off without saying a word to any of the dumbstruck cowboys, even though he had been there for almost a full hour.

Adam Grayson, an early resident of the Creek Nation, made the following comments concerning Bass Reeves:

Bass Reeves, a colored man, was a noted and well-known United States marshal. He was a fearless man when it came to fulfilling his duty as an officer of the law . . . He owned and always rode a sorrel horse which he loved next to his duty. He was known in Oklahoma and in the Indian Territory for his deeds as U.S. marshal for at least thirty-five years. He is said to have missed only one time in capturing his man and that was a man named Hellubee Sammy who lived at that time in what is now the Boley vicinity. Hellubee Sammy owned a large black horse that was a swift runner, and that was the only reason why he was not captured — Sammy's horse outran the U.S. marshal's horse.

Undoubtedly, this was not the only man to elude Reeves, but

most likely one of the few who did. Reeves rode tall in the saddle while on the prairie. He could be easily recognized at long distances. The homesteaders of Pottawatomie County remembered Reeves riding a big red stallion with a white blazed face. He carried a gourd dipper tied to his saddlebag, which he used when he stopped at farmhouses for a drink of well water.

Like most men of his time, Reeves loved horses, and considering his line of work, a good horse was absolutely essential. Because of his height and weight, Reeves needed a horse of majestic size. He often said: "When you get as big as me, a small horse is as worthless as a preacher in a whiskey-joint fight. Just when you need him bad to help you out, he's got to stop and think about it a little bit." When you take into account the fact that Reeves often had to ride fifty to a hundred miles a day in the performance of his duties, a small horse just could not stand up under the constant strain of carrying his great weight over such distances. Because of this, Reeves favored big horses, and he was partial to bays and sorrels. He, along with many of his contemporaries, felt that a bay or sorrel horse had an inherent quality of lasting ability, so vital to fast, continuous travel across the varied landscape of the Indian Territory.

Giving the example of Hellubee Sammy eluding Bass by having a faster horse, Reeves once owned a horse that was famous for its speed. He took great pride in demonstrating this speed, and backing it up with hard money whenever possible.

While riding along the upper reaches of Hellroaring Creek in the Chickasaw Nation, Reeves had the occasion to come upon a man, Allen Thompson. Reeves was on his way to the Creek Nation with a pocketful of warrants, and Thompson was working the brush along the creek for stray cattle. As was the custom of the travelers of that day, Reeves stopped to talk for a short while before riding on.

Reeves was riding a big sorrel gelding, standing almost a full nineteen hands tall, and Thompson was riding a little gray mare hardly bigger than a Spanish mule. Both men admired the other's horse, discussing the finer points of both, and after a few minutes, the question of speed was mentioned. Bass, with a great display of calculated indifference, said that his horse was pretty slow, but he might be able to get a race out of him so long as it was a short one and over good ground, because the sorrel was old and had traveled many a hard mile already that day. Thompson rose to the bait and "allowed his gray might could run just a little bit" if he encouraged her along with the liberal appli-

174

cation of his quirt because, after all, she was only a poor, hard-working cow horse that had been popping cattle out of the brush all day. Chasing cows was mighty poor training for racing speed in a horse, he added.

With each man belittling his horse's ability as a racer, a matched race between the sorrel and the gray was reluctantly arranged. Just to make it interesting, a twenty-dollar gold piece was to be put up by each man to help the winner reconcile the strain and effort his "poor worn out horse" would have to exert in running the race. The loser was to receive the best wishes and deep sympathy of the winner, with maybe just a smattering of heel dust from the winner thrown in for good luck next time.

In short order a two-mile course was picked out. Reeves was to toss a rock over his shoulder into the creek and the splash it made was to be the signal to start. Reeves selected the rock, tossed it back, and then, down the fertile bottom land of Hellroaring Creek, with perhaps not another living soul closer than forty miles, the race began.

Thompson and his little gray were off like "a guinea hen in a hailstorm" to take an extremely easy lead, leaving Reeves and his sorrel "sittin' and wonderin' " what type of cows that gray was used to chasing.

Reeves cut loose with a bellow "louder than any cow-chasing range bull" advertising his availability and gave the sorrel his head. He leaned low in the saddle and shifted his weight as far forward as possible, and the sorrel settled down to the task of catching the upstart gray.

The gray was running easily. Its ears were flat and laid back along its stretched neck, and Thompson was laid so far out over the saddle, chuckling and encouraging the gray, that it was hard to tell where the gray's ears ended and Thompson's began. He and his horse did not intend to lose the race, for this gray mare was one of the fastest horses in the Chickasaw Nation, and Thompson had a reputation to maintain of beating all comers in a matched race.

Reeves's sorrel began to unlimber and answer the challenge of the gray with the long, powerful, ground-eating strides that had served Bass so well in his official capacity as a lawman, and which had won so countless many match races before.

When the gray reached the half-mark, Reeves and his sorrel were back in the race and closing fast on the gray. By the three-quarter-mile mark, the gray didn't stand a chance; she was fast and was truly a horse among horses, but her short-coupled, small size was no match for the long-bodied, rangy sorrel. The sorrel passed the gray so fast that Thompson grunted in disbelief. He spoke to the gray and even used his quirt in an effort to increase her speed, but the daylight between the two horses increased until Thompson felt there was a "Tuesday 'til next Saturday night" difference between them. He sat back and pulled up the gray, letting her finish the race in an easy lope. The size and power of the sorrel were too much for the gray over a two-mile course, and Thompson didn't want to break her heart by letting her finish a race in which she was so greatly overmatched. He simply pulled her up to wait for another day and another race, and above all, a race with another horse.

After a span of many years in which Reeves served as a deputy U.S. marshal, stories echo from yesteryear concerning the many disguises he used in capturing outlaw fugitives. In fact, Reeves was a master of disguise. Sometimes he dressed as a cowboy, a tramp, a gunslinger or outlaw, and he used many aliases. Always dressed neatly when not in disguise, he was noted for his politeness and courteous manner during his everyday discourse among the populace.

The following two stories are examples of Reeves's undercover work while pursuing outlaws in the territory. The times and dates are not known, but the incidents were not forgotten by the pioneers and became part of the legend of Bass Reeves.

The first incident concerns the time when notices were issued offering a $5,000 reward for the capture of two badmen. Reeves decided that he wanted the reward. He studied the many ways in which he might make a capture and finally heard that the two men were somewhere south, near the Texas border. Reeves selected a few men to act as a posse and journeyed to the locality where he felt the outlaws were hiding.

Reeves pitched his camp about twenty-eight miles from the suspected hideout. He established the camp at this distance so that he could take his time in making a plan of procedure for a capture without creating any suspicions, and so that he could look over the lay of the surrounding land. He had made out one plan to see if he could successfully carry it out, and if this failed he was going to try other plans. The first plan was successful. It is said that he used the disguise of a tramp. In doing so he removed the heels from an old pair of shoes, carried a cane, and wore a very floppy old hat in which he had shot three bullet holes. He concealed his handcuffs, pistol, and badge under his clothes. Thus disguised, Reeves started out on foot in the direction of the probable hideout of the two wanted criminals. He walked the twenty-eight miles to reach his destination, the home of the two criminals' mother.

When he arrived at the house, the mother of the two outlaws greeted him. Reeves, playing his part to the hilt, asked for a bite to eat, remarking that he was very hungry and his feet were blistered after walking a very long distance. Reeves told her that this was the first opportunity he had to stop after being pursued by a posse that put three bullet holes in his hat. The woman replied, "I will be glad to give you something to eat." Reeves was invited into the home, where she prepared some food. While he was eating his meal, the woman proceeded to tell the lawman about her two boys, who were also on the run from the law.

After Reeves had finished his meal, he still feigned weariness and requested to stay a while longer. The woman gave the consent and remarked, "It would be a good plan that you and my two boys join forces so that you can be a protection to one another."

After the sunset had faded and the darkness ruled supreme, Reeves thought he heard a sharp whistle from the nearby creek. The old woman went outside and gave an answer. Two riders rode up and had a lengthy conversation with the woman. When finally they came into the house, the mother introduced the new outlaw. The boys agreed to the plan to join forces with the unknown guest for criminal gain.

When they prepared to go to bed, a place in a separate room was made for Reeves. He immediately suggested they all sleep in one room, saying, "Something might happen and if we are separated we couldn't be much protection to one another." They all agreed to sleep in one room, with the boys sleeping on the floor.

While in bed, Reeves kept a watchful eye on the boys. Just as soon as the outlaws were asleep, Reeves left his bed and managed to handcuff the pair without awakening them. He waited until early morning before he awoke the boys, at which time Reeves was ready to leave. He kicked the boys from their sleep and said, "Come on, boys, let's get going from here." When the two boys finally got the sleep out of their eyes, they realized that they were in the hands of the law. When Reeves started out with his prisoners to his camp, the mother followed him for three miles, cursing him and calling him all sorts of vile names. The boys were forced to walk the full twenty-eight miles.

Upon reaching his camp, Reeves found all his possemen waiting for him. He remarked, "Maybe you think my money won't turn green now, boys." In saying this, he meant that he expected to obtain the $5,000 reward.

The next famous story of undercover work took place sometime in the 1890s. Reeves received a tip that some dangerous outlaws were holed up in an abandoned log cabin about a mile east of the saloon town of Keokuk Falls, in Pottawatomie County, Oklahoma Territory. Keokuk Falls in the last decade of the century was one of the wildest, most fierce saloon towns on the border of the Seminole Nation. All the Indian nations being dry, residents had to go across the border into Oklahoma Territory to get whiskey, where saloons were legal. Reeves was one of the few deputy marshals who dared go into the dangerous border-town saloons at Violet Springs, the Corner, Youngs Crossing, and Keokuk Falls. The Wewoka Trading Post, then owned by Governor John F. Brown, Jr., chief of the Seminole Nation, had been robbed, and Bass Reeves was called in to investigate the robbery. The outlaws' trail led to Keokuk Falls. Informants there told him that men such as Reeves described had been in the Red Dog Saloon the night before, and were believed to have ridden east into the Creek Nation. Reeves picked up the trail and located the abandoned cabin. When he got near the cabin he noticed smoke coming out of the chimney. After thinking about his approach, he decided to disguise himself as a tenant farmer.

The next morning, Reeves rented a yoke of flea-bitten, aged oxen hitched to a ramshackle wagon of outdated vintage and usage, and proceeded toward the half-hidden cabin in a cluster of trees. Driving close to the cabin, he deliberately got the wagon hung up on a large tree stump. When the unsuspecting desperadoes came out to help, hoping for the most part to get him away from their quiet hideout, Reeves let them lift the wagon free of the stump. Just as they completed their task, Reeves reached into his faded and patched overalls pockets and came out with two big Colt revolvers. He got the drop on the four careless outlaws. None challenged the Colt authority; the odds were in Bass's hands.

After disarming them and backing them away from their guns on the ground, he gathered their weapons and put them in his wagon. Then, handcuffing them, he chained them together and padlocked them to the wagon wheel, while he recovered the stolen money and the loot from the cabin. The deputy marshal then marched all of them in front of the wagon on foot to the county seat at Tecumseh, a distance of over thirty miles. There they were properly jailed by Sheriff Billy Trousdale, and later taken to the federal jail at Guthrie, where the robbers were convicted.

Reeves claimed that he used detective skills and clever disguises as much as possible to avoid shootouts, although he did admit to having to kill at least fourteen men in the line of duty.

Isa S. Smith, an African-Creek lighthorseman from Canadian Town, made the following statements concerning Reeves:

> Bass Reeves, Colbert, Crowder Nicks and John Garrett were all colored and could arrest anyone colored, Indian or white. They would camp close to a house and ask if any stealing, killing or anything like had been going on in that part of the country. If there had been and you didn't want them to get the guilty person you just said that you didn't know about anything like that.
>
> If the crimes had been against you or your friends you told them about it and where the guilty person would be likely found. They didn't need a writ but just went and arrested the persons and took them to jail.

Harve Lovelday, an early white homesteader, made the following comments about the territory:

> In old Oklahoma the West was West when the six-shooters worked out in the gambling halls and in the saloons of Asher, Avoca, Wanette, Earlsboro, Violet Springs, Corner, and Keokuk Falls about the time of 1889 and 1890. Earlsboro, Violet Springs, Corner, and Keokuk Falls were on the boundry {sic} line between the Pottawatomie country and the Seminole Nation while Asher, Avoca, and Wanette were along the boundry lines between the Pottawtomie country and the Chickasaw Nation . . .
>
> The Western people as man to man answered one another in Western style. The man who answered first was the man who was quick on the draw and on the trigger and all disputes were settled just outside the saloons on the porches or they engaged in fistic fights . . .
>
> These small Western towns were inhabited by Negroes, whites, Indians, half-breeds, gamblers, bootleggers, killers, and any kind of an outcast . . .
>
> Bass Reeves, a coal-black Negro was a U.S. marshal during one time and he was the most feared U.S. marshal that was ever heard of in that country. To any man or any criminal that was subject to ar-

179

rest he did his full duty according to law. He brought his men before the court to be tried fairly but many times he never brought in all the criminals but would kill some of them. He didn't want to spend so much time in chasing down the man who resisted arrest so would shoot him down in his tracks.

All the killings Bass Reeves was involved in were investigated and deemed justified after scrutiny. Any incident where a felon was killed by a deputy marshal was thoroughly investigated by the Fort Smith court. Judge Isaac Parker did not tolerate cold-blooded murder on the side of law or outlaw. There were some deputies who were prosecuted and subsequently served time in prison for unjust killings. But Bass Reeves, although accused of murder on one occasion, was not one of them.

Nancy E. Pruitt, an early resident of the Creek Nation, also had some interesting comments concerning Reeves:

> Bass Reeves and Grant Johnson were colored officers . . . They could talk Creek and the Creeks liked Negroes better than they did whites, [which] I suppose is the reason they had colored officers. This Bass Reeves had the name of being a good officer and when he went after a man he got him. One time he went after two mean Negroes and knew when he left that if he didn't kill them they would kill him, for it would be impossible to bring them back alive. When he found them they were lying under a tree asleep but before he could get to them one awakened and got up. Bass started talking to him and gave him a letter to read. By that time the other one was up. When the first had read the letter Bass told him to let the other one read it. When he turned to give the letter to the other one, Bass shot him and then the second before he could draw. That looks like a cold blooded murder to us now but it was really quick thinking and bravery.

Bass Reeves, like many African-Americans and Native Americans of that era, believed in the powers of the spirit world. Most Indians believed that the spirit power could be gained by certain people or through certain ceremonies.

All traditional African religions recognize the existence of a supreme God. But most emphasize that people should seek help by appealing to lesser gods or the spirits of dead ancestors.

Medicine men were highly sought out and respected by both the Indians and the Indian Freedmen. In many instances, the medicine men were the most venerated persons in a community. D. C. Gideon

180

recounted a story concerning Reeves and a Creek medicine man:

Bass Reeves, the invincible deputy United States marshal related to the writer an instance of the supernatural power at one time exerted over himself by Yah-kee, who made his abode on North Fork. "I was up there," said Bass, "to arrest a lot of men for horse theft, and had two wagon-loads of prisoners encamped in the woods in care of my posse. Among them were two Indians who had each made Yah-kee a present of a pony for medicine the old man had furnished them, guaranteed to render them 'invisible' should the officers attempt to serve a warrant upon them for horse theft. As I also had a warrant for Yah-kee I went back and got him, too, and when we camped for the night I was feeling very stiff and sore, although having felt well all the day. We started for Fort Smith the next morning and although I rode a saddle horse I was unable to keep within sight of the wagons. When I reached their camp at noon they were done eating and the prisoners, shackled together, were lying under the trees asleep. With the greatest difficulty I dismounted, and fell forward against a tree, aching in every limb, and my eyes were so swollen that I could scarcely see. I could eat nothing and seemed possessed of a consuming thirst. Believing that old Yah-kee had bewitched me, I felt that all hope was gone. My knees refused to bear the weight of my body, and feeling that my last hour had come I thought to take a last look upon the man whom I felt was responsible for my present condition. He was lying on his back asleep, and his coat had turned partly over so that a concealed inner pocket was in view. I saw a string dangling from it and made up my mind that it was attached to his 'conjurbag.' Gently I dragged myself to his side and with a jerk drew from his pocket a mole-skin bag, filled with bits of roots, pebbles and tiny rolls of short hair, tied with blue and red strings. I tossed it as far as I could, and saw it float away on the bosom of a creek that flowed alongside the camp. With a start Yah-kee awoke. 'Bass,' said he, 'you stole my conjur-bag.' 'Yes, I did,' said Bass, 'and it is now sailing down the creek.' The old man promised all kinds of pay if I would return it, but I feared it less as it sailed down the creek than when it was in the hands of Yah-kee. 'I can't conjur any more,' said the old man; 'my power is gone. Take off this chain and I will follow you like a dog.' I declined to do this, however, and the prisoners started on. From the moment the bag touched the water I began to feel relieved. I later mounted my horse and when I caught up with the party in the evening I felt as well as ever." Yah-kee told him afterward that if he had not lost his "conjur-bag" Bass would have been dead before they reached Fort Smith; and he believes it, too.

181

This was the last time Yah-kee ever tried to exert this power for evil over any person, and thereafter refused to practice the black art.

According to Reeves, each of his prison wagons was equipped with a long, heavy chain. When a prisoner was captured, he was shackled with old-fashioned brads. At night all the prisoners were shackled in pairs and the shackles passed through a ring in the long chain. One end of the chain was locked around the rear axis of the wagon. In this manner one man could handle thirty prisoners if there was a need. The only precaution was to prevent the prisoners from ever getting within reach of the six-shooters. No guard or cook was allowed to gamble with the prisoners for fear they would lose their six-shooters. Reeves said the first thing a prisoner wanted after they were captured and shackled was to gamble.

Adam Grayson, a Creek Nation resident, said that one time Bass Reeves made camp at what is now Pharoah or Springhill, Oklahoma, in eastern Okfuskee County. It was a custom to hold several prisoners in camp until he had secured more before loading them into wagons for the trip to Fort Smith. At that time, Grayson related, Reeves had a man named Campbell, who stayed all the time in camp with the prisoners, as guard and as the camp cook. All the prisoners were seated on a large log cut especially for this purpose. The prisoners' feet would be shackled together and the shackles pinned to the ground near the end of the log and the rest of the loose shackles pinned to the log itself.

In his free and spare moments, Reeves would walk up and down before the prisoners and preach about the evils of criminal behavior. Reeves hated to think that he took men to prison, but it was his duty to carry out the law, so he would take the time to tell his prisoners the consequences of doing right or wrong.

J. B. Sparks, a white Oklahoma pioneer, said:

Bass Reeves was a Negro, but he was a U.S. marshal and made a brave officer. He was sent to get two outlaws near Atwood. He caught and arrested them and that night he went to Frank Casey's home and had them fix beds in the yard so he could sleep with both prisoners handcuffed to him.

The first newspaper notation concerning Reeves that this author was able to locate has him serving as a guard at the executions of James Diggs and John Postoak at Fort Smith. This event took place on December 20, 1878. James Diggs, a black man, had murdered a cattle-drover, J. C. Gould, in the northern portion of the Indian Territory

182

near the Kansas line, August 4, 1873. John Postoak, an Indian, was convicted on August 16, 1878, for the murder of John Ingley and his wife in the Creek Nation.

Reeves was noted as saying that the high point of his career was the subduing of territory outlaw Bob Dozier because he was successful where so many of his fellow deputies had failed. Reeves had been on the trail of Dozier for several years, but Dozier had managed to stay one step ahead. Bob Dozier was a criminal strictly by choice. He had been a prosperous farmer for years, but the wild criminal life appealed to him so strongly that he made the cold, deliberate decision to give up his farm and a peaceful life and become an outlaw.

As a farmer, Dozier was very successful; as an outlaw, he was even more successful, for several reasons. He was not a specialist who concentrated all his efforts in one particular phase of outlaw operations. He was smart and operated on the theory that diversification was more profitable and much safer. He stole cattle, robbed stores and banks, hijacked cattle buyers carrying large sums of money, held up stagecoaches, ambushed travelers as they crossed the Indian Territory, acted as a fence for stolen jewels, stuck up big money poker games when he could find them, delved into land swindles as well as other confidence schemes, and was the ring leader of a stolen horse operation. Of course, during the rush of these activities, he killed several people, and it was rumored that he even resorted to torture in order to obtain the information his large-scale operations required if they were to be successful.

In some respects, Bob's theories on criminal operations were remarkably astute. Because of his diversified activities, he never enraged any one particular group of people to the extent that they banned together to support and aid the deputy marshals sent out to arrest him. Many people felt that as long as they were not personally involved, they shouldn't cooperate with the deputies and furnish them information about the whereabouts of Bob Dozier. This attitude was widespread, and it may have been bolstered by the common knowledge that Bob always remembered a favor, but he never forgot a traitorous act.

With this disadvantage, the deputy marshals were completely baffled in their efforts to locate and arrest Dozier. He was able to avoid their effort for years, until at last, Bass Reeves took the trail after him.

Reeves knew a great deal about Bob Dozier. He knew what Dozier looked like from the descriptions furnished by his victims, and he understood how Dozier operated to escape capture. With this knowledge, Reeves theorized that a lone wolf pursuit, with perhaps a one-man posse to help, would accomplish more than several deputies banded together. One or two men could move about and not arouse any suspicions that might reach Dozier and scare him off.

For several months, Reeves made no substantial progress in his attempt to arrest Dozier. He never made actual contact with his adversary, but came close enough to keep Dozier constantly on the run. Dozier eventually learned who was hunting him. He sent word to Reeves that if Bass didn't stop hounding him, he was as good as dead. Reeves laughed and sent back the message that at least Dozier would have to quit running to kill him, and he was ready at any time to give Dozier his chance. However, nothing developed from this exchange, and Dozier kept on the move with Reeves getting closer and closer.

Reeves finally picked up Dozier's trail in the upper Cherokee Nation. Reeves was jubilant; this trail was fresh and hot, and he had another man along, as posse, to help him.

Reeves trailed Dozier deeper and deeper into the thickets of the Cherokee Hills, knowing he was only a matter of an hour or two behind Dozier and the one other unknown rider with him. But late in the afternoon, just before dark, a heavy, steady rain began to fall which began to blot the tracks. To make matters worse, heavy lightning and thunder accompanied the rainstorm which made the eerie Cherokee Hills seem even more foreboding.

After sunset, and with all hope of tracking and locating Dozier completely gone, Reeves and his posseman began to look for a dry place to camp for the night. They rode down into a wide, heavily timbered ravine, using the lightning flashes to find their way down its treacherous slopes. The instant they reached the bottom of the ravine, the blast of a gunshot greeted them, and a bullet just missed Reeves's head.

Reeves and his posseman left their horses in a hurry for the cover of the trees, expecting more shots from the hidden ambushers. After a few minutes, Reeves saw a dim shadow of a man slipping from tree to tree. He waited until the shadow was caught between two trees and fired two quick shots. The shadow stopped and fell. This eliminated one of the men, but his two shots had given away his position to a second man who immediately opened fire. Reeves jerked upright, took a reeling step away from the protective shield of the trees, and fell full-length to the ground, facing his attacker. Unknown to his would-be assailant, Reeves waited with his Colt pistol cocked and ready in his hand.

For several minutes the ravine was relatively quiet; only the rain and the crack of lightning could be heard. Bass lay waiting in the mud and rain, fully exposed. Finally, a man stepped from behind a tree, laughing aloud, convinced that Reeves was dead and his posseman frightened away. Reeves smiled to himself as the lightning lit up the man's face. The long trail was over; he was facing outlaw Bob Dozier.

Reeves waited until Dozier was only a few yards away before he raised up and ordered him to stop and drop his gun. Dozier stopped laughing, and moving, his eyes wide with surprise. He hesitated for a moment, then dropped into a crouch and attempted to aim and shoot once again as Reeves lay prone and waiting in the mud for him. Before Dozier could level his gun, Reeves shot first, hitting him in the neck and killing him instantly.

Thus the career of an Indian Territory outlaw, who had laughed for years over the futile attempts of Judge Parker's deputies to capture him, was ended by the greatest manhunter of the territory.

Like the threat sent by Dozier, Reeves was left many threats written on cards along the outlaw trails. These cards were posted on trees for Reeves's special benefit. He did not let any of these threats disturb him. They were not idle boasts, for Reeves escaped numerous assassination attempts on his life during his long career as a peace officer in the territory. At the end of his federal career he had a dozen of these cards in his possession.

On October 17, 1883, the Fort Smith *Weekly Elevator* carried a story concerning a posse action in which Reeves was involved:

Johnson Jacks
The Murderer of Deputy Marshal Beck,
Brought In
On Sunday evening last, about 5 o'clock, Special Deputy C. C. Ayers, with a posse of ten men, was sent over into the Cherokee nation to arrest Johnson Jacks, who so wantonly murdered Deputy U.S. Marshal Addison Beck and young Morrell, a few days ago. The marshal and party made a forced march in the night, arriving in the neighborhood of where the tragedy occurred about daylight. From Dick Anderson, who lives near there, they learned that Jacks, who was badly wounded in the fight with the officers, had been taken to the house of Tom Bearpaw, about half a mile from where Beck was killed and about forty miles from here. The marshals surrounded the cabin, but no resistance was offered, and they quietly loaded Jacks

185

into a wagon and arrived here with him Monday evening late . . .
He is half [N]egro and half Indian. Bark, the man Beck had the writ
for, is still at large and on the scout . . .

The following are the parties that went with Ayers to arrest
Jacks: G. H. Fanin, John Williams, Wiley Cox, Bass Reeves, Geo.
Delaughter, Hiram Moody, Bynum Colbert, John Phillips, Sam
Mingo and one Pittcock.

The year 1884 was one of the most eventful in Bass Reeves's long
and illustrious career as a deputy marshal. The Fort Smith *Weekly Elevator* printed the following story on July 11, 1884:

A Trip Not Entirely Devoid of Interest
We mentioned last week the arrival of Deputy U.S. Marshals
J. H. Mershon and Bass Reeves with a load of prisoners from the
Choctaw and Chickasaw Nations. We find them registered at Jailer
Burns' office as follows: Cash Benton (white), Robert Colbert (Indian), Eli Riddle (negro), assault with intent to kill; Sterling Williams, A. P. McKinney (negroes), Joquis Thawes, Ike Ross, George
Seeley (Indians), Ed. McCurry (white), larceny; Thomas Logan,
Wash Taylor (negroes), Colbert Moore (Indian), J. D. Williams
(white), introducing and selling whiskey in the nation. Colbert
Moore immediately gave bond. Ed McCurry is badly wounded in the
groin, having made such a vigorous resistance when arrested that the
officers were compelled to shoot him. His arrest was made by the Indian police. In the fight, Ed's partner was killed and one of the police wounded in the knee. He is charged with peddling whiskey in
the Territory and also with larceny. He was brought all the way from
near Tishmingo laying on a mattress, in the bottom of a wagon bed,
and stood the trip remarkably well considering the severity of his
wound. On the trip the Marshals killed a man named Webb who was
charged with murder and would not submit to having the writ
served on him . . . Near Fishertown, Mershon attempted to arrest
one Hamilton, a full-blood Creek Indian, on a charge of murder,
when he resisted by firing on the officer and his posse and running.
In the melee Mershon's horse fell with him, and the posse coming up
at full speed behind, ran over the prostrate man and horse, bruising
them both up considerably, while Hamilton escaped to the woods,
where the officers learned he soon afterwards died.

Being a U.S. Marshal may appear to some a regular picnic, but
we don't want any of it in ours.

This particular trip definitely was not a picnic for Bass Reeves.
His shootout with Jim Webb was one of the closest calls he ever had.

The shooting itself was one of the greatest rifle duels ever to take place in Indian Territory history.

Around 1882, Jim Webb, whom Reeves described as having Mexican blood, drifted into the Chickasaw Nation. He went to work for the celebrated rancher, Billy Washington, who at that time was a partner with Dick McLish, a prominent Chickasaw Indian, in an extensive ranch in the southern portion of the Chickasaw Nation. Jim Webb was hired as the foreman of this ranch, with forty-five cowboys under his supervision.

The ranch was isolated, the cowboys were tough, and the cattle were wild and scattered. Jim Webb was an ideal choice as foreman because he ran the ranch with an iron hand. The men he couldn't whip with his fist, he fired, and his gun was always ready to argue any point if anyone was foolish enough to stand up to him. This tendency to argue with a gun led to his clash with Bass Reeves.

Rev. William Steward, a black circuit preacher, had a small ranch adjoining the Washington-McLish Ranch which he operated between his ministerial trips. In the spring of 1883, Reverend Stewart started a grass fire on his ranch which got out of control and spread over into the Washington-McLish range. Jim Webb blew his top and rode over to chastise the preacher, and a bitter but short quarrel started. It ended with Jim Webb killing the preacher.

Reeves was given the writ to arrest Jim Webb for murder. Reeves took the warrant, obtained the services of a white man named Floyd Wilson as his posse, and went deep into the Chickasaw Nation to locate and arrest Webb. Reeves decided to disguise himself as a working cowboy. With his one-man posse, he reached the Washington-McLish Ranch about 8:00 one morning several days later.

When Reeves and Wilson rode up to the ranch house, there were only three men there: Jim Webb, a cowboy named Frank Smith who obviously was a trusted friend of Webb, and the ranch cook. Reeves had never seen Webb, but thought he recognized him from the description he had been given before leaving Fort Smith. To make sure that this man was Webb, however, Reeves and Wilson rode up like any traveling cowboys and asked for breakfast. Webb, however, had not lived as long as he had by being foolish; he was immediately suspicious. When Reeves and Wilson walked up to the porch, both Webb and Smith had their pistols in their hands, holding them nonchalantly at their sides, yet vividly conveying the idea that they were ready for immediate use, if necessary. Reeves began to think of a way he could

187

arrest Webb without someone getting killed.

The ranch house was a typical one for those days, consisting of two large rooms, built of logs, and a long "dog-run" or breezeway completely separating these two rooms. One side served as a kitchen and dining room, and the other served as the bunkhouse. Reeves and Wilson were escorted into the kitchen-dining room side and told to wait until the cook could fix their breakfast.

Reeves sized up the situation and didn't like it a bit. He felt he must do something to ease Webb's suspicions if he was to have any chance at all of arresting Webb. After talking for a few minutes, he asked if he couldn't feed his horses while they were waiting for breakfast. Webb grunted his permission, but he followed Reeves out to the barn, watching Reeves every second with his gun still in his hand. Reeves, talking easily and steadily, fed his and Wilson's horses, loosened their saddle girths, and casually pulled his Winchester from its saddle boot and leaned it against a corn crib, hoping this would convince Webb he was honestly a traveling cowboy just passing through the country.

Reeves was under the impression that Webb had fallen for his ploy, especially after the cook called out that breakfast was ready. Webb did not follow him back into the dining room. But when Webb called Smith out of the room into the dog-run and they began to whisper and gesture toward Reeves and Wilson, Reeves knew that he had failed. Watching Webb and Smith by their reflections in a mirror on the opposite wall, Reeves could see the bench he and his companion would be asked to occupy as soon as the meal was finished. Reeves, in a guarded undertone, told his posseman that he must take care of Smith, and he (Reeves) would get Webb.

Breakfast over, they walked out and sat down on the bench as had been planned by Webb. He stood directly over Reeves, while Smith and Wilson were similarly arranged at the far end of the bench. Both Webb and Smith still had their pistols in their hands. Reeves looked him so steadily in the eye during their brief conversation that Webb had no opportunity to give the signal to Smith to seize the posseman. Reeves simply kept talking and hoping for the best.

After this watchful waiting had continued for a few minutes, with Reeves talking his head off about absolutely nothing, one of those incidents that ordinarily occur only in movies saved the day. Something in the yard attracted Webb's attention for a second. In a twinkling, Reeves had Webb by the throat with his left hand, while his right hand shoved his Colt revolver in Webb's face. "I give up! I give up!" gurgled Webb.

In the meantime, Wilson, so overwhelmed by the suddenness of the attack, was unable to move. He made no attempt to seize Smith. Even as Webb surrendered, Smith whirled and fired two shots at Reeves, but missed with both shots. With Webb completely controlled by his left hand, Reeves instantly wheeled and shot Smith in the stomach. Smith threw up his hands and fell to the floor.

Reeves, never loosening his grip on Webb's throat, ordered Wilson to put the handcuffs on Webb. This was done, and two horses were harnessed to a wagon, into which the wounded man and the prisoner were placed, and the quartet started on the long trip to Fort Smith.

The return trip was uneventful, except that Frank Smith died from his wounds by the time they reached Tishomingo, the Chickasaw capital. Smith was buried there without ceremony, and Reeves and Wilson traveled on to Fort Smith.

Upon reaching Fort Smith, Reeves placed Webb in jail and proceeded to forget all about him. But Webb and Reeves were destined to meet once more before their story was finished.

Webb was given a hearing and bound over for trial. However, he had friends who were hard at work in an effort to save him. After spending almost a year in jail, two such friends, Jim Bywaters and Chris Smith, managed to have him released on a $17,000 bond. But when the time came for Webb's trial, he had disappeared; the bond was forfeited.

Reeves received a new warrant for Webb and traveled back to the Chickasaw Nation. On this trip Reeves once again only had a one-man posse, a man named John Cantrell. They traveled to what was known then as Bywaters' Store, which is now located at Woodford, Oklahoma. When Reeves and his posse came within sight of Bywaters' Store, Cantrell was sent ahead to learn whether Webb was actually there. Cantrell slipped up to the store, and sure enough, there sat Jim Webb near one of the windows on the opposite side of the store. Cantrell eagerly motioned for Reeves to ride on up. As he went dashing up, Webb saw him coming and quickly leaped through the open window, armed with both revolver and Winchester, then ran for his horse that stood about one hundred yards away.

Reeves spurred his horse ahead in time to block Webb from reaching his horse, calling for Webb to surrender several times. Webb, realizing that he was cut off from his horse, turned and ran toward the nearby underbrush. Reeves fell in behind the sprinting Webb, with the horse in a trot, and continued calling for Webb to surrender.

After running about 600 yards, Webb, either completely winded or realizing that escape on foot was impossible, stopped running and made the outlaws' classic, last-ditch attempt to escape arrest. He stopped, turned and, facing Reeves, unlimbered his Winchester, shooting as fast as he could lever ammunition into the rifle and aiming to kill. Webb was determined not to be captured and face the almost certain hanging waiting for him at Fort Smith.

Webb was a good shot. His first shot grazed the saddle horn on the deputy marshal's saddle; his second shot cut a button off Bass's coat; and his third shot cut the bridle reins out of his hand.

During this time, Reeves was pretty busy. He was still calling to Webb to surrender, telling him that he didn't have a chance and might as well give up. Also, when the shooting first started, Reeves's horse got its head down and did its best to jump over the moon, each jump bringing him closer to Webb and his accurate rifle. When Webb shot the bridle out of his hands, Reeves lost complete control of the frightened animal. Reeves ducked his head and made a dive for the ground. Just as he rolled to his feet, Webb's fourth shot clipped the brim of his hat, and that was Webb's final shot.

Reeves gave the following description of the gunfight:

> He [Webb] stepped out into the open, 500 yards away, and commenced shooting with his Winchester. Before I could drop off my horse his first bullet cut a button off my coat and the second cut my bridle rein in two. I shifted my six shooter and grabbed my Winchester and shot twice. He dropped and when I picked him up I found that my two bullets had struck within a half-inch of each other. He shot four times, and every time he shot he kept running up closer to me. He was 500 yards away from me when I killed him.

At the conclusion of the shooting, Jim Bywaters and John Cantrell came running up. They saw Webb lying on the ground, his revolver now in his hand, and heard Webb feebly calling for Reeves to come to him. Bass advanced but, while keeping his Winchester trained on him, told Webb to throw the revolver away. Webb hesitated a moment, then he pitched it away, and the three men walked to the dying man.

Mr. Bywaters later wrote down Webb's dying statement, which read:

190

Give me your hand, Bass. You are a brave, brave man. I want you to accept my revolver and scabbard as a present, and you must accept them. Take it, for with it I have killed eleven men, four of them in the Indian Territory, and I expected you to make the twelfth.

Reeves accepted the gift, and in a few minutes, Webb died. Reeves helped to bury him, collecting his boots to present along with the gun belt as proof that the warrant had been served on Webb. Reeves and Cantrell joined up with Deputy Mershon, who was also serving warrants in the area, and returned to Fort Smith. It had taken a long time and had ended in an unnecessary, bloody battle, but the law had been upheld.

It is interesting to note what the territorial paper, *Indian Champion,* of June 21, 1884, said:

> Deputy Marshal Mershon and posse attempted to arrest Jim Webb near Bywaters' store in the Arbuckle Mountains, on the 15th inst., which resulted in a running fight, in which Webb was wounded and died that night. Webb was boss of Washington's ranch. He was charged with killing a negro for burning the range last winter.

Why Reeves was not given credit in the newspaper can only be left to conjecture. It may have been that publicizing a killing by a well-known black officer was not a popular thing to do. Reeves was well known, respected, and feared in the territory. But publicizing the fact that a black officer killed a white outlaw, even one with some Mexican blood, may not have set well with the local population. There were many residents with Southern sympathies, and at best tolerated the presence of black officers in the territory. It is impossible to know the ethnicity of all the men Reeves killed. But they most likely reflected the racial make-up of the criminal element found in the Indian Territory.

On August 8, 1884, the Muskogee *Indian Journal* had two articles on Bass Reeves:

> Bass Reeves, one of the best Marshals on the force, reported at Atoka, Monday, from the Chickasaw, Pottawotamie {*sic*} and Western Creek country with the following prisoners: One Hanna, Creek, murder; Chub Moore, murder; Jedick Jackson, Jno. Bruner, colored, Jim Mack, Chickasaw, for larceny; Jno. Hoyt, Dr. A. Smith, J. M. McConnell, whites, Alex Baker and Daniel Dorsey, Creeks, all for introducing.

A Thrilling Tragedy

Bass Reeves on his last trip had an experience came near cutting short his usefulness and did send one man where he won't fool with other peoples horses. He had warrants for two men, Frank Buck and John Bruner. While up the Canadian looking for prisoners he came on these men but did not know them. He enquired {sic} for other parties whom he was after and Buck and Bruner volunteered to guide him. At noon all parties camped, and while they were getting dinner he noticed Bruner stealthily pulling his pistol. Suspecting something he stepped behind his horse and around to the front of Bruner and grabbed his pistol before he had time to use it, and at the same time pulled his own. Glancing over his shoulder Buck was seen getting out his weapon, when as quick as a flash Reeves, still holding Bruner's pistol in one hand, threw over his other and shot Buck dead. Bruner was then secured and is now on his way to Fort Smith where he will have to answer to a double charge.

On September 5, 1884, the Fort Smith *Elevator* reported on the same trip made by Reeves:

Deputy U.S. Marshal Bass Reeves came in on Monday last with fifteen prisoners as follows: Chub Moore and one Hanna, alias George Washington, murder; James McJohnson, Zedick Jackson, John Bruner, (negro) Ellick Bruner, (Indian) Isaac Deer, larceny; W. B. Burnett, assault with intent to kill; John Hoyt, John McConnell, Dan Dorsey, John Lodcar, J. A. Smith, Alex Baker, introducing whiskey in Territory; Jack Riddle, violating revenue law.

Chub Moore is charged with being the leader of a party of men who seven years ago hung a negro for an assault upon a white woman in the Chickasaw Nation. In making the arrest on the 7th of August Frank Pierce, acting as posse for Reeves, shot Chub in the right thigh, the ball ranging up, inflicting a severe wound. He was placed in a covered hack on a mattress and made the trip here a distance of some 265 miles, and is now doing remarkably well. He is a full blood Chickasaw. Hanna, the other party charged with murder, is a full blood Creek, and killed a white man on the 24th of February last.

Frank Pierce, who shot Chub Moore, turned out to be a notorious horse thief, and has fled the country to avoid arrest . . .

Before he returned to Fort Smith, Reeves had told Marshal Boles that he had made a shocking discovery. Posseman Frank Pierce was a horse thief. Pierce was alerted to Reeves's discovery and fled before he could be arrested.

The Fort Smith *Elevator* on October 17, 1884, reported:

Bass Reeves, one of the most successful of the marshals "doing business" in the Territory, has been discharged from the force by Marshal Boles. It seems he had a habit of letting a prisoner escape when more could be made than in holding him and that is where the trouble came in.

The marshal could not produce the evidence to substantiate this charge against Reeves, and he was reinstated.

Evidenced by the following article from the *Weekly Elevator* of December 26, 1884, Reeves was back at work:

E. D. Jones was arrested in Franklin County on Wednesday of last week as a fugitive from justice by Deputy Marshal Reeves. He was lodged in the U.S. jail on the following night, and on Friday Chief Deputy C. M. Barnes left with him for Louisville, Ky., where there is an indictment against him for altering a mail contract. He was formerly a Kentucky mail contractor. He has a family in the Blue Grass State. He sent his wife $10 the morning he left.

Two events that happened earlier in 1884 were even more significant on Reeves's law enforcement career than those already discussed.

Reeves was quoted as saying the closest that he ever came to losing his life occurred in 1884 on one occasion while riding the Seminole whiskey trail, looking for four men — two white and two black. Reeves was ambushed by three brothers named Brunter, for whom he also had warrants. The Brunter brothers had been accused of horse stealing, robbery, and several unsolved murders in the Indian Territory. The word had gotten to the brothers that the deputy was looking for them. They now had Reeves right where they wanted him: in their gun sights.

Reeves was made to dismount at gunpoint and told to keep his hands away from his guns. At this point, Reeves quickly struck up a conversation and proceeded to show the outlaws the warrants for their arrest. To add insult to injury, Reeves wanted to know the day of the month so he could make a record to the government! With three guns trained on him, the brothers thought that the deputy was out of his mind. They told Reeves, "You are just ready to turn in now," but they were laughing too hard to be very alert. The outlaws relaxed their guard for the merest instant and that was all the time Reeves needed. He whipped out his Colt revolver and killed two of the men as quick as lightning. While he was in the act of shooting those two he grabbed the gun barrel of the third. He was able to hold the gun away from his body while the outlaw pulled off three harmless shots. Reeves proceeded to hit this outlaw in the head with his pistol and killed him instantly. There would be no fees to collect on three dead men, but there would be three fewer outlaws to plague the Indian Territory.

The second incident, and the most far-reaching in terms of economic debt placed on Bass Reeves, was the accidental shooting of his cook on April 10, 1884. This was the most controversial event of Reeves's career. The popular story was that while Reeves was making his circuit through the Chickasaw Nation, he got into a serious argument with his black cook, William Leach. It is said that Leach threw hot grease on Reeves's favorite dog, at which point the furious, indignant, and cursing Reeves pulled his gun and killed the man, who proceeded to fall forward into the campfire. Still fuming, Reeves supposedly left the body in the fire until it was charred. Reeves refuted this version of the story.

It wasn't until January 19, 1886, that a warrant was secured by Deputy U.S. Marshal Frair for Reeves's arrest. Reeves was indicted in the August term, 1886, at which time he was relieved of duties and had to post a bond of $3,000 to remain free. This was done, and Reeves was never placed in jail. Besides posting bond, Reeves hired the most expensive lawyers in Fort Smith to serve as defense counsel. It was said that Reeves was of considerable wealth until this trial, which depleted most of his life savings.

During the course of the trial Reeves was able to prove that the killing of Leach was accidental. Reeves testified that it occurred while he was cleaning his Winchester and a bullet became lodged in the barrel. In the course of trying to remove the bullet the rifle misfired, striking Leach in the neck. Leach did not die immediately. Medical attention was sought, but to no avail. Reeves and Leach did have a minor argument beforehand concerning a stray dog licking on Reeves's meal pan.

The trial took place in October of 1887 and on October 21, the Fort Smith *Weekly Elevator* reported the following:

> At the close of our last report ex-Deputy Marshal Bass Reeves was on trial for murder. His case went to the jury Saturday, and they remained out until Sunday evening when they returned a verdict of not guilty.

After being found not guilty, Reeves's commission was restored as a deputy marshal. Financially, Reeves would never recover from this ordeal.

Up until he was relieved of duty for the trial, Reeves was busy rounding up outlaws or attempting to, as the following article from the *Elevator,* March 27, 1885, relates:

Deputy U.S. Marshal Bass Reeves found a negro man in jail at Gainesville, Texas, last week that he was sure was John Williams, the murderer of Constable Houck, of Van Buren. The Texas authorities turned him over to Bass, who brought him to Van Buren by rail, but he proved to be the wrong man. A Gainesville correspondent of the Fort Worth *Gazette* says Bass paid $100 reward to the Texas officers to get possession of the man. If that's the case Bass is loser.

Being a highly visible black deputy, Reeves also received his share of accusation and innuendo from the territory press. Reeves was figuratively on trial throughout the duration of his career. On April 24, 1885, the *Elevator* reported:

A Gainesville, Texas dispatch reports a fight between Texas officers and cattle thieves from the nation, a few days ago in which Frank Pierce, alias Roberts, one of the thieves, was killed. Pierce is the man who was acting as posse for Deputy Marshal Bass Reeves some time since, and shot Chub Moore, who was brought to this place and died of his wound in the U.S. jail. It has been frequently charged by correspondents to the Indian papers that Pierce was a thief and that Bass was in with him, though Marshal Boles has been unable to substantiate the charges against Reeves. The above indicates that the reports about Pierce must have been correct. Later advices say that the four thieves who were with Pierce, were "rounded up" in the Territory by a lot of cowboys who killed all four of them. The names of the thieves are not given.

In another vein the same newspaper reported on May 29, 1885:

Deputy Bass Reeves came in Sunday from an extended trip through the Territory bringing seventeen prisoners, who were registered at the jailer's office as follows: Jonas Stake, Two-a-nuck-ey, one Wiley, (Indians) charged with murder; Chas. Cosy, one Feglin, arson; Ben Bowlegs alias Ben Billy alias Williams, (Indian) John Pickett, larceny; Robert Ken-a-wah, Joseph Dorsey, one Hawkins, Robert Kelly, Wolf alias Ya-gha, Barney alias Hills Harjo, one Winnie, one

Siller, one Jennie, (Indians) Adam Brady (negro), introducing and selling whiskey in Territory. John Pickett gave bond.

The *Elevator* reported another trip on July 31, 1885:

Deputy Bass Reeves came in same evening with eleven prisoners as follows: Thomas Post, one Walaska, and Wm. Gibson, assault with intent to kill; Arthur Copiah, Abe Lincoln, Miss Adeline Grayson and Sally Copiah, alias Long Sally, introducing whiskey in Indian country; J. E. Adams, Jake Island, Andy Alton and one Smith, larceny. Island, Alton, Lincoln and Smith gave bond. The others went to jail.

The Muskogee *Indian Journal* on October 22, 1885, gave a description and history of the United States court at Fort Smith. The following was included concerning the court and the deputies in the territory:

This court is without doubt the largest criminal court in the United States. It is a district court with circuit court powers. Its jurisdiction extends over sixteen counties in Western Arkansas and the five civilized tribes of Indians . . .
The Deputy U.S. Marshals for Creek and Cherokee Nations are Andrew Smith, Elias Andrews, W. F. Jones, Bud T. Kell and Sam Sixkiller; for Choctaw Nation, Tyner Hughes, John Farr, Sam Wingo and J. W. Searle; for Chickasaw Nation, J. H. Mershon and John Williams; Seminole, Creek and Chickasaw Nations, Bass Reeves. There are many local deputies scattered throughout the district . . .

On October 30, 1885, the *Elevator* gave notice of Reeves's arrival in Fort Smith with yet another group of lawbreakers in tow:

U.S. Marshal, Bass Reeves, came in on Monday evening last with 17 prisoners, among whom were Hens Posey and one Deldrick, charged with murder. The others are John Robinson, assault with intent to kill; Robert Johnson, Wiley Kelly, Colbert Lasley and old man Cintop, larceny. The balance are all whiskey cases.

Charles W. Mooney, a native of Pottawatomie County, Oklahoma, wrote a biographical book about his father, Dr. Jesse Mooney. In the book, Mooney tells how his father was one of the first country doctors in the Indian Territory. In 1888, Dr. Jesse Mooney reportedly was the personal physician of the infamous Belle Starr.

196

On one occasion upon visiting Belle Starr's home, near present-day Eufaula, Oklahoma, Dr. Mooney and his wife, Ella, were interrupted by the barking of Belle's Great Dane. The dog was giving notice of a lone rider approaching the house. Mooney's mother recollected the event as such:

> He was a big, broad shouldered man, riding high in his saddle, was clean shaven except for a bushy mustache. As he rode into the clearing in front of Belle's house, they saw he was a Negro wearing a Deputy U.S. Marshal's badge pinned on his shirt.
>
> "It's Bass Reeves," Belle said, as she walked out her cabin door and called off the dog.
>
> "Howdy, Miss Belle," the Deputy said politely, dismounting.
>
> "What brings you this way, Bass?" Belle asked.
>
> "Jest ridin' through and thought I'd stop, but didn't know you had company."
>
> "That's alright, Bass yore welcome any time yore near here. This is Doc Mooney and his wife, Ella," Belle said.
>
> "Pleased to meetcha," the Deputy responded, tipping his hat politely. "Your Uncle Isaac told me about you, Doctor. I've know'd him a long time."
>
> "Bass Reeves here is one of the few Deputy Marshals I trust," Belle remarked to Jesse and Ella. "He's been a friend of mine for several years . . ."
>
> "Jest thought I'd warn you," the Deputy said, "I'm on the trail of Bob and Grat Dalton. They may be headed this way."
>
> "Much a-bliged, Bass. But them rascals won't be comin' round here for no help. Bob Dalton knows what I think of him," Belle remarked.
>
> When Deputy Bass Reeves rode away, Belle told Jesse and Ella all about him. She explained that it was unusual for her, who had fought for the Confederacy, to be a friend of a Negro. But Bass Reeves was a dedicated, fearless Deputy U.S. Marshal. He would "shoot it out" if necessary, and made a reputation throughout the Indian Nations as a lawman second to none. Many times he had been "called out" for a showdown by drunken gunslingers at rambunctious saloons in old Oklahoma Territory.

Mooney also stated that Bass Reeves often rode by to visit Belle Starr at her home. Always carrying his own gourd dipper tied to his saddlebag, he would drink from her water well during each visit, at which time Belle would tell him to stop by any time he was in the vicinity of Youngers Bend.

Some of the best horses to be found in the West were located in the Indian Territory; even today Oklahoma is one of the top horse-raising states. Almost every Indian had at least one or two excellent horses, because good horses to an Indian were more than mere animals: they were an absolute necessity and were generally accumulated in large numbers to represent Indian wealth. Because of this abundance of good horses, horse thieves were very active in the Indian Territory.

In the late '80s one of Reeves's tasks was to bring in a notorious horse thief named Tom Story. In serving this warrant he didn't have to spend days on the trail, but waited for the outlaw to come to him.

One of the very first bands of horse thieves, whose sole purpose was to make away with stock alone in the Indian Territory, was the Tom Story gang. The gang made their headquarters somewhere on the banks of the Red River in the Chickasaw Nation. From 1884 until 1889 this outfit made their range the entire Indian country, robbing by wholesale and disposing of the stock in Texas. Among Story's men were Pegleg Jim, Kinch West, and "Long" Henry, all experts in the fine art of stealing and disposing of horses.

In 1889, Tom Story and his gang reversed their operation and stole a herd of horses and mules from George Delaney, who lived in North Texas. The gang stole his herd and drove them north across the Red River into the Indian Territory in search of a market.

When he discovered his herd gone, Delaney began to investigate on his own. Somehow, he learned that Tom Story had stolen his horses and mules and was expected to return to Texas in only a few days. Delaney immediately contacted the marshal's office at Paris, Texas, and a warrant was issued for the arrest of Tom Story on the suspicion of horse stealing. Bass Reeves at that time was serving in Paris as a deputy marshal, and was given the warrant.

Reeves met Delaney and convinced him that if Tom Story was actually the man they wanted, and if he was returning to Texas, the best thing for them to do was wait for him along the way. Delaney agreed with this plan, and when Reeves decided that Story would cross Red River at the Delaware Bend Crossing (near present-day Interstate 35, once called the Old Spanish Trail), Delaney agreed to go along as posse and wait for Story to return.

Reeves and Delaney made their camp close to the Delaware Bend Crossing on Red River, deep in the brush that paralleled the trail across this ford. They fished and even hunted a little while waiting for Story. After about four days of this vacation, they learned from a man

198

crossing the river, who knew Tom Story, that he could be expected late the next day.

As a result, Reeves was waiting for him in the brush on one side of the trail when Tom Story came riding across the ford, leading two of Delaney's finest mules which he had failed to sell.

When Story rode up, Reeves stepped out of the brush onto the trail and challenged him. Story dropped the lead ropes of the mules in surprise. Reeves told him that he had a warrant for his arrest, and right then and there, Tom Story committed suicide. He attempted to draw his gun on Bass, thinking he had an even chance to beat him as Reeves still had his gun in its holster. But Story's gun hadn't cleared leather before the deputy marshal's Colt was "out and barking." Story was dead before he hit the ground.

Reeves and Delaney buried Tom Story, and Delaney left for home, taking his two mules along. With his mission accomplished, Reeves went back to Paris, and the Story gang quickly disintegrated, each going their separate ways, never to be heard from again.

During the early 1890s another incident of note took place while Reeves was assigned to the Paris, Texas, federal office.

In Lamar County, Texas, near Paris, Jarrett Burns, a black man, got into a quarrel with his white neighbor named John Ashley. The feuding came to a head when Ashley shot and killed Burns. Then Ashley's horses and mules began dying and eventually all his stock died. Next his house was burned. Ashley's friends believed Jarrett's relatives and friends had poisoned his stock and set fire to his home.

The general consensus was that Ashley's friends came to his assistance in retaliation. Several blacks were taken out and hanged on trees in the vicinity of Little Sandy Creek and Jefferson Road. More threats were made that more blacks would be hanged as soon as they were found.

The majority of African-Americans in the community left that area after Sheriff Gunn arrested about half a dozen and put them in jail, charged with being implicated in burning Ashley's home. Later, Sheriff Gunn heard that the blacks would be taken from the jail and hanged, a threat not to be taken lightly.

There were many federal prisoners in the jail at that time, besides the county prisoners. U.S. Marshal Dickerson summoned his deputies to Paris to protect the jail. It was reported that more than sixty deputies were assembled. With this group of deputies was one conspicuous black deputy, Bass Reeves, who evidently stood out due to his size and color. The mob never made an attempt on the jail, and cooler heads prevailed.

On March 6, 1890, the *Muskogee Phoenix* told of Reeves arriving in Fort Smith with a load of prisoners:

> Bass Reeves came in from the Seminole Nation with Robert Wolfe, "One" Jesse, "One" Walda, "One" Ulta, "One" Kinder, Tom Bruner, Joe Bruner and Thomas Payne, all charged with larceny. — *Times.*

On his next manhunt into the interior searching for criminals, Reeves had the good fortune to capture one of the most feared Seminole outlaws in Indian Territory history. *The Arkansas Gazette* of Little Rock, on April 29, 1890, reported the capture:

HE'S A BAD INDIAN
Capture of a Seminole Who Has "Seven Men"
to His Credit

Special to The Arkansas Gazette.

Fort Smith. April 28. — Deputy United States Marshal Bass Reaves {sic} brought in twelve prisoners from the Indian country today, among them To-sa-lo-nah, alias Greenleaf, a Seminole Indian who is wanted here on three separate charges of murder and who has been an outlaw for the past eighteen years, this being the first time he was ever arrested. About nine years ago he murdered a white man named Davis in the Chickasaw Nation, shooting him from the brush.

A few days later he murdered a man named Bateman in the same locality, shooting him down as he was plowing in a field. Bateman's body lay where it fell four days, and when the murderer fired the shot, the horse his victim was plowing with ran away, the plow struck a stump the point was broken off and is still sticking there. After this he murdered the mail rider near old Fort Washita. He robbed all his victims. All of this time his business has been whiskey peddling, and every marshal that has ridden in the Seminole, Creek, and Chickasaw country has carried writs for him. Since killing the white men above mentioned he has killed four men of his own tribe, all of whom have assisted deputy marshals in hunting him. The last one he killed was Barna Maha. He first shot him down and put twenty-four bullets into his body. For some time past it has been impossible for an officer to get any one to assist in hunting him as it was almost sure death to do so unless the hunt was successful. Reaves was in his neighborhood and learned that Greenleaf had just come into the country with a load of whiskey. He located him at night, got near enough and when he was selling his liquor to hear the Indians whooping and firing off their pistols. He waited until near daylight and then moved up close to the house. Just at daylight he and his posse charged up, jumped the fence, and before Greenleaf got fairly awake had him covered with their guns and he surrendered. After his capture people who had known him long doubted it and flocked to see if it was really so, some riding as far as eighteen miles to convince themselves of his identity.

July 4, 1890, the Fort Smith *Elevator* gave notice of the lawman's arrival with prisoners for the jail:

Deputy Bass Reeves came in Friday with William Roberts, charged with murder; William Trammell, William Cully, Robert Albert, Thomas Jefferson, Wilson Knight and Thomas Knight, all charged with introducing and selling liquor in Indian country. Cully and Jefferson gave bond.

The same newspaper gave the following inclusion of the deputy's activities on September 26, 1890:

Muskogee, I.T., Sept. 22. — Deputy U.S. Marshal Bass Reeves arrested Jim Barnett here on Saturday, charged with larceny of horses. Barnett will be taken to Fort Smith for examination.

It was at this time in Reeves's career when he came up against one of the most dangerous men in territory history. Reeves was one of the deputies who led a posse against the infamous Cherokee outlaw Ned Christie. The *Vinita Chieftain* reported on November 27, 1890, the following:

That Visit To Christy
The *Muldrow Register* has the following account of the raid recently made by the marshals upon the home of Ned Christie:
On Tuesday last U.S. Deputy Marshal Bass Reeves, of Fort Smith, with his posse, made an attack on the house of Ned Christie in the Flint district, who is, perhaps, the most notorious outlaw and desperado in the Indian Territory, and the outlaw's stronghold was burned to the ground. Supposing that the owner had been killed or wounded and was consumed in the building, the news went out that he had met a violent death. But Christie has turned up alive, and may cause trouble yet; is said to be on the war path fiercer than ever and vows vengeance on the marshal and his posse.
Ned Christie is perhaps the most desperate character in the ter-

201

ritory and there is a large reward offered on his head. He has killed a number of men, among whom might be mentioned the Squirrel brothers, also considered "tough men." He is said to be a dead shot, has eluded the officers of the law for about four years and says he will not be taken alive.

Christie did live up to his boast that he wouldn't be taken alive, but he didn't get his revenge on Bass Reeves. There were many reports after the raid exclaiming that Christie had killed him. The rumors that Reeves was killed in action continued for a good part of a year. Listed below are newspaper articles concerning reports and retractions of stories printed concerning these allegations:

Fort Smith, Ark., January 26. — Word reached here to-night of the killing of Deputy United States Marshal Bass Reeves, near Tahlequah, I.T., by Ned Christie, a well known outlaw. Reeves was a negro and well known in this city . . .

— Deputy Marshal Bass Reeves was killed Monday by Ned Christie near Tahlequah. Christie is the outlaw wanted for the murder of Dan Maples several years ago. He is one of the toughest characters in the Territory. He has had two cabins burnt by Officers within a few months in a fruitless effort to capture him.

— It is reported in the *Republic* from Tahlequah and in the *Dallas News* from Muskogee that Bass Reeves was killed Saturday near Tahlequah, while attemtping to make an arrest. It is thought here that it is a mistake, as Bass was in Eufaula last week and with two wagons and supplies for several days and went west.

— The report that Bass Reeves had been killed by Ned Christie in Flint District, Cherokee Nation last week, was without foundation. Reeves was 150 miles away from the reported place of killing at the time of the alleged killing.

Later in the year the Eufaula *Indian Journal* printed the following:

Deputy Marshal Bass Reeves lacks lots of being dead, as was reported recently from Muskogee to the *Dallas News*. He turned up Saturday from the west with two wagon loads of prisoners going to Ft. Smith. He had twelve prisoners in all. Eight for whiskey vending, three for larceny and one for murder. Two of whom were United States citizens from Oklahoma, a white man and a negro. They had crossed the line and were selling fire water to Indians.

202

On May 28, 1891, the *Muskogee Phoenix* told of the following arrest made by the invincible Reeves:

Sunday night, about 12:30, officers Bass Reeves and Wiley McIntosh arrested W. H. McDonald and one Cords, charged with killing John Irvins, the man found murdered in Blue creek {*sic*}, twelve miles west of Wagoner some two weeks ago. The officers had spotted the men some time and arrested them at their house near Blue creek. The evidence against the two men is very strong. They were known to have threatened the life of Irvins and cannot well account for themselves at the time the crime was committed. Our readers are familiar with the particulars of the finding of Irvins body in the creek with a bullet hole in his head. The men were taken to Fort Smith and jailed.

On May 27, 1892, the Fort Smith *Elevator* reported:

Charles Smith and William James, whiskey cases and Joe Fulsome, larceny were brought in by Bass Reeves from the Creek Nation. Smith and James both gave bond . . .

The infamous Christian Gang that killed Oklahoma City Police Chief Milt Jones in 1895 created quite a commotion in the Indian nations. It was known that the gang rode east into the nations to evade the law. On one of the manhunts, black Deputy U.S. Marshals Bass Reeves and Bill Colbert were members of a posse in pursuit of the gang. The *Daily Ardmoreite* carried a report:

Paris, Tex., June 9. Deputy Marshals Brockington, Chancellor, Gibbs, Reeves, Colbert and Lewis Williams, have returned from a trip into the Creek nation, where they went to try and capture the Christian gang. They trailed them to their rendezvous on the Deep Fork of the Canadian in the western part of the nation. As they approached the place which consisted of two cabins built of heavy logs with port holes, a negro named Will Stevenson came out and made fight. Brockington, Reeves and Williams had one cabin covered and Chancellor, Gibbs and Colbert the one Stevenson was in. When Stevenson attempted to shoot the officers fired, wounding him so that he only lived a short time. Dick Sanger, the negro in the other cabin, was with much difficulty induced to surrender. After capturing Sanger it was learned that the Creek authorities had offered a reward for him and Stevenson for robbing a man of $15,000 a few days before, and he was turned over to them. The Christian gang had been at the place only a short time before the arrival of the officers but had left. The cabins were in an unfrequented part of the country and were made for the purpose of defense. Had Stevenson not been killed at the beginning the officers would have had a hard fight.

In reflecting on his career, Reeves said he never made a thirty-day trip and back with less than $400 worth of fees and expense money. As an example, one time he went to Mud Creek and brought back sixteen prisoners at one time and the fees amounted to $700 while the total overall expense to him was less than $300. The most rewarding financial trip Reeves ever made was when he captured seventeen prisoners in Comanche County, in which Fort Sill is located, and took them to Fort Smith. The fees for the trip amounted to $900. Reeves said on his manhunts he was allowed to take a posseman, a guard, and a cook. The posseman and guard drew three dollars a day, and the cook twenty dollars a month. The deputy paid his own expenses and got all the fees. After 1898 the fee system was ended and new deputies were started at a flat $900-a-year salary.

There was some criticism from clerks in the Department of Justice at Fort Smith that Reeves could not properly fill out the official marshal's reports, but his superior skills as a deputy marshal more than compensated for his educational shortcomings.

Reeves was never exposed to a formal education, and as a result, he never learned to read or write. This fact complicated matters when he was given a stack of subpoenas to serve on the numerous witnesses the courts required during a regular court session, because in most cases, the people who were to be served with a subpoena could not read or write either.

Reeves approached the problem with several different methods. First, he would study each separate subpoena until he could associate the symbols of a written name with the sounds of the name as it was spoken. Second, he would have someone read the entire subpoena to him until he memorized which name belonged to a particular subpoena. After going through this ritual, he would take to the trail to locate the subpoenaed persons.

When he located a man or woman that answered to one of the names he had memorized, Reeves would search through his stack of subpoenas until he located the one with the proper symbols, thrust it into the person's hands, and gruffly command, "Read it." If the person could read, they had nothing to worry about, but if they couldn't, Reeves was forced to locate someone who could read to insure the right party had been served.

Locating someone who could read was not always an easy task. There were two factors involved that must be considered. Reeves had to keep the person he located in tow because many of them had a tendency to disappear as they had no desire whatsoever to participate in any trial. Appearing as a witness in a trial generally entailed making a long trip over rough country, losing several days and possibly weeks of work, and there was always the danger of reprisals if the person they were testifying against was acquitted. As a result, Reeves often had to resort to actual threats to keep the person he located with him until he found somebody who could read.

For another thing, the subpoenaed persons Reeves located were usually to be found in the most isolated and thinly populated areas in the entire territory. This meant sometimes riding as far as a hundred miles before finding somebody who could read. This long ride strictly was not due to the fact that people were scarce, but more for the reason that even a basic education was rather rare during frontier times in many areas of the Indian Territory.

As a possible third minor factor, only incidentally contributing to his difficulty, the weather almost invariably turned unfavorable when Reeves was out on the range on subpoena service. He even went as far as to warn the other deputies, "Get ready for bad weather, boys. I got a stack of subpoenas to serve, so Mother Nature is bound to go crazy. Hope I don't drown or freeze before I get back."

In spite of these difficulties, Reeves always served the subpoenas he was issued, and was proud of the fact that he never made a mistake of serving one on the wrong man. Many of the courts he rode for specifically asked for Reeves to serve their subpoenas because of his dependability.

On November 17, 1896, Judge Isaac Parker died in Fort Smith. It was obvious to some that he had worked himself to death. Many people proclaimed him the greatest judge in the history of the West. The most touching tribute was paid by Pleasant Porter, principal chief of the Creeks, who, in behalf of all the tribes of the nations, placed upon his grave a simple garland of wild flowers. Parker had always considered Bass Reeves one of his favorite deputies if not one of his most dependable.

As stated earlier, in 1889 a congressional act had established courts for the Indian Territory besides the one in Fort Smith. The Congressional Act of 1895, which replaced the Act of 1889, created three district courts in the Indian Territory. This act gave the three courts limited jurisdiction in judicial matters, for they could not be assigned cases in civil suits involving more than $100 and could not be involved in criminal cases that required the death penalty or sentences of hard labor.

By the act of June 28, 1898 (the Curtis Law), the tribal courts were abolished. Thenceforth, all legal actions, cases, and causes of every class and kind whatsoever were brought before the federal courts in the Indian Territory.

Bass Reeves was transferred to Muskogee, which was the seat of the Northern District Federal Court, and worked under U.S. Marshal Leo Bennett. Previously, Bennett had served as Union Agency Indian agent in Muskogee; he also founded the *Muskogee Phoenix* newspaper.

During this era a large white population of homesteaders moved into the Indian Territory as more and more Indian land opened up for white settlement. Many Indians and Indian Freedmen opposed the land allotment program carried out by the Dawes Commission. Racial tension became acute at various times in Oklahoma and Indian Territories. Sometimes these actions and attitudes induced action by the deputy marshals. These conflicts became more noticeable after 1900.

Of the three districts, the Northern and Central had the largest number of black deputies. In 1901 the *Muskogee Phoenix* reprinted an article (from the *Ardmore Appeal*) concerning a black deputy marshal encountering conflict in the Southern District:

That Pauls Valley Incident

The action of the [N]egro deputy, Jack Walters, at Pauls Valley a few days ago has justly called forth the censure and condemnation of the people of that city upon his head, upon Captain Jno. S. Hammer, who appointed him, and upon Office Deputy A. M. Foss, whose encouragement he received.

When [N]egroes are appointed as United States Deputy Marshals with full power to arrest white people it is indeed high time to call a halt. Even though there is no legal right to demand such a thing, yet the feelings of the people of this whole country demand it.

The white citizens of the Southern District have no objections to [N]egro deputies appointed so long as they arrest only men of their color, but when swaggering [N]egroes armed with Winchesters and vested with authority to arrest, so far overstep the people's customs as to attempt to arrest a white man merely because he had made the remark to a friend that no "d--- negro deputy could arrest him," it is time for the installation of new public officials who have the interest of the people at heart.

206

Yet the [N]egro was not as much to blame as was his superiors who have stood by him even to the extent of endorsing what he had done.

The citizens of Pauls Valley did right in condemning such contemptible and unwarranted conduct by the [N]egro and in censuring Marshal Hammer for allowing a [N]egro the privileges which he exercised.

The *Muskogee Phoenix* made the following reply to the article:

Capt. John S. Hammer, U.S. Marshal for the Southern District, has brought down upon his head the wrath of the *Ardmore Appeal* and of many citizens of Pauls Valley by appointing a [N]egro to the office of deputy marshal . . .

. . . He might try the plan of sending a politely worded note to the malefactor, requesting him to come to jail . . .

Bass Reeves continued to be an important deputy in the territory. Research showed he avoided racial conflict, if possible, and concentrated on black and Indian lawbreakers at the time. Working out of Muskogee, which had a large black and Indian population, he had the leverage to do so, whereas black deputy Grant Johnson, one of the few lawmen in the Eufaula area, didn't. By the late 1890s the white population had grown to over 200,000, after only a total of 60,000 in the Indian Territory in 1885.

A white resident, Merril A. Nelson, of the Indian Territory during this period, told this story about Reeves:

One time a Negro deputy by the name Bass Reeves had the choice of some routine work or of capturing a black man who had killed a fellow for a bale of cotton. Reeves said, "Let Sherman and Adams go to Muskogee and serve the papers," he said he did not want to get mixed up with white folks. "I will go and get this man or bring his boots." When we returned he had his man in the wagon. "What happened," we asked. "Well, he got in a log cabin and started firing at me, so I had to kill him," said the colored officer.

Another white resident, I. F. Williams, said:

Bass Reeves was a bad Negro and wasn't afraid to come out after the bad ones. He didn't bother much about the white outlaws but worried after the Creek and Cherokee Negroes and Indians. The United States officers arrested them when they stole or did anything against the whites.

207

He would sometimes make the arrest alone and bring the prisoners to the wagon in which they would be chained. I saw him one time when he had three prisoners who brought him a reward of $1,000.00.

He tried to hire me to go and guard the wagon, but I wouldn't go with him because he was a Negro and I didn't think a white man should work under a Negro. It sounds like it would be a soft job to guard some prisoners who were chained to a wagon, but it was really as dangerous [as] to capture them. Sometimes the prisoners had been surprised and caught without a fight but a marshal never knew exactly what would happen when he started after some men. After he got them in the wagon, the guards had to be careful or two or three of the friends of the prisoners would come up and throw guns on the guards and release the prisoners.

On March 24, 1898, the *Muskogee Phoenix* carried a story in which Bass Reeves was called in to investigate a triple killing caused by a white mob:

A MOB'S HORRIBLE WORK

A few miles north of Muskogee, between the Arkansas and Verdigris [R]ivers, is a strip of country that has been the scene of many a dark deed and brutal murders in years that are past. It has at different times within recent years been the rendezvous of desperate and daring outlaws and criminals . . .

Ed Chalmers, a state-raised [N]egro was living in a little hut not far from Wybark with a white woman by the name of Mary Headley. They were said to be married and certainly claimed to their neighbors that they were man and wife. So far as is known they were both harmless and peaceable residents and were industrious farmers. The fact that a white woman and a [N]egro man were married and were living as man and wife grated on the nerves of some of the residents of this section . . . A few of the near residents, all supposed to be white persons, assembled Saturday night and during the rain and storm proceeded to the humble home . . . and literally murdered them in cold blood . . . The white woman was shot to death in her bed and her [N]egro consort was shot all to pieces, though he lived until nine o'clock Sunday morning . . . Before he died . . . he made a dying statement in which he named several parties as the guilty ones.

Early Sunday morning a messenger came running into Muskogee and informed the officers that a man and woman had been killed across the river . . . Deputy Marshal Bass Reeves was at once dispatched to the scene of the triple tragedy — the man who was found at the [railroad] track was evidently shot at the house where the two other parties were killed — and instructed to find out all the facts as far as possible . . .

The *Muskogee Weekly Phoenix* on March 30, 1899, described a fugitive capture Reeves just missed:

Aaron Grayson, who was charged with assault to kill, while being pursued very closely by Deputy Bass Reeves, swam the Verdigris [R]iver in order to escape being arrested.

The *Muskogee Evening Times* of September 25, 1901, carried a story of Reeves arresting a group of men, one of whom was a peace officer gone bad:

Three Landed by Deputy Reeves.
Sometime ago Orlando Dobson a deputy marshal and Bill Vann, his posseman, raised, it is charged, all sorts of disturbance over at Okmulgee. Dobson skipped out, likewise Vann was in . . . leaving for a hiding place. The marshal's office got news of Vann and that he was scouting over about Ft. Gibson. Deputy Bass Reeves was sent out for him and he "cotched" him. Reeves also caught two colored fellows John Wolf and J. C. McElway. The latter is a powerful [N]egro and has two charges of whiskey, one charge of carrying a concealed weapons, and one of wife beating, against him. All of them were taken to jail this morning where they will await trial.

Much of Reeves's work in the early 1900s was fairly regular and sometimes unintentionally humorous. The era of riding the range on horseback was slowly coming to an end. The following articles give an example:

Deputy Bass Reeves came in Sunday with Ed Walker. Walker is a colored gentleman who sometimes preaches, or as he puts it, he is an exhauster of the scriptures. His time and mind is not wholly given to the sacred book and its teachings, however, for occasionally he finds time to make love to the fair sex of his own color with satisfactory results to himself. In one particular, Walker is a Mormon, at least he believes in that doctrine to the extent that a man is entitled to as many wives as he can get, and for having more than one darling to love, obey and worship him, he was lodged in the U.S. jail to await the action of the court.

William Bussie, charged with assault to kill was brought in Thursday by Bass Reeves and lodged in jail.

209

Bass Reeves Saturday brought in one Charley Wright charged with being perniciously active in trying to destroy his neighbors' hogs by dogging and otherwise mutilating them.

The *Chickasaw Enterprise* on November 28, 1901, printed a feature story on Reeves:

> Negro Deputy Marshal at Muskogee
> A Good One.
> Muskogee, I.T., Nov. 20 — Bass Reeves, a [N]egro deputy marshal, working for the Muskogee court, claims that he has been a deputy for twenty-seven years; that during that time he has arrested more than three thousand men and women. He has, according to his statement, during that time killed twelve men . . .
> . . . He also says that a Seminole Indian is the hardest man to arrest of any class of people he ever met; that he is always ready, and if given a ghost of a chance he will shoot you and run . . .

In an interview with the Oklahoma City *Weekly Times-Journal* in 1907, Reeves expressed some of the same sentiments concerning Seminole outlaws:

> . . . The old deputy says the worst criminals and the hardest to catch are the Seminole Indians and Negroes. They stick together better, fight quicker and fight to kill. A Seminole on the scout is always on horseback, never sleeps until after midnight and gets up with the sun; every minute he is not asleep he is on his horse. He does not get off to eat. Riding up to a house he says "hombux," which means he wants something to eat. He is given a piece of meat and bread, and sits in his saddle and eats it, watching all the time for an expected foe.

By 1900, Reeves had remarried, to a woman named Winnie, and lived with three sons and one stepdaughter in Muskogee.

Very few men possessed his devotion to duty and respect for the law. He did not know the meaning of the word "fear" and never showed excitement under pressure. To him the supreme document was a "writ" or a warrant for an arrest. No circumstances could cause him to deviate from serving this instrument of the court. This attitude extended to his own family. Although there is no exact date regarding the following, the event occurred late in Reeves's career. The apprehension of his son was well known, as it is recorded in his obituary notice.

One of his sons, Benjamin, had married a beautiful black girl who was a native of the Indian Territory. They set up house in Muskogee and were very happy at first, but Benny's work kept him away from home so much that this happiness was relatively short-lived.

Benny realized that something was wrong with his marriage, for his wife was drifting further and further away from him. He began to work harder than ever before in the hope that providing his wife with all the luxuries he could provide would win her back. His idea was commendable, but it actually compounded the problem; by working harder, he was away from home even more. The situation progressed steadily from a small problem until it reached the point where Benny felt he had to try something else. He returned home from work unexpectedly one day to talk things over with his wife, and caught her with another man.

Benny was hurt and mad, but he didn't do anything. He and his wife were reconciled, with Benny completely forgiving her because he honestly felt that he was directly responsible for the whole problem by being away from home so much. Immediately, he found a new job that allowed him to spend more time at home. Their home life improved after this incident, and his wife seemed more satisfied and happier.

Benny and his father were very close; they had no secrets between them. One day, over a congenial glass of Forty-Rod, Benny explained to Bass the trouble he and his wife had experienced and asked how he would have acted, given the circumstances. The father's answer was short and to the point. He is quoted as saying: "I'd have shot the hell out of the man and whipped the living God out of her." This succinct advice must have made a lasting impression on Benny.

Shortly after telling his father about the previous troubles, Benny came home from work and found his wife again with another man. In the melee that followed, the man Benny had caught in his place escaped, bloody and beaten, but otherwise unharmed. However, in a hysterical rage, he killed his wife. Realizing what he had done, he ran away into the hills of the Indian Territory.

Naturally, since a crime had been committed, a warrant was issued for the arrest of Benny with the charge of murder. However, since the warrant called for the arrest of the son of Bass Reeves, the court and Marshal Leo Bennett of the Muskogee federal court were at a loss over what to do. Marshal Bennett wanted to send a deputy after Benny, but he also wanted to bring him in alive if he could. In addition to this, everyone concerned hated to go after the son of a man as respected and

211

well liked as Bass Reeves, particularly when the circumstances leading to the crime were considered. For two days the warrant lay on Marshal Bennett's desk, with all of the deputies fearing that they would be chosen to serve it. Bass, himself, eventually solved the problem.

The elder Reeves was visibly shaken by what had happened. Perhaps he remembered the advice he gave Benny and felt responsible. Whatever he thought, Reeves went to Marshal Bennett and demanded the warrant. Reeves told the marshal that it was his son who was wanted, and that it was his responsibility to bring him in to Muskogee. Bennett reluctantly gave Bass the warrant, and he left town on another manhunt — probably the hardest he ever performed.

Almost two weeks passed before Bass returned to Muskogee with Benny. He turned him over to the marshal, and Benny was bound over for trial.

During the trial, the damning fact that Benny had bolted and went "on the scout" condemned him. He was convicted, sentenced to prison, and was quickly transferred to the federal prison at Leavenworth, Kansas. Benny stood up under the ordeal of his trial quite well; he didn't plead or whine in an attempt to influence the court toward leniency. He admitted killing his wife and then running away, never clearly elaborating on the reasons why he did it. Bass stood by him every moment, right up to the time that Benny boarded the train for Leavenworth.

When Benny reached Leavenworth, he was resigned to serving his full sentence. He became a model prisoner, establishing a perfect record unmarred by any prison demerits. This became an extremely important point in the events that followed.

Many influential people in Muskogee eventually learned what actually led to the murder, and they felt that Benny had not been treated fairly. A citizens' petition was drafted and circulated expressing the opinions of this group; it was presented to the proper authorities in an attempt to obtain Benny's pardon. This petition, coupled with his exemplary prison record, resulted in a full pardon and Benny's subsequent release from prison. Benny returned to Muskogee and became one of the city's most popular barbers.

Perhaps the one thought that best expresses the sentiments of the early citizens of Muskogee can be summed up by the expression so many people used when asked to sign the petition for Benny's release. They generally answered, "Sure, I'll be happy to sign it. He's got the blood."

In the early 1900s, racial violence occurred in both Oklahoma and Indian Territories, in various towns such as Stroud, Chandler, Lawton, and Shawnee.

At Sapulpa, in the Creek Nation, a white mob in 1901 ordered all African-Americans to leave town. When the blacks refused, they were driven from their homes. The next year a race riot broke out at Braggs, which was located near Muskogee. When the whites, who had been suffering from a series of petty thefts by blacks, caught one, they horsewhipped him. The African-Americans retaliated by marching on the white settlement with the intention of getting revenge. In the ensuing fight, one white man and five blacks were wounded. When further trouble was expected, deputy marshals were dispatched to the town from Muskogee. Bass Reeves was among them.

The *Cherokee Advocate* from Tahlequah, I.T., on Saturday, May 31, 1902, reported on the uprising:

Twenty-Four Men Arrested

Muskogee, May 20 — Deputy United States Marshals Adams and Reeves came in from Braggs today with twenty-four prisoners who are charged with taking part in the race war.

The deputies made the arrests without resistance. All prisoners were bound over and will be tried in the United States court tomorrow. — *Ardmore Appeal.*

The *Muskogee Weekly Phoenix* on July 3, 1902, printed an article about the reappointment of deputy marshals:

From Wednesday's Daily.

All of Marshal Bennett's field deputies are in town. They were summoned by their chief to be present today and take the oath of office as deputy marshals in the new Western district. Following are the field deputies and their place of residence:

David Adams, Muskogee; John L. Brown, Webbers Falls; R. D. Faught, Sapulpa; Ed N. Fink, Waleetka; Grant Johnson, Eufaula; W. Frank Jones, Checotah; Henry C. Kaase, Holdenville; John W. Matthews, Choska; John S. O'Brien, Wagoner; Bass Reeves, Muskogee; H. A. Thompson, Tulsa . . .

That Reeves had a every acute memory can be attested to by the following newspaper story:

Deputy United States marshal John Cordell arrived in Muskogee Monday with two prisoners, Barney Fixico, and an Indian named

"Wild Cat," who was charged with the murder of Billy Culley, a prominent Seminole on February 3. Deputy Marshal Bass Reeves immediately identified "Wild Cat" as a prisoner who had escaped from him twenty years ago while the two were on their way to Fort Smith. It was supposed that "Wild Cat" was long since dead.

Throughout his career Reeves insisted that he never started a fight or drew first blood in a fight. Reeves swore that he never shot a man or at him until the other fellow started the fight; this, he swore, was true in all the fourteen deaths in which he was involved while he was a deputy marshal.

On the eve of Oklahoma statehood, Deputy Marshal Reeves was as active as ever. He was still making arrests and the local criminals were making attempts on his life — hardly anything new. About 10:00 on the night of November 13, 1906, somewhere north of Wybark, Indian Territory, Reeves was shot at while crossing under the railroad trestle. The would-be assassin's bullet sent showers of splinters over his head. Reeves shot from his buggy but missed his attacker(s). Since he had writs for a large number of criminals in the area, he felt he knew who had tried to kill him, but there was no hurry; he would capture whoever did the shooting sooner or later.

Charles Davis, a former resident of the Creek Nation, said Reeves had a unique and effective method of serving warrants around Muskogee. Reeves would on many occasions attend African-American churches on Sundays to serve warrants. He would notify the suspected felons thusly: "I have a warrant for you; but would you mind coming to the marshal's office in Muskogee tomorrow? I don't know what it is for. You better go see about it. If I have to arrest you, they will take you to Fort Smith, and you will be away from your family." Who would argue with such a logical request?

The last day Bass Reeves served as a deputy U.S. marshal was November 16, 1907, the first day of statehood for Oklahoma. Local courts would take care of the enforcement of laws which the federal courts formerly had jurisdiction over. The new government of Oklahoma moved swiftly to pass legislation to separate blacks and whites. The very first bill that came before the Oklahoma Senate provided for "Jim Crow" in public transportation. The bill, eventually passed by the first Oklahoma legislature, required separate railway cars for black and white passengers and provided a penalty for those who disobeyed the law. Subsequently, the legislature completed the "Jim Crow Code" with laws that prohibited marriage between blacks and whites, and which carried out the constitutional provision for separate schools.

This would certainly be a different land from the one in which Reeves had worked during the past three decades.

Reeves was getting up in age and needed a rest. He was still youthful in appearance — looking more like a man of fifty than sixty-nine — but the strain of thirty-two years as a deputy marshal was beginning to show and his health was breaking. He had spent too many nights sleeping on the ground in the wet and cold, and the countless days and nights spent in the saddle on manhunts had contributed to this condition. Reeves now walked with a cane, without a limp, to help support himself.

Some newspapers reported that Reeves had been wounded in earlier gun battles, but this was erroneous. In talking with former residents of the Indian Territory, they said Reeves was never shot, and his obituary notice reported that he was never wounded during his long tenure as a peace officer.

Bass Reeves was the only deputy U.S. marshal, that this author is aware of, who started with the inception of Judge Parker's court and worked with the federal police up to statehood in 1907.

At the age of sixty-nine, Reeves accepted a position with the municipal police force of Muskogee, Oklahoma, as a beat officer. The *Western Age* of Langston, Oklahoma, made the following announcement:

NEGRO DEPUTY U.S. MARSHAL: A POLICEMAN
Muskogee, Okla., Jan. 2 — Former Deputy United States Marshal Bass Reeves a giant [N]egro, who was in many battles with outlaws in the wild days of Indian Territory and during Judge Parker's reign at Fort Smith, is on the Muskogee police force . . .

He is now over 70 years old and walks with a cane . . . He is as quick of trigger, however, as in the days when gunmen were in demand.

Reeves was given a beat, patrolling the area of the Ritz Theater, north to Fourth Street between the courthouse to the "Katy" Railroad tracks. He later relished the record he established on his beat. For the nearly two-year period that Reeves patrolled this area, there was not even a minor crime committed on his beat.

It was said that while walking the streets of Muskogee, Reeves was always cautious. If someone called his name, he would always put his back flat against a wall before looking around to respond. He al-

215

ways took with him a sidekick, who would carry a satchel full of pistols. Reeves would also wear a shoulder holster with pistol, besides a pistol on his hip.

After serving on the police force for almost two years, the old man's health took a turn for the worse. He became seriously ill and had to permanently retire to his home. The *Muskogee Times-Democrat* on November 19, 1909, commented on the lawman's health:

> Bass Reeves, a deputy United States marshal in old Indian Territory for over thirty years, is very ill at his home in the Fourth ward and is not expected to live.
>
> Reeves was a deputy under Leo Bennett in the last years of the federal regime in Oklahoma, and also served in the old days of Judge Parker at Fort Smith.
>
> In the early days when the Indian country was over-rid[d]en with outlaws, Reeves was sent to go through the Indian country and gather up criminals which were tried at Fort Smith. These trips lasted sometimes for months and Reeves would herd into Fort Smith, often single handed, bands of men charged with crimes from bootlegging to murder. He was paid fees in those days which sometimes amounted to thousands of dollars for a single trip . . .
>
> The veteran [N]egro deputy never quailed in facing any man. Chief Ledbetter says of the old man that he is one of the bravest men this country has ever known.
>
> He was honest and fearless, and a terror to the bootleggers. He was as polite as an old-time slave to the white people and most loyal to his superiors.
>
> His son shot and killed his own wife and Reeves, enforcing the law, arrested his own son. The young [N]egro was sent to the penitentiary.
>
> While the old man is slowly sinking, Bud Ledbetter, who for years in the government service with Reeves, is caring for the old man the best he can and is a daily visitor at the Reeves home. Police Judge Walrond, who was United States district attorney while Reeves was an officer, also calls on the old [N]egro.
>
> "While Reeves could neither read or write," said Judge Walrond today, "he had a faculty of telling what warrants to serve any one and never made a mistake. Reeves carried a batch of warrants in his pocket and when his superior officer asked him to produce it the old man would run through them and never fail to pick out the one desired . . ."

Reeves died on Wednesday, January 12, 1910. He was buried at

216

Muskogee with great ceremony. It was a large funeral with literally hundreds of old friends and admirers — Indian, black, and white — in attendance. Reeves is reported to be buried in the old Union Agency cemetery in Muskogee.

How good of a gunfighter was Bass Reeves? Bill O'Neal, in his book *Encyclopedia of Western Gunfighters,* has constructed a statistical chart of gunfighters, showing the number of killings, number of gunfights, and number of possible assists (posse or gang action). The top three persons on O'Neal's chart are murderers, the highest ranked individual with twelve killings. The top peace officer is (Wild) Bill Hickock, with seven killings. If we take the word of Reeves and the local Indian Territory press that he killed fourteen men, he would have to rank very high on O'Neal's chart. It is not known how many gunfights Reeves had or how many possible assisted killings within a posse action he was involved in. But given the fact he worked for over thirty years, and considering the conditions of the Indian Territory, to say he had more than a few fights with outlaws is not unreasonable. But Reeves did not glorify having to shoot people; he was more proud of his detective skills.

Bass Reeves was truly a man of contradictions. He was the humblest and gentlest of men, yet he killed fourteen. He was easygoing and good-natured, yet he could erupt with great physical violence when a situation demanded it. He was a devoted father, yet he could seek and arrest his own son when the law was violated.

After conducting extensive research, this author believes Bass Reeves was the most outstanding peace officer of his era. Given the historical and social context Reeves worked in and his accomplishments in his line of endeavor, the man was a phenomenon. Bass Reeves was one of the greatest frontier heroes this country has ever produced — a true giant of the American West.

217

CHAPTER 17

Grant Johnson:
The Freedman Marshal

The second most important African-American deputy U.S. marshal in the Indian Territory was Grant Johnson. He was the son of Alex Johnson, a Chickasaw Freedman, and Miley, a Creek Freedwoman. It was generally believed that Johnson was born somewhere in North Texas. Speculation has centered on such towns as Denison, Sherman, Bells, or Bonham as being Johnson's birthplace.

Johnson was not very large in stature. One early resident of Oklahoma, Ezra Golson of Arcadia, grew up in Eufaula. He remembered Johnson as standing about five feet eight inches in height; he wore a white hat with a black bandana around his neck, carried two pistols on his hip, and rode a black horse with a Winchester attached to the saddle. He also remembered Johnson as being fond of smoking cigars. This recollection by Golson was of Johnson late in his career, when he was a member of the Eufaula, Oklahoma, Police Department.

Another early Indian Territory resident who remembered Johnson when he worked for the federal office said Johnson wore a large, wide-brimmed white hat and rode a big bay horse with a black mane. Johnson may have been of medium stature, and only 160 pounds, but he made a big impression on everyone who came into contact with him in his capacity as a peace officer.

Johnson was a quiet, reserved man — one who gave the impression of being almost shy in the company of strangers. He had an easy-going manner and very delicate features. His cheekbones were high with a slightly broadened nose separating them. His firm, determined jaw gave balance to clear, brown, fearless eyes, all framed on a light brown face. Johnson's physical strength and fortitude belied his small-boned, medium-built body. He was a man of the frontier who had confidence in his ability to do a job well.

According to a Eufaula *Indian Journal* article in 1901, Johnson at that time had held a deputy U.S. marshal's commission for fourteen years. This meant he would have entered federal service in 1887. Johnson began his career working out of the Fort Smith federal office. In 1895, Judge Isaac Parker described Grant Johnson as one of the best deputy marshals that he had known or worked with in the Indian Territory. Deputy Johnson's last commission from Judge Parker's Fort Smith court was dated July 1896.

Under the Act of 1889 there was still a high volume of transporting prisoners to Fort Smith for trial. When the Act of 1895, which created three districts in Indian Territory, went into effect, Johnson worked out of Eufaula, I.T., because he was reassigned to the Northern District of Indian Territory, where he remained until 1906.

The people in the territory sometimes erroneously called Johnson the "mulatto from Eufaula," which was incorrect because he was an African-Indian, or they would refer to him as the "Creek Freedman Marshal," which was correct. In being a Creek Freedman, Johnson was aware of the customs and language, which he spoke fluently, of the Creek Nation.

Johnson frequently worked with other peace officers; his work with Bass Reeves was a legend in the Indian Territory. An arrest Johnson made early in his career was done in tandem with Bass Reeves. The fugitive was a white man who would later become a Eufaula peace officer. Abner Brasfield had killed one Bill Hamm at Harrison, Arkansas, for which he was sentenced to twenty-one years in the Arkansas State Penitentiary. Brasfield appealed, but during the appeal in 1886 he escaped to the Indian Territory, where he wrote letters to his family, postmarked at Eufaula, Creek Nation. Brasfield's family moved to Eufaula on March 4, 1890.

Bill Brasfield, Abner's brother, gave an account of what was to follow:

> We hadn't been in this primitive setting but a few days when early one morning three men on horses rode up to the house. My

brother, Abner, sat on the middle horse, his hands handcuffed to the saddlehorn, and his feet fastened by a chain that crossed under the horse's belly. On a horse on each side of him sat a Negro United States Marshal, Grant Johnson and Bass Reeves. They would not let Abner dismount; just gave him time to say a few words. They had caught him at Brooken which is twelve miles to the east of Eufaula; they were taking him to Little Rock. When brother Abner broke jail at Harrison, a $1,500.00 reward had been placed on his head.

We followed them into town and once in Eufaula, Johnson and Reeves turned my brother over to Andy Duren, as a guard while they went in search of breakfast. Duren was a deputy placed at Eufaula to keep watch over the inhabitants of its dozen or so residences, two stores, post office and depot. It was in front of the post office that Abner was permitted to dismount, his hands having been uncuffed and his feet unshackled. However, from my place on the sidewalk beside my father, I would catch glimpses of Abner through the crowd that milled about. Abner stood beside his horse, handcuffs dangling from one wrist, and the chain still attached to his ankle. Duren stood nearby.

A few minutes later a well known horse and rider appeared and the crowd parted to let them through. The horse was black, weighing about eleven hundred and eighty-five pounds and went by the name of Niger. He had never been out run in several years of competitive territorial horse races. His rider was his owner and my cousin, Abner Brasfield, and it was after my cousin Abner that my brother was named. Cousin Abner, then nearly sixty years of age, dismounted within a few feet of brother Abner, but Niger walked up by brother Abner's side. In my mind leaped the thought that brother Abner would try to make his get away on Niger. I later learned that almost everyone else thought the same thing but that's where we all were fooled, including Andy Duren.

Into Niger's saddle bag went brother Abner's hand and when it came out it brought with it a .45 Colt which we had aforetime named "Old Martha." Cousin Abner lived at Brooken and hearing of brother Abner's arrest had hurried by our house after "Old Martha." This .45 Colt had been named "Old Martha" after cousin Abner's wife who had given it to us.

The handcuffs still hanging from one wrist and the chain dragging, brother Abner backed away from the deputy sheriff. The crowd, by the way had suddenly diminished. Duren told brother Abner to stop. Where upon brother Abner retorted, "Go to h--l." The deputy jerked his gun and fired without taking careful aim. Duren's shot went wild and brother Abner's shot knocked the gun from Duren's hand severing the thumb from the hand. The deputy dived through the post office door. (This building still stands just across the street west of Belt's store in the present town of Eufaula.) Brother Abner took two parting shots at the door through which the deputy had disappeared. His bullets embedded themselves in the woodwork of the door.

When Johnson and Reeves arrived on the scene a minute later, father and cousin Abner were placed under arrest and taken to Fort Smith; they were accused of plotting brother Abner's escape. When the others of us reached home we found brother Abner seated in a chair on the porch with a Winchester between his knees. He had forced a neighbor to cut his chain and handcuffs off.

Dad and cousin Abner made bond and came back home; made three or four trips to Fort Smith for trial but it was never held and the charges against them were finally dismissed. Brother Abner stayed around for a few days and then went to Texas. Two years went by before we saw him again. At that time he returned and gave himself up to Grant Johnson. A detective in Texas had broken brother Abner's arm with a shot. Brother Abner served four years in the Arkansas prison at Little Rock and the Governor pardoned him.

For several years before statehood brother Abner served on the law force at Eufaula . . .

W. R. Mulkey, a Cherokee Indian resident of the territory, said: "Bass Reeves (colored), Grant Johnson (colored) never used devious means for arrest."

In referring to early Eufaula, John Hubble, C. E. Foley, and Lizzie Gibson said that Deputy U.S. Marshal Grant Johnson was the only law officer in the area during the formative years of the town. James M. Calhoun said: "Grant Johnson, a mulatto [N]egro, of Eufaula, was the best marshal they [Eufaula] ever had . . ."

In 1890, Grant Johnson had a self-preservation gun battle with a notorious outlaw named Jake Stanley. Bill Brasfield described what happened during the fight:

I recall hearing of a gun battle between Jake Stanley, outlaw, and Grant Johnson, United States Marshal. Stanley had stolen quite a bit in and around Eufaula. One day he was seen leaving town in a wagon. Johnson followed on horseback and a little way out of town caught up with the Indian-Negro outlaw. Stanley halted his team and using his wagon to hide behind returned the United States Marshal's fire. Johnson fired from his saddle. Sitting on his horse he made a good target. Stanley . . . aimed at his head. Johnson had to head back to town, doing so after two of the bullets sent his way by the outlaw had found their way through his hat.

On July 4, 1890, the Fort Smith *Elevator* carried a report on an arrest made by Johnson: "Deputy Grant Johnson brought in Amos Hill, charged with introducing, etc."

The *Muskogee Phoenix* on August 27, 1891, reported the following.

Deputy Grant Johnson went out west a few miles last Thursday and arrested D. A. Lane, a lad about 18 years old, charged with attempting to pass counterfeit money. He was carried to Fort Smith had his examination trial and plead guilty to the charge. His bond was fixed at $500 for him to appear at the October term of court, but he failed to make it and now languishes in the Ft. Smith jail. — *Eufaula Journal.*

A humorous note concerning Johnson was found in the Eufaula *Indian Journal* on December 24, 1891:

Grant Johnson went down to Muskogee and bagged a whiskey peddler Tuesday. The prisoner came near escaping Tuesday night, and he and the marshal had a fine quarter mile heat foot race all to themselves.

Like all good lawmen in the Indian Territory, Johnson had alert mental facilities, and on many occasions had to use quick thinking. The Emancipation Day celebration was a big affair in Eufaula, and during one of these he showed his ability at public relations. The African-American population always held two picnics — one at each end of town. Johnson could not possibly be in both places at the same time, but he did own two horses, a black one and a white one. Early on the morning of the picnic he tied one horse to a tree at one end of town so it would be in full view of the crowd. When the festivities began later in the day, Johnson rode to the other end of town and mingled with the crowd. The people at the opposite end of town assumed Johnson was somewhere in the crowd, because his horse was in plain sight of everyone. Johnson was in the meantime at the other end of town keeping the peace. That turned out to be one of the quietest Emancipation Day celebrations Eufaula witnessed.

On April 21, 1892, the *Muskogee Phoenix* reported on activity by Johnson:

Deputy Grant Johnson caught a young man by the name of Chahe-

222

negee, about forty-five miles west of Eufaula last week and one Albert Malbin about six miles above Muskogee. Chahenegee is charged with breaking into a house and stealing a pistol, and Malbin is charged with selling whiskey. Both prisoners have been turned over to the United States Court at Fort Smith. — *Eufaula Journal.*

Johnson's tenacity for capturing horse thieves was highlighted in the *Phoenix* on October 5, 1893:

Horse Thieves Captured
Grant Johnson, Deputy U.S. Marshal, came in last night from the Creek nation with Frank and Geo. Curtis, who are charged with stealing horses and lodged them in jail. The Curtis brothers stole a lot of horses, some time ago from B. A. and W. J. Aldridge, of Iron Bridge in the Choctaw nation. Johnson got on the track of the thieves and followed them eighty miles before he captured them. He had the rare good fortune to recover the horses and return them to their owners. — *Ft. Smith Record.*

On August 23, 1894, the *Muskogee Phoenix* reported an unusual arrest for horse theft by Johnson:

Deputy Grant Johnson came in Wednesday morning with a boy about ten years old and very small for his age, whom he arrested near Webbers Falls for stealing horses. The boy is a pitiful looking little fellow and only weighs sixty pounds. He says he was persuaded to steal a mare and colt and sell them by older persons. Grant says he was ashamed to arrest him as he looked so innocent and pitiful. — *Indian Journal.*

The *Muskogee Phoenix* carried the following articles concerning Johnson's police work on the following dates in 1894:

September 22
Deputy Grant Johnson today placed in jail John Pierce and Bill Davis, charged with killing an Indian named Russell between Webbers Falls and Briartown in August. Russell had been to Webbers Falls and was on his way home when two white men held him up. It is thought one of them became frightened and nervous and that he shot Russell without intending to do so. This theory is strengthened by the fact that they ran off as soon as the shot was fired and did not wait to rob their victim, whom they had stopped for that purpose.

December 19
Monday, Deputy Grant Johnson arrested two brigands in the

Younger bend, on the Canadian [R]iver, near Brooken. Jim French was not one of them, though a horse thought to be Jim French's was captured. They had in their possession a number of blankets that correspond with the blankets taken from Lafayette Bros.' store at the recent robbery. The prisoners acknowledge that they are bandits and it is expected that they will make important disclosures.

December 22

BANDITS CAUGHT

Eufaula, I.T., Dec. 19 — Deputy Marshal Johnson arrived last night with Columbus Rose, a Cherokee Indian, and John Morrow, a white man, charged with robbing J. M. Lentz's store at Golconda, and Featherstone's store, at Featherstone, I.T., a few nights ago. They also attempted to rob the store of J. R. Pearce, at Texanna, Tuesday night, but were fired upon by A. J. Powell, a clerk in the store, and driven off, taking only a saddle and a pair of boots.

Rose is supposed to be the man who killed Postmaster Russell at Briartown last July, for which crime John Pearce was arrested not long since. Johnson also has John Pearce under arrest for horse stealing. Rose and Pearce were captured at Younger Bend, in the Cherokee nation, and Morrow was captured at Enterprise, in the Choctaw nation.

The marshal and posse left again tonight in search of the remainder of the gang, which is supposed to be in the mountains of the Choctaw nation, southeast of Eufaula, and will very likely capture the whole outfit, consisting of eight or ten men. Rose has confessed to being implicated in the Featherstone and Golconda robberies.

An arrest Johnson made in early 1895 came as a surprise to the prisoner-to-be, Amos McIntosh, a Creek Indian. McIntosh had a few months earlier killed Lee Atkins, also a Creek, who held a commission as a deputy U.S. marshal. However, he was not in the discharge of his duty when he was killed. There arose, then, the question of which court would have jurisdiction over the case — that of the Creek Nation or that of the United States government. The latter legal body decided to try the case.

Johnson had been given the writ for McIntosh's arrest, but didn't move on it right away. He realized that McIntosh had been to Eufaula several times to shop. Johnson's lack of haste lulled the killer into a sense of false security. McIntosh rode into Eufaula on a Monday, January 21, 1895, dismounted, and walked into the Grayson Brothers general store, where he purchased a shroud and a coffin for his wife, who had died the day before. Walking casually up to the counter,

224

Johnson arrested McIntosh while he was paying for his purchase. It must have been a trying moment for McIntosh, who had been about town for a number of weeks during which no attempt was made to capture him. Johnson accompanied McIntosh to his home where he let him remain until after the funeral the following day. On the next day, Wednesday, January 23, 1895, Johnson left for Fort Smith with his prisoner.

About a month later, Johnson was in Muskogee and there, in a saloon with Deputy George Lawson, he arrested a white man, Wade Chamberlee, who was implicated in the Blackstone train robbery. Chamberlee, about thirty years of age with a known criminal past, was arrested earlier at Verdigris Bottom. Later, he was arraigned at the Muskogee Court for harboring outlaws. However, Chamberlee was released after his preliminary hearing. Then new evidence was presented, and a grand jury indicted him on February 11, 1895. The next day he rode into town and had a long conversation with Deputy Johnson while neither man had any knowledge of the indictment. Later, Deputy Lawson was given the writ for Chamberlee's arrest and asked Johnson if he knew the man well enough to point him out. After a good laugh over the incident, both deputies arrested Chamberlee while he was in one of Muskogee's finest saloons.

One afternoon Deputy Johnson took Elijah Conger into his confidence and told him of his plan to catch the leader of an illegal whiskey business, a man named Cook who lived near Eufaula. Conger arranged a big card game, invited Cook, and asked him to bring plenty of whiskey to the game. Cook, however, sent his sons to the game instead. When Johnson rode up and knocked on the door, the boys panicked and ran. The deputy quickly caught them and hastily traveled to their father's home so he could conduct a search. Conger and the other card players searched for Cook's whiskey while Johnson held Cook at gunpoint. Cook's friends, who conducted the search, failed to tell the deputy about the whiskey hidden in the loft and the flour barrel. Not to be outwitted, Johnson took Cook to Fort Smith anyway. Both stayed in the town sixty days, awaiting trial, until Cook was finally released due to insufficient evidence.

One of the best attended festivities in the Indian Nations of the Five Civilized Tribes was the ball games. These games were part of the traditional Native American customs. Sometimes the games would get out of hand, with contestants fighting among themselves. The *Muskogee Phoenix* on September 7, 1899, reported an incident where Deputy

Johnson had to intercede during a fracas:

The big Indian ball game that was advertised to come off last Wednesday between the Eufaula and Okfuskee "towns" resulted in a free-for-all fight between the two teams and the game was declared off. When the ball was the first tossed up the scrapping began and continued for three or more minutes, when Deputy Marshal Grant Johnson, of Eufaula, got in among them and caused them to scatter by shooting in the ground. — *Checotah Enquirer.*

For many years Johnson was the only law officer in the Eufaula area. At the turn of the century, when race relations were not exactly cordial in some parts of the Indian Territory, Grant Johnson was a highly respected lawman. Many of the whites of the area commended the way he handled his duties and admired his personal demeanor. The following articles are from the *Muskogee Phoenix* late in 1900:

October 11
Shooting Affray
Tuesday night about 9:30 o'clock Will Howell and W. R. Houston, both colored, got into a row in a gambling house on the west side, Eufaula, over five cents in a game. Howell drew a gun and shot Houston through the right lung. Howell skipped out promptly and has not been heard from since. Houston is dangerously wounded and may die.

The man Howell is a bad darkey. He was fined last week by the mayor for fighting.

Later: Howell was captured by Grant Johnson across the Canadian east of town about dark yesterday evening. He will be tried before the commissioner today. — *Eufaula Journal.*

October 18
Grant Johnson took Rush Phillips to Muskogee Saturday bound over for attempt at train wrecking. Monday he took to Muskogee, Lee Knight and McCarty on similar charges for trial before the Muskogee Commissioner, Judge Marshal being unable to attend to the case on account of death to his wife. — *Journal.*

December 13
Deputy Grant Johnson arrested and took to Muskogee Friday night John Shields, charged with assault and robbery. Shields is the [N]egro who, with Henry James, was arrested for the robbery of Charley Smith about a month ago. Lack of evidence caused his release but additional evidence has been produced and the grand jury

226

has found a bill. — *Eufaula Gazette.*

The most famous gunfight Grant Johnson ever had took place in Eufaula, I.T., in December of 1900. The following article from the Eufaula *Indian Journal* gives a description of the events:

John Tiger Goes To War
He Shoots Four Men and Reaps Some
Lead Himself

Christmas morning about 11 o'clock John Tiger, a fullblood Indian living two or three miles east of Eufaula, left his buggy in charge of his wife near the Tully store and sauntered down Main [S]treet to where L. B. Roper was standing in a crowd near the Sorbe restaurant. Tiger was drinking and had in his hand a fence pailing. He approached Roper and some words passed between them the result of which was that Roper wrenched the paling from Tiger's hand and struck him over the head with it. Tiger was not knocked down. He turned with the remark, "That is all right," and walked back 150 yards to his buggy. Here an altercation occurred between Tiger and his wife over the possession of a grip containing a pistol. The man finally got possession of the weapon, a 45 calibre six-shooter, and started down Foley [A]venue shooting at all the inhabitants in sight. He threw down on Bill Bumgarner first and accused him of being Roper. Bill denied it and pushed his hands heavenward in witness that he was "only old Bill Bumgarner, your friend, John." The warrior was convinced but turned to Dave Porter and shot him in the back without comment. Porter fell and as he went down he drew his pistol which went off in the air.

Tiger next turned his attention to an old man, a mover, who was on his way to buy bread at the Sorbe restaurant. The old man ran but Tiger shot him through the head and he fell. The first two, Porter and the mover, are now dead.

Tiger then opened fire on a surveyor named Clemens, but Clemens ran so crooked and fell down so opportunily that he was only shot through the pants leg. Having fallen, Tiger apparently thought he was dead for he next shot Jesse Beck just above the hips. Beck is in a critical condition — expected to die.

Buddie Taylor next acquired a bullet in the fleshy part of his thigh — not serious.

Tiger's pistol being now empty he ran across the railroad track for his home east of town. He had hardly kicked up a cloud of dust and disappeared in it when deputy United States marshal Grant Johnson came up, cut loose a horse from a hitch rack, and with Abner Brasfield as posseman, started in pursuit.

227

They overtook Tiger a short distance down Belt [A]venue. When the bad man saw he would be overtaken he climbed over a fence and got behind a tree. As Grant Johnson came along, his horse running and bucking, Tiger shot at him, but missed because, it is supposed, of his bucking and curving horse. Not so Grant, for his first shot broke Tiger's left arm. Tiger's second shot also missed, and he having only slipped two cartridges in his pistol, threw the empty gun away at the command of the officer and was lead back to town where Dr. Tolleson dressed his head and shattered arm.

Drs. West, Benson and Counterman were busy dressing the wounds of his victims.

Tiger was lodged in Muskogee jail the same afternoon, Grant Johnson and Constable Milam taking him up on the Flyer.

The affair is a very bad business and is deplored by every citizen of Eufaula. Tiger was not a resident of this town and the people he shot were innocent men who had nothing to do with his row with Roper and were not even in the crowd when the first trouble occurred. Mayor Foley, who saw the first trouble, had in the meantime gone through the crowd on Main [S]treet and disarmed every man. The shooting took place on Foley [A]venue just around the corner and Tiger never saw Roper after the original difficulty. He seemed to think just anybody would do and murdered accordingly. The people were very indignant over the coldblooded slaughter and there was some wild talk of lynching but better advice prevailed and Tiger will be hanged by the legally constituted authorities.

The Abner Brasfield mentioned in the previous newspaper article is the same person Johnson along with Bass Reeves arrested years earlier.

J. S. (Shorty) Brown, a Eufaula resident at the time of the Tiger shootout, was an eyewitness, and gave an account of what happened in an interview years later:

John Tiger, a Creek Indian, came to town one day in 1899. He was very drunk and his wife had to drive the team part of the way. Upon reaching Eufaula, John stopped in front of a small restaurant. He had two guns, a Winchester, the other a six-shooter, and being too drunk to know what he was doing, he picked up his guns and began firing at the people on the street. Before the "law" could stop him he had killed three men and there was a small boy some distance from him who had some of his waist buttons shot from his pants. Tiger saw the United States Marshal, Grant Johnson, who was a Negro, coming and knew that his game was up so he ran for a short distance, then stumbled over a low fence. He then started firing with his six-

228

shooter at the marshal. There were two large trees between John Tiger and Grant Johnson and each one took to a tree for protection. While fighting the bullets could be heard hitting the trees. The marshal shot Tiger in the right arm and captured him. The people in Eufaula were in a panic and wanted to string John Tiger up but Mr. Foley quieted the mob and prevented them from lynching John Tiger.

The *Indian Journal* on January 25, 1901, stated:

The people of Eufaula made a purse a few days since and sent it to Grant Johnson as a mark of their appreciation of the prompt and courageous manner in which he arrested John Tiger on Christmas day and also for his effective work in preserving the public peace during the excitement that followed the lamentable occurrences of that day. A man cannot be paid in cash for this kind of work. Duty is all that prompts a man under such circumstances. This present to Grant is not, therefore, a reward but a mark of appreciation of duty well done the reward for which is only the sense duty well done.

The same newspaper ran another article the same day concerning Johnson arresting outlaws in the territory:

Deputy Marshal Grant Johnson brought in Monday John and Arthur Indsley from near Texanna charged with introducing and selling whiskey. Also charged with horse stealing. They were held by Judge Marshall to await action of the grand jury.

Being a law officer often placed Johnson in a kill-or-be-killed situation. Death was always a possibility for a law officer in the Indian Territory. Some lawmen would shoot to kill; some even shot first — the questioning would come later. But Johnson was the type of man who would rather wound a man than kill him in the line of duty. This serious and rather quiet man felt that life was a very dear gift to any man and used almost any peaceable method to arrest a criminal and cause the least injury humanly possible under the circumstances.

Johnson was forced to kill his first desperado in 1901 in Eufaula. If Johnson would have had any type of options except to save his own life, he wouldn't have shot the man. The Eufaula *Indian Journal* described the shooting:

HIS FIRST KILL
Grant Johnson, Deputy Marshal,
Kills Frank Wilson

229

Monday afternoon about 3:30 Frank Wilson and Wade Smith, both colored, engaged in a quarrel near the old Lucand photograph gallery on the East side, Eufaula. Wilson drew a pistol and fired two shots at Smith who fled.

Deputy Marshal Grant Johnson, a few minutes later started after Wilson to arrest him. Wilson fled and the officer pursued on horseback, calling to him to stop and firing in the air to empathize his demand. The fugitive notified the officer that he would die before he would surrender and leveled his pistol at Johnson who then fired. Wilson was shot through the stomach and then fell.

A few minutes later Wade Smith ran up with a shotgun which he had procured somewhere and wanted to shoot the prostrate man but was stopped by the officer. Wilson was given good medical attention but died Tuesday.

Grant Johnson has been a deputy United States marshal in these parts for fourteen years and has arrested more bad men than any officer in the Indian Territory. He has never before killed a man and has been forced to wound but one or two others. The people of Eufaula owe much to him for he has kept the peace in this town when the bad man was real bona fide bad man and numerous. His reward in cash has been slight. He has risked his life a hundred times in the interest of peace and held his hand when nine other officers out of ten would have killed. He has made no more than a living out of his office and the work is hard and dangerous. If merit can be rewarded among the deputies of the northern district, Johnson should be given a rewarding promotion of some sort for his 14 years of hard service.

As much as the service of Johnson and other black deputies merited reward, there was none forthcoming. There was never an African-American appointed as a United States marshal in the Indian Territory, nor was there one appointed chief deputy marshal. It is not known just how much the existing Southern sentiment and influence had on the appointment of blacks to the higher positions, but the marshal's and chief deputy's job both represented prestige and power.

The performance of Grant Johnson and Bass Reeves as law officers was not surpassed by any deputy marshals that worked the Indian Territory.

At the turn of the century, there was considerable trouble with a disgruntled group of Indians in the Creek Nation. The leader of the "hostiles" was Chitto Harjo, commonly called Crazy Snake. His followers included several hundred full-blood Creeks known as the Snake faction, who sought to resurrect the defunct Creek Nation. This group included some Creek Freedmen. The hostility came to be known as the Crazy Snake Uprising.

The roots for the uprising reached back to long-standing complaints by Chitto Harjo and the full-blood Creeks against the government's dissolution of the Creek Nation as a sovereign entity. The Curtis Act of 1898 unilaterally abolished the Creek, Cherokee, Choctaw, and Chickasaw Nations. In an attempt to salvage as much for themselves as possible, the Creeks on May 25, 1901, ratified what they felt was a more acceptable agreement. When the Snake faction of full-blood Creeks continued to resist enrollment and to refuse to sign for individual allotments of land, the government enrolled them anyway and assigned them random land allotments.

In the fall of 1900 the Snake faction met at Hickory Ground, a traditional gathering spot in McIntosh County, about six miles south of the town of Henryetta. The Snakes elected a principal chief, a second chief, a two-house legislature, and a court. They tried to bring back the old laws of the Creek Nation, which had been suspended by the Curtis Act, and appointed a police force to enforce them. The full-bloods then sent an ultimatum to President William McKinley, posted their laws throughout the countryside, and confiscated large numbers of allotment certificates from the Creeks who had received them. The Snake Indians began whipping Creeks who willingly took allotments, employed whites, or rented lands to persons who were not citizens of the Creek Nation. This turn of events caused the federal government to intercede.

Grant Johnson would play an important part in the quelling of this uprising by the Snake faction. The *Tahlequah Arrow* carried an article where Johnson gave an appraisal of the situation in the Creek Nation:

INDIANS CAUSING TROUBLE
Snake Band of Indians May Have to Be
Suppressed With Soldiers

A press dispatch from Eufaula states that the [S]nake band of Creek Indians, better known as the disaffected Creeks, are in open insurrection against the regular Creek government in this district, in fact, in several districts west of Eufaula. They are riding the country in bands of fifty, arresting peaceable Indians whom they claim have broken the ancient laws and traditions of the tribe. They try these men before their insurrectionary tribunals at Hickory Ground and whip them according to an ancient Creek law. One man was killed resisting arrest. They are seizing cattle for non-payment of fines.

"The country," said the deputy United States marshal, Grant Johnson, who just returned from the scene of trouble, "is in an uproar and trouble of a serious nature is looked for. The peaceable Indians have appealed to the United States authorites and it is expected that only soldiers can settle the affair without bloodshed. The Snake bands are composed of the most ignorant and stubborn class of full-blood Creeks. They are armed with Winchesters and have given it out that they will re-establish their ancient form of government. In fact, they have a new chief and a new council, etc. The general opinion is that soldiers will be required to overthrow these insurrectionists."

The Eighth U.S. Cavalry was eventually called out, and peace was restored when federal marshals arrested nearly one hundred Indians. The leader, Chitto Harjo, was arrested by Deputy Marshal Johnson. The *Indian Journal* carried an account of the arrest:

Crazy Snake and Followers in
Eufaula Under Arrest.

All Eufaula had a good square look at the noted chief of the Snake Indians Monday afternoon when Deputy United States Marshal Grant Johnson and posse brought him and eleven of the faithful into town from Hickory Ground. The marshal marched the prisoners straight to the M.K.&T. depot. where he corralled them until the arrival of the north-bound flyer. The marshal stated that the Snakes made no resistance when captured, and had behaved well during the overland trip to Eufaula.

During the hour or so that passed before the train arrived, the depot platform swarmed with people curious to catch a glimpse of Crazy Snake, the bad "Injin," who has been a disturbing element to the peace and dignity of the country and the federal courts for two years. He sat apparently indifferent to all that was going on about him, with his black slouch hat slightly pulled down over his eyes. Once he remarked: "I wonder what kind of animal they think I am?" After a while he added: "I don't know why we have been arrested and taken from our families at a time when our families can least spare us. We'll not suffer, perhaps, but they will. Food is scarce, and how are women to get it? We were peaceably assembled counseling among ourselves for our own good. We meant nobody harm. Why should we be taken to jail for this? We have not laid waste nor plundered. No home is vacant, and no field lying untilled because of our mischief. Rather our homes are vacant and our fields are lying untilled. We believe that if the United States officials understood our wants and needs as we understand them, we would not be regarded as outlaws, but as friends to be helped and pitied . . ."

The Eufaula *Indian Journal* carried two articles concerning the arrest by Deputy Johnson of the Snake Indians on March 7, 1902:

INDIANS GIVEN A HAIR CUT
Government Trying New Methods with Crazy
Snake Malcontents — Important Documents Found.

Twelve of the Crazy Snake faction, who were captured by United States Deputy Marshal Grant Johnson, near Hickory Ground, the place where they have been holding council, were placed in jail at Muscogee. The most important one of the capture was Chitto Harjo, or Crazy Snake. There were seven Creeks, four Seminoles and one Choctaw among them.

Some important documents were found, among which was an agreement entered into by representatives of the five tribes in which they bind themselves to agitate the people until a government is established in conformity with the treaty of 1832. Another document was relative to the government of the Creeks under Lah-tah Micco, the chief of the Snake band. It will be remembered that Lah-tah Micco was captured a few days ago, but made his escape.

The compact above referred to was signed by Lah-tah Micco on the part of the Creeks, Yaha Hocochie on the part of the Seminoles, Soletawa on the part of the Cherokees, Samuel Yokes on the part of the Chickasaws, Daniel Bell on the part of the Choctawa . . .

CRAZY SNAKE A PRISONER
His Band Captured and Threatened Uprising
is Ended.

Deputy Marshal Grant Johnson arrived at Eufaula, from the northern part of the Choctaw nation, the other day, with twelve Snake Indian leaders, among them Crazy Snake himself and the second Chief Wako-Hoyo, who escaped from Henrietta. The band was surprised in camp by Johnson and a posse.

The twelve prisoners, among whom is Alex. Archibald, the Choctaw leader of Snakes, were taken to Muscogee along with their captured Winchesters.

All the Creek leaders of prominence are now in custody save Lah-to-Micco, who escaped after being captured near Henrietta.

Shortly after this episode, Deputy Johnson was given new orders pertaining to the Snake Indians. This dictum was printed in the *Indian Journal*, March 21, 1902:

U.S. MARSHAL'S INSTRUCTIONS.

Deputy Marshal Grant Johnson has been instructed to make no further arrests upon warrants issued against the members of the so-called Snake government, as negotiations are pending by which it is hoped that a renunciation of said government may be made. He has also been instructed to inform the Snake Indians or their friends of his instructions and to assure them that they can go to Muskogee and enroll and file without molestation.

Chitto Harjo and several of the Snake faction eventually got an opportunity to travel to Washington, D.C., to lobby for a recognition of the Creek Treaty of 1832. This venture did appease them for a while, but was doomed from the first. Grant Johnson had done his job well, carrying out his orders to the letter; no more could be asked of him. After statehood there were again problems concerning the Snake faction, for which the Oklahoma National Guard had to be called in for police action.

The Eufaula *Indian Journal*, on May 8, 1903, reported yet another arrest of a Snake Indian by Deputy Johnson:

A Prophet Arrested For the Larceny
of a Wagon and is Bound Over

Wachache, the great Snake prophet and healer, was arrested at his home near Lenna Wednesday by Deputy Marshal Johnson.

The prophet is charged with the larceny of a wagon belonging to one of his own clique. Commissioner Marshall fixed his bond at $1,000 in default of which he was committed to jail at Muskogee pending a preliminary hearing.

It seems that Wachache did not go and steal the wagon by stealth but took charge of it after it was on his premises and refused to give it up, claiming that the Great Spirit had authorized him to take possession of it and destroy it as a device of evil.

In the spring of 1902 Wachache began business by making a bonfire of all his earthly plunder except a few things even a savage can not live without. He then proclaimed himself a prophet and medicine man having divine authority.

Immediately he was surrounded by credulous fullbloods in great numbers and his erstwhile obscure and lowly log cabin on Limbo [C]reek became the Mecca of pilgrims . . .

He prophesied. He built the fires and led in the "stomp"

dance. He made the faithful drink medicine and fast and bathe in the holy water frequently. His followers increased in numbers and at times the white renters in the neighborhood became alarmed and murmured, but at last became reconciled, believing Wachache harmless . . .

A few months later Grant Johnson was investigating a murder which was reported by the *Muskogee Phoenix* on July 23, 1903:

A KILLING AT EUFAULA
Bert Tucker, Jealous of his Wife, Kills the Man Whom She Loves.

Special to the *Phoenix*.

Eufaula, July 18. — Jim Berea, a half blood Cherokee Indian, was shot and killed this morning at the home of John Davis, three miles south of this place, by Bert Tucker, a young farmer. The cause of the tragedy was jealousy on the part of Tucker, who claims that his victim had been paying attention to his wife. Tucker went to Eufaula and surrendered to Grant Johnson, deputy U.S. marshal . . . When Tucker went to the Davis home yesterday morning, where his wife had gone to stay all night, he found the half-blood there. He had warned him before, and when the Indian saw the farmer coming, he fled toward the barn. Tucker pursued him and shot him five times, once through the body. The Indian's death was almost instantaneous.

Johnson on occasion worked with the also well-known white deputy marshal, J. F. "Bud" Ledbetter, of Muskogee. On December 5, 1904, they captured Indian outlaws Jim Tiger and "Fish" at Mellette, fifteen miles east of Eufaula. That arrest culminated a manhunt conducted by nearly a hundred deputies as a result of the murder of Deputy Marshal E. Fink near Weleetka on November 20.

Deputy Fink had trailed the Indian outlaws in their endeavor to transport illegal whiskey. When Fink ordered the Indians to surrender, Tiger, who was mounted with his back to the peace officer, suddenly turned in his saddle and fired his gun, killing officer Fink. In searching for the killers, marshals arrested every pair of Indians they found at the nearby railroad station. When Johnson and Ledbetter finally captured Tiger and Fish, the marshals told each that the other had confessed; that he was innocent and the other guilty, whereupon both men confessed to the murder and were tried at Muskogee.

In October of 1905, Grant Johnson went on a manhunt for three murderers. The *Muskogee Democrat* reported the capture:

THREE INDIANS ARRESTED FOR MURDER
OF HARJO

Eufaula, I.T., Oct. 18 — (Special) — Deputy Marshal Grant Johnson yesterday brought in Simpson Tiger, Turner Foster and Burney Jackson, all full blood Snake Indians, charged with murdering Tobasola Harjo also a Snake Indian on September 4th, at midnight. The Snakes had camped about 15 miles west of Eufaula and were participating in a dance the night before the great Indian ball game. At the dance about 12 o'clock at night the three above named Indians, it is charged, started the row in hopes of implicating a prominent member of the Creek council. He seeing their object sebexed, which in Creek means, flew the coop, and Tobasola Harjo was killed by crushing his skull and cutting up his body. The three prisoners were bound over to await the action of the grand jury, by Hon. H. L. Marshall, United States Commissioner.

Grant Johnson and Bud Ledbetter worked well together and had an understanding concerning each other's territory. They were both known as good "field men," responsible to Marshal Bennett of the Muskogee federal office. Ledbetter was stationed in Muskogee and Johnson in Eufaula, both towns connected by the M.K.&T. Railroad. Something happened between them that caused friction in their relationship. Perhaps this came between the years 1904 and 1906; several incidents indicated that such a situation existed. The most serious incident occurred when Ledbetter decided Johnson was not strict enough in enforcing the liquor laws. Ledbetter made an unannounced trip to Eufaula where he raided a number of drugstores (which served also as illegal bars), destroyed all the whiskey he seized in the raids, and arrested several men for gambling. Ledbetter made his report and was satisfied that he had cleaned up Eufaula; he left for Muskogee. Johnson was incensed over the report and the activities of his colleague from Muskogee. The very same day, Johnson boarded the afternoon train and went to Muskogee. He moved nonchalantly around the town staking out several gambling houses. That night Johnson raided four crap games, and arrested and jailed twelve men. The local drug stores also received a visit from Johnson and lost some of their liquor merchandise without hope of compensation. Johnson thus got his revenge on Ledbetter for invading his "territory."

On February 9, 1906, Johnson was informed by U.S. Marshal Leo Bennett at Muskogee that he would not be reappointed as a deputy U.S. marshal. Bennett accused Johnson of being too lax in the suppression of bootlegging. There were people in the territory who felt Johnson was not reappointed due to Ledbetter's influence in Muskogee and the ill feelings generated by the raiding incidents of their respective towns. The clash between Johnson and Ledbetter didn't appear to be racial, but one of personalities. Johnson was a proud man and would not step down to anyone. The manner in which he accomplished his assignments gave evidence that he was not an ordinary deputy. Even Johnson's signatures were unusual for frontier lawmen; they were examples of excellent penmanship. In nearly twenty years as a deputy U.S. marshal, Johnson had a distinguished record as peace officer for his bravery during his years of service with the Justice Department and took great pride in protecting his assigned district.

After his dismissal, Johnson made the newspapers one more time. The *Muskogee Times-Democrat* carried the incident on October 4, 1909:

Knife Used on Grant Johnson, an Old Deputy Marshal at Eufaula

Eufaula, Okla., Oct. 4. — (Special) — Grant Johnson, for many years a deputy United States marshal, and a good one, was badly wounded at Bond Switch by being stabbed in the neck by Robert Watson. Johnson is now at his home east of Eufaula and Watson is in jail awaiting the outcome of the wound.

Johnson recovered from the inflicted injury and was employed for a number of years by the city of Eufaula as a policeman. His regular patrol was the African-American section of the town where, as always, he kept the peace with a quiet dignity. He was especially good at keeping youngsters out of trouble, and they all respected him.

In regards to Johnson's personal life, his marriage produced one child, a son, John Johnson. John inherited his father's fierce pride. In World War I, John won the Purple Heart in combat in France on May 12, 1918. John was discharged from the army with the rank of staff sergeant. Grant was justly proud of his son, who was a true hero in his father's image.

The end of the trail came for Johnson on April 9, 1929. He was buried near Eufaula in the African-American cemetery. In performing his law enforcement duties, Grant Johnson was highly efficient and remarkably accountable. No more could be asked of any peace officer then or now.

CHAPTER 18

Zeke Miller:
Outstanding Legacy

In the Reader's Digest publication, *Story of the Great American West,* one African-American is included among the peace officers in the section entitled "Law and Order in the West." As being one of the ten lawmen highlighted, the following is printed:

> *Zeke Miller.* A black man, he served as a deputy U.S. marshal for the central district of Indian Territory from 1894 to 1907. Although he hunted down numerous outlaws, Miller never had to shoot a man to make an arrest, nor was he ever injured on duty.

Zeke Miller was the third most important African-American deputy marshal to ride the outlaw trail in the Indian Territory. Miller, like Bass Reeves, was not an Indian Freedman, like many of the black officers. Miller was originally from Ohio, where he worked as a mine inspector.

In appearance, Miller was a very light-complected black man. His granddaughter, Mrs. Mae Lois Stewart, feels he may have been buried in the white cemetery of Alderson, Oklahoma, because his headstone cannot be found in the black cemetery.

When Miller decided to relocate to the Indian Territory, friends recommended him for the job of deputy U.S. marshal. Even without a background in police work, his reputation gained him the appointment. Although there may be some controversy now as to whether he was truly black, and undoubtedly looking at his picture he could have "passed," he was known in the territory as an African-American peace officer. William Taylor, a resident of the Choctaw Nation, said:

I knew a few United States deputy marshals. I think John Simpson was one. He was an Indian. Zeke Miller and Bob Fortune were marshals; they were colored. And John Chambers, a white man, was a marshal. The United States marshal was about the only contact we had then with the United States Government; the Choctaws had their own government and laws. White people and Negroes who weren't Freedmen or intermarried with the Indians, were just about without any laws except for the marshals. Of course, the towns had their own legal set-ups, but they had jurisdiction only within their city limits . . .

William J. Layne, who earlier in the book described the capture of the black outlaw Step Ody, also talked about the arresting marshals of Ody, and others in the vicinity, including Miller:

Bill Ellis captured him. Bill was a deputy United States marshal; the first one to be stationed at Hartshorne. The United States marshal from Wilburton, Robert "Poorboy" Fortune, was with him. Ellis was a white man but Fortune was a Negro. A lot of the marshals in the Territory were Negroes then, maybe because we had a Republican president. Zeke Miller, the marshal stationed at Alderson then, was a Negro.

Miller worked very closely with fellow African-American deputy marshals Neely Factor and Robert Fortune, who were also assigned to the central district. They all worked in the McAlester, I.T., area. Factor was interviewed about one of their manhunts:

Neely Factor . . . was one of the early peace officers in the Indian Territory, and during the period of his service many bands of outlaws roamed throughout the Territory. One of these bands had located themselves in an old house near the mining town of Adamson. Factor was instructed to spy on the gang and report their activities to his superiors and also try and find out when the entire gang might be captured. For several days he watched the house and finally reported his findings to Zeke Miller, a fellow officer, then Miller sent a couple of his men to aid Factor in his vigil. One morning, after watching the place all night, the trio were nearly discovered by a member of the band who came wandering aimlessly about the

239

meadow where the officers were lying in the tall grass. The man, however, was not suspicious and after sitting on the rail fence awhile he went back to the cabin.

At last the officers decided it was time to act so they sent word to their superior officer and that night he arrived with a posse. It was decided to try to take the outlaws about nine o'clock and at that hour the posse began to advance on the house. Before they could get very close, however, the outlaws, warned by the barking of their dogs, immediately began firing when they found out that the officers were closing in on them. It was a fierce fight while it lasted but realizing that they were outnumbered and at a disadvantage the outlaws at last called out that they would surrender. They were instructed by the officers to come out of the house with their hands in the air and carrying no weapons. The bandits complied and it wasn't long before they were being taken into town and to the Federal jail at McAlester.

Miller was never injured in the line of duty, nor did he ever have to shoot a man. Members of his posse shot several outlaws, but Miller retired from government service in 1907 without ever having to shoot anyone. This reluctance on his part to use his weapon obviously did not lower his efficiency; if it had, he would not have been allowed to hold his post as long as he did.

Miller never became cold and callous toward the men he had to arrest. Once there was a bank robbery in his area and Miller organized a small posse and set out after three robbers, only this time they used a railroad handcar instead of the more common mode of travel — the reliable horse. They caught the robbers still carrying the loot and returned them and the money. One of them was a very young man, hardly more than a boy, and when the three were sentenced to the penitentiary, Miller took it upon himself to correspond with the young offender and sent him books and reading material so that he might educate himself, thereby encouraging him to find a better way of life. Miller evidently had a very good heart toward his fellow man.

According to Crockett Lee, a former deputy U.S. marshal in the Choctaw Nation, Miller was involved in some controversy on at least one occasion:

In 1901, we almost had a race war at the little mining town of Bache, which was about eight miles east of McAlester. Dave Tatum, a white man, was missing and had last been seen in the barbershop of Charley Williams, a colored barber. The white people thought that Williams had murdered Tatum who had robbed a poker game a short while before and was out on bond. Zeke Miller, a deputized Negro, had started a search for Tatum's body in the Negroes' houses and being unsuccessful had demanded that all of the houses of the whites be searched also. The Negroes had been mad at the action of Miller and now the white people were all in an uproar against him. To try and avert a clash between the two factions I was ordered to Bache out of McAlester and when I arrived the first thing I did was to hunt up Miller. He was still searching houses and I ordered him to stop that. I then went to the home of Dave Tatum and had a talk with his wife. Following this I passed the word around for everyone in Bache to attend a mass meeting at the company store at a certain hour. Here it was explained to them that Dave Tatum had probably skipped his bond and was alive. This seemed to satisfy the crowd and ended the hard feelings . . .

It is evident that Miller had more good days than bad as a peace officer. *The Daily Oklahoman,* on April 23, 1939, carried a story which included comments on Miller:

. . . The M.K.T. Railway Co., officials highly praised Miller and his posse of Negroes, when four hours after an early day train robbery near Caney, Miller captured the entire gang and their ill-gotten loot . . . Those were the days when the Doolin, Christian and Dalton gangs of outlaws infested the hills of what is now eastern Oklahoma . . .

One of the best synopses of Miller's career as a peace officer comes from Kay Teall:

For several years during his career as a Deputy Marshal, Miller rode a large black stallion and he and his horse developed that kind of sensitivity to each other that sometimes occurs between men who love and respect animals and the animals they keep. On a number of different occasions, the horse saved him from injury or possibly, death. Once he rode home late at night and as they approached the house, the horse became very nervous and excited. Miller trusted the horse's instincts and stayed back from the house. The cause for the horse's behavior was discovered when the hired man responded to Miller's shouts; there was a man waiting in ambush for Miller, ready to kill him. He was captured and Miller's faith in the horse was confirmed.

For a man with a wife and children, a deputy's salary did not go too far so Miller also ran a farm where he raised cattle and horses, and a small general store, both of which were left to the charge of his

241

family and hired help during his frequent absences. Catching an out-law was not a simple task; there were no real roads, only trails and almost all travel was by horse. The biggest problem was with horse and cattle thieves. Much of his time was taken in tracking them down and trying to recover the loss. There were times when he stayed on the trail of lawbreakers for several days.

One day while he was searching for an outlaw gang, a group of men rode up to the house looking for him. They seemed friendly and Mrs. Miller, with typical frontier hospitality, invited them to rest and water their horses. While the horses were refreshing themselves, the men confided to Mrs. Miller that they were hungry and she promptly invited them to eat and spread a hearty meal for them. The men ate with great relish — "as though they hadn't had a meal in a week" — and then insisted on paying Mrs. Miller for the food before they rode away into the night. When Miller returned, his wife told him about the visitors he had while he was away. Miller questioned her carefully, asking for a description of the men; then, with only a hint of a smile, he told her that they were the very men for whom he had been searching!

Miller's first headquarters was at Alderson, but was later moved to McAlester in the Choctaw Nation. These places, due to the territorial judicial system, served merely as depositories for captured criminals until they could be taken to the federal court at Fort Smith. When statehood came, Zeke Miller resigned as a deputy marshal and became a full-time businessman. He opened a timber company, contracting business with various mining companies in the McAlester area. Zeke Miller died of Bright's disease in 1909. Miller left behind an outstanding legacy as a peace officer of the Indian Territory.

CHAPTER 19

Others Who Wore the Star

In *Bill Doolin, Outlaw O.T.*, Hanes describes deputy U.S. marshal Rufus Cannon as an African-Cherokee who worked quite frequently with Deputy U.S. Marshal Heck Thomas.

The great-granddaughter of Rufus Cannon has stated that Cannon's father was a black man, an ex-slave from Arkansas, and that his mother was a white woman. (It is quite possible that Cannon's mother was a mixed-blood Cherokee.)

As noted earlier, Deputy Marshals Rufus Cannon and Ike Rogers had a running gunfight with Henry Starr, Ed Newcome, and Jesse Jackson, on January 20, 1893. In the course of the fight, Starr and Newcome escaped, but Cannon shot off the right arm of Jackson and he surrendered. Jackson was soon picked up in Bartlesville by Deputy Marshal Heck Thomas on charges of robbing a Santa Fe Railway train on November 8, 1892, at Wharton, O.T. During the course of this particular train robbery, Jackson's cohort was a white man named Ernest Lewis, who was mistaken for the notorious Oklahoma Territory outlaw Bill Doolin.

The Fort Smith National Historic Site has records that show Rufus Cannon received deputy marshal commissions on September 15, 1892, and June 1, 1893, from the Fort Smith court under Judge Parker.

On September 22, 1894, the *Muskogee Phoenix* carried a story concerning a shooting in which Cannon was involved:

About a year and a half ago, Rufus Cannon and W. L. Stamphill, deputies under Marshal Yoes, had a fight near Wewoka with a portion of the Woodard gang. Joe Pierce was killed and his friends claimed that his killing was unjustifiable. They attempted to have the deputies indicted for murder, but failed. The special grand jury, which convened last month, took up the case again and returned indictments against both. Stamphill was in the city and surrendered at once. Rufus Cannon was out in the Seminole [N]ation, but came in today and gave himself up to C. J. Lamb. Both had admitted to bond and are confident of their acquittal.

Evidently, Cannon was acquitted. He was back in the employ of the U.S. marshal service when he arrested William "Old Man" Christian, the father of the notorious Christian brothers, and lawman Bill Carr on July 22, 1895, in Pottawatomie County, Oklahoma Territory. Christian and Carr were implicated in the Oklahoma City jailbreak of the Christian brothers, Bob and Bill. The *Oklahoma Daily Times-Journal* reported:

. . . the old man was captured in the brush, he running onto Deputy Marshal Rufe Cannon by accident . . . Cannon had been hunting the Christians for several days, and was within half a mile of Deputy Owens and posse when he came upon Carr and put him under arrest also.

In 1896, when Heck Thomas was closing in on Bill Doolin, Deputy Marshal Rufus Cannon, who had captured the train robber Jesse Jackson and handed him over to Thomas, came over from the Indian Nations and joined his posse. The posse was camped on Dry Creek, northwest of Chandler, on August 23. Shortly afterwards the posse brought Doolin's outlaw career to an abrupt end. All the posse members received reward monies for the death of Doolin except Cannon. It was said that by being an auxiliary deputy marshal in a posse, he was not eligible for reward. Possemen shared any rewards collected unless they were paid as regular peace officers, in which case they received no part of the reward. The reward money in such cases was usually divided equally among the members of the posse, and this was one of the reasons the deputy marshals often did not look favorably on large posses. As an example, Bass Reeves kept his posse as small as possible. It is reported that Heck Thomas shared some of his reward money with Cannon.

Not much more is known about this "colorful" lawman. He did live a full life, reaching the ripe age of 105. Cannon lived his last years in Kansas City.

The following story from the Fort Smith *Weekly Elevator* of April 15, 1887, concerns a shootout in which a young African-American, Crowder Nicks, played a prominent role. At the time Nicks did not hold a deputy marshal commission, but his outstanding action in this incident undoubtedly helped him receive one.

WM. FIELDS MURDERED
The Successor of Sam Sixkiller Shot
While in the Discharge of His Duty.
The U.S. Indian Police Again Without
a Captain
James Cunnieus, His Slayer Lodged in Jail.
He Pleads Guilty of the Murder.

United States Marshal Carroll received a dispatch on Monday morning last stating that Capt. Will Fields, of the United States Indian Police, had been killed the day previous by Jim Cumming, whom he was endeavoring to arrest for larceny. This startling intelligence created a profound sensation among the many friends of Fields in this city, and more especially in court circles, and Mr. Carroll immediately wired to Muskogee for particulars, and in reply received a telegram that the murderer was under arrest, had acknowledged that he was guilty, and would be forthwith started to this place in charge Deputy Marshal Bud Kell.

That active young marshal arrived here on Wednesday with the murderer, whose true name is James Cunnieus; also with Nark Cunnieus, brother of James, and Ed Leeper, whom Fields had under arrest when killed. From Marshal Kell we got the following particulars of how poor Will Fields lost his life: It appears that Jim and Nark Cunnieus and Ed Leeper, who is a young fellow, broke into a Missouri Pacific freight car and stole some 800 pounds of flour and three caddies of tobacco, which they carried to their camp, where they were engaged in making railroad ties. Old man Leeper, the father of Ed was apprised of the theft, and not approving of such conduct, reported the matter to Fields, who was a detective on the road as well as a deputy marshal. He secured writs for them, and on Sunday morning last arrested young Leeper and Nark Cunnieus nine miles northeast of Eufaula, Creek Nation. Leaving them in charge of other parties, he took with him a colored man named Crowdy [Crowder]

Nicks and proceeded to a camp fifteen miles from Eufaula for the purpose of arresting Jim Cunnieus. Fields and Crowdy approached the camp on foot and met Cunnieus who was riding a mule and was armed with a shotgun and revolver. Fields "threw down" on him with a Winchester, saying, "Jim, I've got a writ for you, throw down your gun," but the words had scarcely issued from his lips when Cunnieus fired on him, inflicting a scalp wound, and as quick as a flash jumped from his mule and converted the animal into a breast work. As he dismounted Fields fired on him, when Cunnieus returned the shot with the remaining barrel of his gun, putting turkey shot in the left breast of the brave officer, the balls being scattered from his waist to his neck, and falling to the ground he almost instantly expired. This all happened almost in an instant, and as soon as Cunnieus fired the last shot from his gun he threw it down and drew a revolver and began shooting at Crowdy Nicks, who returned the fire, and the two men kept up a running fight for a distance of a quarter of a mile through the woods, when Crowdy finally put a ball through the left thigh of his antagonist . . . and he soon threw down his pistol and surrendered to the plunky [N]egro. During the skirmish they exchanged forty or fifty shots, and Crowdy's clothes were perforated with bullets in several places.

Cunnieus was born and raised near Decauter, Wise [C]ounty, Texas, and from there moved to Washington Territory, where it is said he is wanted on two charges of murder. From there he went into the Indian Territory, where he claims to have lived since June last.

The tragedy created great excitement at Eufaula, and in fact throughout the Territory. The friends of Cunnieus threatened to rescue him, and the people of Eufaula and vicinity were in for hanging him. The killing occurred between 12 and 1 o'clock, and a telegram was sent to Muskogee summoning Bud Kell to the scene. When he arrived there he found the excitement intense, and fearing the prisoner would be lynched he boarded the first train with him on Monday morning had him safely locked in jail at Muskogee. Here excitement soon became general and lynching was strongly talked of, but Kell kept his man well guarded and got off with him early on Tuesday morning by stage for this place. At Webber's Falls he was met by a crowd of men, one of whom had a rope, but this vigilant officer hurried on through and no violence was attempted.

. . . William Fields, the murdered man, was a brave and generous officer; a man who was highly esteemed by every one acquainted with him, and greatly admired for his manly, unassuming, genial disposition — in short, he was an honest, honorable, high-toned gentleman. His tragic death adds another bloody page to the history of Indian Territory.

On the 25th of January last Capt. Sam Sixkiller was murdered at Muskogee, and a few days later Fields, who was his trusted 1st lieutenant, was appointed to the position made vacant by his death, and now his mutilated body has been laid away at Atoka, where his wife's relatives reside. His bright career having been brought to a sudden and dreadful close, while the life of a young wife and mother has been rendered desolate by the hand of a murderous thief and vagabond whose own life is hardly worth the taking.

Crowdy Nicks, the [N]egro, who displayed such bravery in arresting the murderer single handed, deserves great praise for his act, and in appreciation of it a contribution of $151 was gotten up on his arrival here and presented to him as a reward. The citizens of the Territory should double the amount.

Not much is known about Crowder Nicks's career as a deputy marshal. The Eufaula *Indian Journal* did carry two short articles concerning his police work during the month of January 1890:

Jan 16
The whiskey peddler that was shot in the head by Crowder Nix *{sic},* deputy marshal, near Eufaula, just before Christmas, died in Fort Smith a few days ago. Nix *{sic}* is out on small bond, and will no doubt be justified at his trial upon the grounds that he was acting in the discharge of his duty.

Jan 30
Crowder Nix *{sic}* captured in the Choctaw nation last Tuesday the horse that was stolen from Mr. Hubble some time ago. The thief who stole him is still at large.

There have also been few territory newspaper articles found concerning African-American Deputy U.S. Marshal Bill Colbert. He was stationed at Atoka, I.T., which was located near Boggy Depot in the Choctaw Nation. The *Muskogee Phoenix* carried an incident involving Colbert on September 24, 1891:

Bill Colbert, a [N]egro marshal, shot Bill Alexander, another [N]egro, at Atoka, Saturday morning, while trying to arrest him. Alexander died in the afternoon. Further trouble is feared.

On March 15, 1894, the *Muskogee Phoenix* reported another shooting in which Deputy Colbert was involved:

There was at least one fairly well-known African-American deputy U.S. marshal who held a commission in Oklahoma Territory. The
territorial seat was located at Guthrie, but prisoners were taken to the
federal jail in Wichita, Kansas, until the Guthrie Federal Jail was completed in 1891. The Osage Nation was under the jurisdiction of the
Guthrie court, which is where Charlie Pettit was headquartered. Pettit
was called a "colored giant" who worked the Osage country. He is
mentioned in *Bill Doolin, Outlaw O.T.* as a deputy under the administration of Marshal E. D. Nix. Described as a "large Negro," he supposedly took a warrant to Ingalls, O.T., to serve on Bill Doolin; however, when confronted by the outlaw, the deputy allegedly backed
down and left town.

In the autobiography of former Oklahoma lawman Frank Eaton,
there is a passage concerning Eaton assisting Pettit in making an arrest
in Pawhuska:

> Charlie Nida and I gathered up our stock and started back
> home. When we got to the Osage Agency — it was called Pawhuska
> by that time — we camped and put our stock in the livery stable at
> the wagon yard.
>
> We were just leaving the livery barn when I saw Charlie Pettit
> walking up to me. Charlie was a big Negro Deputy United States
> Marshal, from the Wichita Court.
>
> "Frank," he said, "Ernest Lewis is up at the hotel and I have a
> warrant for him. He may have a gang up there. Come up and help
> me get him."
>
> We started up to the hotel together. Lewis was sitting on the
> porch. He started like he was going to make a gunplay, but I put my
> hand on my gun and shook my head at him and he stopped. He and
> I had played with guns and he knew I was the best shot.
>
> "Sorry, Mr. Lewis," Pettit said, "but I have a warrant for you
> and it's a fugitive warrant."
>
> By that he meant that Lewis was paid for if anything went

248

wrong. He had committed a crime that was punishable by death. Pettit's orders were to bring him in dead or alive.

"Unbuckle your gun belt carefully and drop your gun," Pettit told him. Lewis unbuckled his gun and handed the whole outfit to me. Pettit reached for his handcuffs and just then the whole window burst out on him with shotgun shells. I covered Lewis and started for the door and at the same time Pettit went in through the window. Inside the window stood Lewis's wife with a gun in her hands! She had shot both barrels of the shotgun at once and blown the whole window clear out onto the porch floor. Pettit grabbed the gun barrel, then saw it was a woman.

"Madam," he said taking off his hat, "them things get a person hurt. You should be more careful."

Pettit put his handcuffs on Mr. Lewis and my handcuffs on Ernest. He took the prisoners to Guthrie, where he put them in the Federal jail . . .

The following citation was found in the *Pawhuska Wah-Sha-She News,* concerning a Pettit arrest dated April 20, 1895: "Deputy Pettit brought in Perrin Rich, charged with introducing and his trial was set for Tuesday, next."

In regards to the actions of black Deputy U.S. Marshal Jack Walters of Pauls Valley, I.T., who was mentioned in the section on Bass Reeves, the *Chickasaw Enterprise* in 1901 printed articles concerning the aforementioned problem and his police work in the Chickasaw Nation:

Tempest In a Teapot

Jack Walters a [N]egro deputy marshal, appointed especially to look after the wild [N]egroes on Wild Horse [Creek], happened to be the only deputy at hand Monday of last week when word of the shooting of Mr. Shelton was brought in. He promptly organized a posse and on Thursday captured and brought in Bob McGee one of the murderers. On Saturday McGee was remanded to the jail at Ardmore by Judge Pfeiffer. The prisoner was asked by Mr. Foss if he was willing to have Jack Walters take him and replied that: "Jack had arrested him and had treated him right and he would rather go to jail with Jack than anybody else." As Jack was entitled to the fees for the trip, he was sent with the prisoner.

At the depot a bystander resented the idea of a [N]egro being in charge of a white man and used abusive language toward Jack, who resented the insult and placed him under arrest for a short time, making him subside at the point of a gun. A warrant was sworn out in the mayor's court against Walters for disturbing the peace. After Mr. Foss had been telephoned for and took charge of the prisoner, Jack went with City Marshal Martin to the Mayor's court and gave bond for appearance at a trial, which was held Monday, at which time a fine of $10 and costs was assessed against him. The case was promptly appealed to the U.S. District Court by the defendant.

After the train had gone taking Walters and his prisoner to Ardmore, a public meeting was called at the opera house, which was very large and enthusiastic. Speeches were made by Rev. Hunkapillar, Moman Pruiett, R. T. Jones, C. O. Barton and others and a commitee {sic} of twenty-five was appointed to draft resolutions protesting against the employment of a [N]egro on the marshal's force and demanding the immediate dismissal of Walters.

It is understood that Marshal Hammer sustains and will retain his deputy.

Stolen From Sheriff

A few days ago deputy Jack Walters found a suspicious character down on Wild Horse [Creek] trying to sell a team of mules. He arrested him on suspicion and brought him to jail. This morning a card was received from Tom McClure, Sheriff of Wise [C]ounty, Texas, describing the mules and giving brands. They had been stolen from the Sheriff himself.

On Saturday, Sheriff T. F. McClure of Wise Co., Texas came up and took Arch Wheeler back with him on a charge of horse stealing. The owner of the stolen mule team came along and identified them and drove them home. On Sunday a man named Jos. Jobes, from the same county came in on the train and laid claim to a buckskin horse which had also been found in possession of Arch Wheeler; but after some close questioning on the part of the officers he returned to Texas without the horse. Jack Walters will get the $25.00 reward for the capture, which was a clever piece of work.

African-American and Native American peace officers of the Indian and Oklahoma Territories had as distinguished careers as any lawmen in the history of the American West. It is hoped that their contributions to the growth of this nation are not forgotten. These deputy U.S. marshals and Indian lighthorse policemen wrote a page in American history that gave conviction to the words "truth" and "justice."

Appendix: Modern Day Lawmen

It is interesting to take a look at Oklahoma's Native American and African-American executive law enforcement officers in the year of 1988. Black and Indian police officers can be found throughout the state. Some black and white officers in the state have Native American ancestry in their respective family lineage. Officers highlighted here hold high administrative offices within various municipal, state, and federal police departments.

CHIEF JOHN COLEY

The only Native American found to hold an executive police administrative position in the fall of 1988 was Chief John Coley of Wewoka. Chief Coley, half white and half Seminole Indian, served four years in the U.S. Navy and received a bachelor of arts degree from East Central University at Ada, Oklahoma. Prior to working for the city of Wewoka, Chief Coley worked for the Oklahoma Department of Corrections as a case manager at Lexington Prison in Lexington, Oklahoma. At the time of publication of this book he had worked for more than five years for the Wewoka Police Department, where he held the positions of police officer, detective, and assistant chief of police. John Coley had been chief of police for four years.

CHIEF HUNTER MIXON

The police chief of Seminole, Oklahoma, in 1988 was Hunter Mixon. Born and reared in Stroud, Oklahoma, to Hunter and Della Mixon on November 10, 1950, he was the youngest of seven children.

Hunter began his education in an all-black elementary school named "South Stroud." On entering fourth grade, the elementary schools in Stroud became integrated. After finishing high school, Mixon went to Oklahoma State Tech at Okmulgee, Oklahoma. Majoring in building construction in 1972, he returned to Stroud.

In 1973, Mixon became the first African-American ever to serve on the Stroud Police Department. He served with the department for five years and advanced from patrolman to sergeant. After leaving Stroud, Mixon served on the Lincoln County Sheriff's Department for six months.

On March 25, 1977, Mixon went to work for the Drumright Police Department, where after three months he advanced to assistant chief of police. After three more months as assistant chief, Mixon went on to become chief of police. He was the first African-American police chief Drumright ever had and held the position for eight years. Of the total of eleven years in Drumright residency, Mixon served three of them as a bodyguard for one of Drumright's most prominent citizens, W. J. "Snookie" Taylor.

Mixon returned to the Drumright Police Department in 1985 as chief and in April 1988, was hired as chief of police for Seminole, Oklahoma. Chief Mixon was also the first African-American to ever serve in that capacity with the Seminole Police Department.

SHERIFF J. C. BURRIS

The county sheriff of historic Logan County, as of 1988, was J. C. Burris. The Logan County seat is located at Guthrie, Oklahoma. Sheriff Burris, originally from Idabel, Oklahoma, has two sons serving on the Oklahoma Highway Patrol. This makes the Burris family one of the foremost families in law enforcement within the state of Oklahoma. After serving six years as elected sheriff of Logan County, Sheriff Burris ran unopposed in the 1988 election. He was the first African-American ever to be elected a county sheriff in the state of Oklahoma.

1st LT. RODNEY U. BURRIS

The highest ranking African-American of the Oklahoma Highway Patrol in 1988 was 1st Lt. Rodney U. Burris. Lieutenant Burris was born in Oklahoma City, Oklahoma, to J. C. and Faye Burris, the third of five sons, on August 26, 1953. Lieutenant Burris grew up in the historical black town of Langston, Oklahoma, which is located forty-five miles northeast of Oklahoma City. His formal education consisted of elementary school at Langston, secondary school at Guthrie High School in Guthrie, and later Langston University.

Lieutenant Burris is married to Earlene (Kennerson) and has one daughter, Yulonda. The Burrises reside in Guthrie.

Burris's law enforcement career began as an officer with the Langston University Security Police. From there he went to the Guthrie Police Department, where he was one of only two black police officers. At both Langston University and the Guthrie Police Department, Burris attained the rank of sergeant.

In January 1978, he began his career with the Oklahoma Highway Patrol. As one of three African-American cadets in the Thirty-sixth Oklahoma Highway Patrol Academy, Burris was commissioned a state trooper after sixteen weeks of intensive training in May 1978. His first assignment was in Washington County in northeastern Oklahoma. After four and a half years as a road trooper, Burris was transferred to the Training Division, where he instructed Basic Accident Investigation, Advanced Accident Investigation, Technical Accident Investigation, Emergency Vehicle Operation, Radar Operation, Basic Police School (Traffic), and Report Writing.

Burris was promoted to the rank of second lieutenant in 1984, becoming only the third African-American promoted to this rank in the forty-eight-year history of the patrol. He was assigned to supervise a ten-man sector of the interstate system of Oklahoma City. Burris was subsequently assigned to supervise an eleven-man sector consisting of Logan and Canadian counties of Troop A Rural. In the summer of 1988, Burris became the first African-American trooper to attain the rank of first lieutenant. He is troop commander of Troop A Rural, which consists of commanding six counties of central Oklahoma, with a command strength of thirty-two uniformed members (three second lieutenants and twenty-nine troopers) and three civilian personnel.

Burris's father is the sheriff of Logan County, and his younger brother, J. C., Jr., graduated from the Forty-third Oklahoma Highway Patrol Academy, Summer 1988. This marks the first time that two African-American brothers have served together on the Oklahoma Highway Patrol.

CAPT. ROBERT MUSGROVE

The highest ranking African-American on the Ardmore Police Department is Capt. Robert Musgrove. The captain, a 1961 graduate of Ardmore's Douglass High School, received an associate degree in education from Murray State College in Tishomingo. He also attended East Central State University in Ada.

Captain Musgrove's law enforcement career began while he was serving in the U.S. Army. He spent his time in Germany as a military police officer.

In 1967, Captain Musgrove joined the Ardmore Police Department as a patrol officer. He has worked his way up the ranks and in 1988 served as a supervisor within the department.

Musgrove and his wife, Joyce, along with their five children reside in the city of Ardmore.

MAJ. BOBBY LEE BUSBY

Bobby Lee Busby was born on January 25, 1937, in Depew, Oklahoma, where he grew up on a farm. He graduated from Depew and Bristow, Oklahoma, high schools. From 1956 to 1959, Busby was a member of the U.S. Army Military Police, where he attained the rank of E-4.

In 1961, Busby became a warrants officer for the Municipal Criminal Court, Tulsa, Oklahoma. In this capacity he served warrants and other processes for the court. He worked there until 1969, when he graduated from the Tulsa Police Academy and began work as a patrol officer.

In 1973, Busby was promoted to investigator for the Tulsa Police Department. From 1973 to 1976, Busby cleared more cases by arrest and prosecution than any other investigator in the department. In 1976, Busby was promoted to senior investigator, where he supervised a squad of six burglary investigators. Busby was promoted to the rank of lieutenant in 1980 and assumed command of a shift composed of forty-six officers, five sergeants, and four corporals.

In 1984, Busby became the first African-American to be promoted to the rank of major within the Tulsa, Oklahoma, Police Department. He was assigned to watch commander's duties, which included acting as chief during the chief's absence. In 1986, Major Busby was assigned to Field Operations Support Division (FOSD). He assumed command of Airport Security, Helicopter Unit, Canine (K-9) Unit, Special Operations Team, Bomb Squad, Dignitary Security, Motorcycle Unit, Equipment Control, Property Room, Special Events, Community Service Officers, Warrant Squad, and the FOSD administrative personnel.

In September 1988, Major Busby took charge of Uniform Division South/West of the Tulsa Police Department. He obtained a degree from Tulsa Junior College in 1973, and attended the FBI National Academy in 1982. In 1988, Major Busby was the highest ranking African-American officer of the Tulsa, Oklahoma, Police Department.

MAJ. M. T. BERRY

Although holding the rank of major on the Oklahoma City Police Department, M. T. Berry also holds the name of Major. His given name at birth was Major Tally Berry, Jr. Born in Eufaula, Oklahoma, on September 16, 1950, he is married with four children. He holds an associates degree in law enforcement from Oklahoma State University, and a bachelor's degree in criminal justice administration from Central State University, located in Edmond,

254

Oklahoma. Berry also graduated from the 123rd session of the FBI National Academy.

Berry began his police career on September 1, 1970, at the age of nineteen, when he became a member of the Oklahoma City Police Department's Community Service Officer Program. This was a federally funded program for underprivileged youth between the ages of eighteen and twenty-one. Berry was the first African-American to graduate from the program and the only African-American to continue with the department which participated in the program. On September 21, 1971, Berry was promoted to the rank of police officer and served in that capacity until January 1977, at which time he was promoted to detective and assigned to Recruiting and Internal Affairs. In September 1978, Berry was promoted to the rank of sergeant and served as a supervisor in Recruiting/Internal Affairs and the Traffic Division.

In August 1981, Berry was promoted to lieutenant and assigned to supervise the Internal Affairs/Recruiting Unit. He was the first African-American in the history of the Oklahoma City Police Department to hold this assignment.

In April 1985, Berry was promoted to captain and assigned as the public information officer for the police department, again the first of his race to hold this position with the department. In August 1987, Berry was promoted to the rank of major and assigned as the executive officer in charge of all uniformed field operations of the Oklahoma City Police Department.

Major Berry, in 1988, was the highest ranking African-American of the Oklahoma City Police Department. The only African-American to achieve a chief's rank with the Oklahoma City Police Department was Assistant Chief Gerald Emmett, who retired after thirty years of service in 1984.

CHIEF DEPUTY RAYMOND VAN PUTTEN

In 1988 the chief deputy United States marshal for the Western District of Oklahoma, based in Oklahoma City, was an African-American named Raymond Van Putten. He graduated from Wichita State University in 1974 with a bachelor's degree in administration of justice and in 1983 received a master's in forensic science and criminal justice.

Van Putten began his law enforcement career with the Wichita, Kansas, Police Department. Later he worked with the United States Immigration Service before joining the United States Marshals Service, where he was promoted to supervisor by 1983. In 1985 he was promoted to supervisory criminal investigator and assigned to San Diego, California. Van Putten was promoted to chief deputy U.S. marshal in 1986 and reassigned to Oklahoma City.

He is a member of the American Management Association, Metropolitan Chiefs of Police in Oklahoma, and the International Association of Chiefs of Police (IACP).

A hundred years after the era of the Oklahoma gunfighters, these gentlemen are carrying on in the fine tradition of Sam Sixkiller, Bass Reeves, and Grant Johnson.

Glossary

ball: Gun-play in which two antagonists or two factions have a shootout. When a person said, "The ball had commenced," it meant someone had fired the first shot in a fight.

bullwacker: Driver of an oxen team.

cowhand: A more commonly used term than "cowboy" in the early West.

cowtown: A town at or near a railroad to which herds of cattle were driven to be shipped to market.

drop: When a gunman has the "drop," he has his weapon out and aimed at his adversary first. Sometimes the man with the drop shot first, missed, and got killed.

Freedman: An African-American who was held in bondage by one of the Five Civilized Tribes, or descendant of such persons.

hack: A one-horse buggy.

homesteader: One who accepts a government grant of 160 acres of free public lands on condition that they live on the land and improve it.

introducing: To bring illegal alcohol into the Indian Territory.

mixed-blood Indian: An offspring of white and Indian parents, very common in the Five Tribes.

peace officer: A deputy U.S. marshal or sheriff or deputy sheriff; that is, federal or county officers. The Indian police of Indian Territory were peace officers because their jurisdiction included a whole Indian nation.

road agents: Term used for stagecoach robbers.

rustler: A horse or cattle thief; quite numerous in the Indian Territory.

section: Comprises one square mile or 640 acres of land. Allotments of land to Indians and Freedmen were in quarter sections (160 acres), eighths (80 acres), and sixteenths (40 acres).

scout: The phrase "on the scout" means hiding out or on the dodge from lawmen. Said of a criminal for whom a warrant is out and peace officers or police are looking for them.

State Negro: A term used by Indian Freedmen for African-Americans who came into Indian Territory from bordering states. Also called state-raised.

tree: Verb, meaning to intimidate the citizens and officers of an area so badly that the officers fear to make an arrest even for murder. The outlaw would have the settlers and officers so frightened, or buffaloed, they would be "treed."

wrangler: A ranch hand who is an expert at handling horses.

Bibliography

Books

Aldrich, Gene. *Black Heritage of Oklahoma.* (Edmond, OK: Thompson Book and Supply Co., 1973)
Blacks in the Westward Movement. Anacostia Neighborhood Museum. (Washington, DC: Smithsonian Institution Press, 1975)
Bontemps, Arna, and Jack Conroy. *Anyplace But Here.* (New York: Hill and Wang, 1966)
Calhoun, Sharon C., and Billie J. English. *Oklahoma Heritage.* (Maysville, OK: Holt, Calhoun & Clark Pub., Inc., 1984)
Croy, Homer. *He Hanged Them High.* (New York: Duell, Sloan, and Pearce, 1952)
————. *Trigger Marshal.* (New York: Duell, Sloan, and Pearce, 1958)
Cunningham, Eugene. *Triggernometry: A Gallery of Gunfighters.* (New York: The Press of the Pioneers, Inc., 1934)
Drago, Harry Sinclair. *Outlaws on Horseback.* (New York: Dodd, Mead & Co., 1964)
Durham, Philip, and Everett L. Jones. *The Negro Cowboys.* (Lincoln: University of Nebraska Press, 1983)
Eaton, Frank. *Pistol Pete: Veteran of the Old West.* (Perkins, OK: Evans Publication, 1979)
Foreman, Grant. *The Five Civilized Tribes.* (Norman: University of Oklahoma Press, 1934)
Franklin, Jimmie Lewis. *Journey Toward Hope: A History of Blacks in Oklahoma.* (Norman: University of Oklahoma Press, 1982)
Gideon, D. C. *Indian Territory; Descriptive, Biographical and Genealogical, Landed Estates, County Seats — General History of the Territory.* (New York: Lewis Publishing Co., 1901)
Gregory, Jack, and Renard Strickland. *Hell on the Border.* Indian Heritage Edition. (Muskogee, OK: Indian Heritage Publications, 1971)
Guns and the Gunfighters. Editors of Guns & Ammo. (New York: Bonanza Books, 1982)

259

Hagan, William T. *Indian Police and Judges: Experiments in Acculturation and Control.* (Lincoln: University of Nebraska Press, 1980)

Halliburton, Rudi. *Red over Black: Black Slavery Among the Cherokee Indians.* (Westport, CT: Greenwood Press, 1977)

Hanes, Colonel Bailey C. *Bill Pickett: Bulldogger.* (Norman: University of Oklahoma Press, 1977)

Harman, S. W. *Hell on the Border.* (Fort Smith, AR: The Phoenix Publishing Co., 1898)

Katz, William Loren. *Black Indians: A Hidden Heritage.* (New York: Atheneum, 1986)

———. *Black People Who Made the Old West.* (New York: Crowell, 1977)

———. *The Black West.* (Seattle: Open Hand Publishing Inc., 1987)

Lake, Stuart N. *Wyatt Earp, Frontier Marshal.* (New York: Houghton Mifflin Co., 1931)

Leckie, William H. *The Buffalo Soldiers: A Narrative of the Negro Cavalry in the West.* (Norman: University of Oklahoma Press, 1967)

Littlefield, Daniel, Jr. *Africans and Seminoles: From Emancipation to American Citizenship.* (Westport, CT: Greenwood Press, 1977)

———. *The Cherokee Freedmen: From Emancipation to American Citizenship.* (Westport, CT: Greenwood Press, 1978)

Love, Nat. *The Life and Adventures of Nat Love.* (Baltimore: Black Classic Press, 1988)

Masterson, V. V. *The Katy Railroad and the Last Frontier.* (Norman: University of Oklahoma Press, 1952; Columbia: University of Missouri Press, 1988)

McReynolds, Edwin. *The Seminoles.* (Norman: University of Oklahoma Press, 1957)

Miller, Tuskhoma Brown. *Este-Cate (Red Man).* (Wewoka, OK: Seminole Nation Historical Society, 1982)

Monaghan, Jay. *Civil War on the Western Border, 1854–1865.* (Lincoln: University of Nebraska Press, 1984)

Mooney, Charles W. *Localized History of Pottawatomie County, Oklahoma, to 1907.* (Midwest, OK: Thunderbird Industries, 1971)

Morrison, James D. *The Social History of the Choctaw Nation.* Edited by James C. Milligan and David L. Norris. (Durant, OK: Creative Informatics)

Nash, Jay Robert. *Blood Letters and Badmen.* Vol. 1 & 2. (New York: Warner Books, 1975)

O'Neal, Bill. *Encyclopedia of Western Gunfighters.* (Norman: University of Oklahoma Press, 1979)

Parker, Doris Whitail. *Footprints of the Osage Reservation.* 3 volumes. (Pawhuska, OK: Pawhuska Oklahoma Genealogy Society)

Porter, Kenneth. *The Negro on the American Frontier.* (New York: The New

York Times with Grove Press, 1971)

Prassel, Frank Richard. *The Western Peace Officer.* (Norman: University of Oklahoma Press, 1972)

Savage, W. Sherman. *Blacks in the West.* (Westport, CT: Greenwood Press, 1976)

Shirley, Glenn. *Heck Thomas, Frontier Marshal.* (Norman: University of Oklahoma Press, 1981)

————. *Henry Starr. Last of the Real Badmen.* (New York: McKay Publishing Co., 1965)

————. *Law West of Fort Smith: A History of Frontier Justice in the Indian Territory. 1834–1896.* (Lincoln: University of Nebraska Press, 1968)

————. *Toughest of Them All.* (Albuquerque: University of New Mexico Press, 1953)

————. *West of Hell's Fringe: Crime, Criminals, and the Federal Peace Officer in Oklahoma Territory, 1889–1907.* (Norman: University of Oklahoma Press, 1978)

Starr, Helen, and O. E. Hill. *Footprints in the Indian Nation.* (Muskogee, OK: Hoffman Printing Co., 1974)

Steele, Phillip. *The Last Cherokee Warriors.* (Gretna, LA: Pelican Publishing Co., 1987)

Stewart, Paul W., and William Y. Ponce. *Black Cowboys.* (Broomfield, CO: Phillips Publishing, 1986)

Teall, Kay. *Black History in Oklahoma.* (Oklahoma City: Oklahoma City Public Schools, 1971)

Thoburn, Joseph B. *A Standard History of Oklahoma.* Vol. 2. (New York, Chicago: American Historical Society, 1916)

Tolson, Arthur L. *The Black Oklahomans, a History: 1541–1972.* (New Orleans: Edwards Printing Co., 1973)

Trachtman, Paul. *The Gunfighters.* (New York: Time-Life Books, 1974)

Waldman, Carl. *Atlas of the North American Indian.* (New York, Oxford: Facts on File Public, 1985)

Washington, Nathaniel J. *Historical Development of the Negro in Oklahoma.* (Tulsa: Dexter Publishing Co., 1948)

Wellman, Paul I. *Dynasty of Western Outlaws.* (Lincoln: University of Nebraska Press, 1986)

West, C. W. "Dub." *Outlaws and Peace Officers of Indian Territory.* (Muskogee, OK: Muskogee Publishing Co., 1987)

Wright, J. Leitch, Jr. *The Only Land They Knew.* (New York: The Free Press, 1981)

————. *Creek and Seminoles: The Destruction and Regeneration of the Muscogulge People.* (Lincoln: University of Nebraska Press, 1987)

Articles

Austerman, Wayne R. "The Black Scalp Hunters." *Real West* (June 1986).
Ernst, Robert R. "Sam Sixkiller: Tragic Life of an Indian Lawman." *Frontier Times* (October 1984).
Foreman, Carolyn Thomas. "The Light-Horse in the Indian Territory." *Chronicles of Oklahoma* (Spring 1956).
Hill, Mozell C. "The All-Negro Communities of Oklahoma: The Natural History of a Social Movement." *Journal of Negro History* 31 (July 1946).
Jeltz, Wyatt F. "The Relations of Negroes and Choctaw and Chickasaw Indians." *Journal of Negro History* 33 (January 1948).
Littlefield, Daniel, Jr., and Lonnie E. Underhill. "Negro Marshals in the Indian Territory." *Journal of Negro History* 56 (April 1971).
————. "The Crazy Snake Uprising of 1909: A Red, Black or White Affair?" *Arizona and the West* 20, no. 4 (Winter 1978).
Mooney, Charles W. "Bass Reeves, Black Deputy U.S. Marshal." *Real West* (July 1976).
Porter, Kenneth Wiggins. "Negroes and Indians on the Texas Frontier, 1836–1876." *Journal of Negro History* (October 1956).
Shirley, Glenn. "James Ledbetter: Hero of a Hundred Battles with Nary a Scratch." *Real West* (January 1973).
Tolson, Arthur L. "Black Towns of Oklahoma." *Black Scholar*. (April 1970).
Walker, Wayne T. "Captain Sam Sixkiller — Indian Policeman." *Golden West* (November 1969).
Williams, Nudie E. "Bass Reeves: Lawman in the Western Ozarks." *Negro History Bulletin* (April/May/June, 1979).
————. "Black Men who wore White Hats: Grant Johnson, United States Deputy Marshal." *Red River Valley Historical Review* (Summer 1980).
————. "Black Men Who Wore the Star." *Chronicles of Oklahoma* (Spring 1981).
"The Light Horse Indian Lawmen." *Great West* (Fall 1981).
"Report on the Five Civilized Tribes, 1897, by the Kansas City Star." *Chronicles of Oklahoma* 48, no. 4.
"Milestones of Progress." United States Marshal's Service, Office of Equal Employment Opportunity.

Manuscripts

Duke, Doris. Papers. Western History Collection, University of Oklahoma Library, Norman, OK.
Indian-Pioneer Papers. 112 volumes. Archives and Manuscript Division, Ok-

lahoma Historical Society, Oklahoma City, OK.

Fronterhouse, Richard D. "Bass Reeves: The Forgotten Lawman." Unpublished seminar paper, 1960. Western History Collections, University of Oklahoma Library, Norman, OK.

Williams, Nudie E. "A History of the American Southwest: Black United States Deputy Marshals in the Indian Territory, 1875–1907." Unpublished M.A. thesis, Oklahoma State University Library, Stillwater, OK.

Newspapers

Vinita Weekly Indian Chieftain
Muskogee Indian Journal
Northwest Arkansas Times
Eufaula Indian Journal
Fort Smith Weekly Elevator
Daily Oklahoman
Muskogee Weekly Phoenix
Muskogee Daily Phoenix
The Weekly Times-Journal
   (Oklahoma City)
Chickasaw Enterprise

Tahlequah Arrow
The Western Age
Cherokee Advocate
Muskogee Evening Times
Arkansas Gazette
Daily Ardmoreite
The Paris News
Muskogee Times Democrat
The Langston City Herald
Muskogee Cimitar

Television

Through the Looking Glass Darkly. Produced by Bob Dotson, July 1973. WKY, Oklahoma City, OK.

Interviews

March 1990 — Joe Younger, Oklahoma City, OK.

October 1988 — Hortense Love, Chicago, IL.

September 1988 — Lucille Taylor, Pocola, OK.

July 1988 — John W. Simmons, Oklahoma City, OK.

June 1988 — Ezra Golson, Arcadia, OK.

June 1988 — Pliney Twine, Muskogee, OK.

May 1988 — Mrs. Melvin Coe, Denison, TX.

August 1988 — Haskell Shoeboot, Denver, CO.

Indian Pioneer Papers, Oklahoma Historical Society, Archives and Manuscript Division Interviews:

Bill Brasfield	Merrill A. Nelson
Alec Berryhill	Carrie Pitman
Carrie Cyrus	Nancy E. Pruitt
C. E. Foley	Isa S. Smith
Lizzie Gibson	J. B. Sparks
Ashley W. Guffey	William Lee Starr
John H. Hannon	Maud Brown Surrell
Herbert W. Hicks	Burl Taylor
John H. Hubble	William Taylor
Robert Johnson	James W. Turley
William Frank Jones	Jim Vaughn
William J. Layne	Clarence O. Warren
Crockett Lee	E. H. Whitmire
Harve Lovelday	I. F. Williams

Correspondence

Guy Nichols, park ranger, Fort Smith National Historic Site, July 1988.
Haskel Shoeboot, Denver, CO.
Robert Ernst, consultant, U.S. Marshal's Service, Stillwater, OK, 1987–1989.
U.S. Marshals Vertical File: Bass Reeves, Oklahoma Historical Society Library.

Main Street, Fort Gibson, Indian Territory, 1898–1899.
— Courtesy Archives and Manuscripts Division,
Oklahoma Historical Society

Saturday street scene in Muskogee, I.T., ca. 1899.
— Courtesy Archives and Manuscripts Division,
Oklahoma Historical Society

African-American-operated ferry on the Arkansas River near Fort Gibson, I.T., ca. 1899.

— Courtesy Archives and Manuscripts Division, Oklahoma Historical Society

Seminole Indian camp in the Indian Territory.

— Courtesy Archives and Manuscripts Division, Oklahoma Historical Society

Street scene of Indian Freedmen camp during Dawes Commission enrollment at Fort Gibson, I.T.

— Courtesy Archives and Manuscripts Division, Oklahoma Historical Society

Freedmen shooting fish with bow and arrow in the Choctaw Nation, 1902.

— Courtesy Archives and Manuscripts Division, Oklahoma Historical Society

Standing left to right: Coody Johnson and Okchar Harjo, aides. Sitting: Hul-putta Micco, principal chief of the Seminole Nation, 1901–1905.
— Courtesy Archives and Manuscripts Division,
Oklahoma Historical Society

African-Americans conversing in the streets of Vinita, I.T., ca. 1900.
— Courtesy Archives and Manuscripts Division,
Oklahoma Historical Society

African-Americans on horseback at Muskogee, I.T., ca. 1900.
— Courtesy Archives and Manuscripts Division,
Oklahoma Historical Society

Horses and wagons in waiting at Muskogee, ca. 1899.
— Courtesy Archives and Manuscripts Division,
Oklahoma Historical Society

Cherokee outlaw Ned Christie.
— Courtesy Archives and Manuscripts Division,
Oklahoma Historical Society

Crawford Goldsby, alias Cherokee Bill.
— Courtesy Western History Collections,
University of Oklahoma Library

Cherokee Bill with mother, Mrs. Ellen Lynch.

Shortly after his capture, Cherokee Bill posed with his captors at Wagoner, I.T. Left to right: (5) Zeke Crittenden, (4) Dick Crittenden, Bill, (2) Clint Scales, (1) Ike Rogers, and (3) Bill Smith.

Cherokee outlaw Henry Starr and family.
— Courtesy Archives and Manuscripts Division,
Oklahoma Historical Society

The Rufus Buck Gang the day before their execution. From left to right:
Maoma July, Sam Sampson, Rufus Buck, Lucky Davis, and Louis Davis.
— Courtesy Fort Smith National Historic Site,
National Park Service

Creek "Snake Faction" Indians, led by Chief Chitto Harjo (Creek for Crazy Snake), under arrest in November 1900.

Chief Crazy Snake, standing far right, and followers under arrest at Muskogee, I.T.

Buss Luckey, Freedman outlaw, served fifteen years in the federal penitentiary at Columbus, Ohio, for participating in the Blackstone Switch train robbery.
— Courtesy author's collection

Indian Police of Anadarko Agency, Oklahoma Territory, 1894.
— Courtesy Archives and Manuscripts Division, Oklahoma Historical Society

Standing on the right, Capt. Peter Conser with members of the Choctaw
Lighthorse Police.

Choctaw Lighthorsemen on patrol.

Choctaw Lighthorsemen at Antlers, I.T., in 1893.
— Courtesy Western History Collections,
University of Oklahoma Library

Seminole Chief John Chupco (seated, center), the Seminole council, and
Lighthorse police.
— Courtesy Archives and Manuscripts Division,
Oklahoma Historical Society

Lighthorsemen, Seminole Nation, Wewoka, I.T.
— Courtesy Archives and Manuscripts Division,
Oklahoma Historical Society

Fort Smith Courthouse and Jail.
— Courtesy Fort Smith National Historic Site,
National Park Service

George Winston, bailiff, Fort Smith Federal Court.
— Courtesy author's collection

Sam Sixkiller, captain of the Union Agency Indian Police and deputy U.S. marshal.

— Courtesy Archives and Manuscripts Division,
Oklahoma Historical Society

Rufus Cannon, African-American deputy U.S. marshal, on his ninety-ninth birthday.

An African-American deputy U.S. marshal Jim Roth on duty in the Oklahoma Territory in 1902.

Baz (Bass) Reeves, deputy U.S. marshal for thirty-two years in the Indian Territory.

Left to right: Amos Maytubby, Creek Lighthorseman; Zeke Miller, Neely Factor, Bob Fortune, all African-American deputy U.S. marshals. From *The Black Dispatch*. March 25, 1937. Neely Factor said this about the picture: "We were on our way to Deadman's Crossing when we had that picture made. Near Coal Creek we captured one murderer and two horse thieves. We captured them after surrounding their home in a community which consisted of twenty or thirty Indians. Their names were Wesley Hembry and Felix McClish. We captured, just a little later, another murderer, a white man who was later convicted and sent to the penitentiary."

Picture of Muskogee Police Department on March 11, 1908. Building draped in honor of L. F. Harvey, a policeman murdered by Jesse Cox. First on left, front row, is Bass Reeves, hired as policeman, January 1908, at the age of sixty-nine. Third from left, front row, is Policeman Paul Smith, who saved lawman Bud Ledbetter's life.

— Courtesy Daniel F. Littlefield, Jr., Collection

Picture of the U.S. Marshal's office at Muskogee on November 16, 1907, the first day of statehood for Oklahoma. On the far left is Bass Reeves. The tall man in front is Bud Ledbetter. In the rear center is U.S. Marshal Leo E. Bennett.

— Courtesy Archives and Manuscripts Division,
Oklahoma Historical Society

Grant Johnson, Creek Freedman and deputy U.S. marshal, front center. Reunion photograph of the deputy marshals who worked the Northern District of Indian Territory in 1897.

— Courtesy Archives and Manuscripts Division, Oklahoma Historical Society

On April 19, 1894, Silon Lewis was sentenced to be shot for the murder of Joe Haklotybbi. He was given his freedom, without bond, until execution day. On November 5 he appeared at Moshalatubbe Courthouse, near Red Oak, Indian Territory, sat down on a blanket, and calmly signified he was ready. Lewis was shot through his lung because his heartbeat was on the right side of his breast. Guards are shown smothering him as the sheriff stands by with a Winchester.

— Courtesy Choctaw Nation Museum

Picture of the last Seminole execution at the Execution Tree in Wewoka, I.T.
— Courtesy Archives and Manuscripts Division,
Oklahoma Historical Society

Sheriff J. C. Burris, Logan County, Oklahoma.

1st Lt. Rodney U. Burris, Oklahoma Highway Patrol.

John Coley, chief of police, Wewoka, Oklahoma.

Hunter Mixon, chief of police, Seminole, Oklahoma.

Maj. Bobby Lee Busby, Tulsa Police Department.

Maj. M. T. Berry, Oklahoma City Police Department.

The Lighthorse Administration of the Creek Nation. Left to right: Marsey Scott, Washington Cummings, Randall Chorette, Tony Lowe, Daniel Checotah, Jimmy Nixon, and Lighthorse Manager Richard Larney. Okmulgee, 1988. Prior to this position Larney was chief of police at Henryetta, having served with that police department for twenty-seven years.

— Courtesy Creek Nation, Oklahoma

A Choctaw Negro and his Indian wife.
— Courtesy Wilburton, Oklahoma,
Chamber of Commerce

Political prisoners of Gaines County.

— Courtesy Wilburton, Oklahoma,
Chamber of Commerce

Choctaw Justice — 1892. A Choctaw Freedman named Sam Bird had killed three people and fled the scene, going on "scout" for several years, but was finally captured. He confessed to his crime and was sentenced to death. In the picture, Bird is the man seated in the back of the front wagon. His coffin is in the wagon behind. He refused to ride in the wagon with his coffin. The entourage is about to start to the execution ground.

— Courtesy Wilburton, Oklahoma,
Chamber of Commerce

Deputy U.S. Marshal Robert Fortune at his home in Wilburton, I.T., 1904. Bob Fortune, who moved to Wilburton in 1900, served as a deputy marshal in the Indian Territory for twelve years. After statehood he worked at the state prison in McAlester. His nickname was "Poorboy."

— Courtesy Wilburton, Oklahoma, Chamber of Commerce

William (Bill) M. Colbert (1835–1933), deputy U.S. marshal and Choctaw Freedman, was stationed at Atoka, Choctaw Nation, I.T.

— Courtesy Donna Harris

Index

295

300

302

303